FOUNDING ACTS

FOUNDING ACTS

Constitutional Origins in a Democratic Age

Serdar Tekin

PENN

UNIVERSITY OF PENNSYLVANIA PRESS

PHILADELPHIA

Copyright © 2016 University of Pennsylvania Press

All rights reserved. Except for brief quotations used for purposes of review or scholarly citation, none of this book may be reproduced in any form by any means without written permission from the publisher.

Published by
University of Pennsylvania Press
Philadelphia, Pennsylvania 19104-4112
www.upenn.edu/pennpress

Printed in the United States of America on acid-free paper
1 3 5 7 9 10 8 6 4 2

Library of Congress Cataloging-in-Publication Data
ISBN 978-0-8122-4828-9

Contents

Introduction. The Problem of Democratic Founding — 1

Chapter 1. Origins and Foundations: Two Features of the Modern Constitution — 15

Chapter 2. The Paradox of Democratic Founding: Canonical Statements and Contemporary Perspectives — 34

Chapter 3. The People and the Lawgiver: Rousseau on the Possibility of Democratic Founding — 57

Chapter 4. Building a Homeland: Founding and Identity in Hannah Arendt's Jewish Writings — 77

Chapter 5. Revolution and Constitution: The Legitimacy of Beginning in Question — 94

Chapter 6. Law and Democracy in Founding Moments: Deliberative Constitution-Making — 119

Conclusion. "The Act by Which a People Is a People" — 144

Notes — 159

Index — 191

Acknowledgments — 195

FOUNDING ACTS

Introduction

The Problem of Democratic Founding

> ... it would be well to examine the act by which a people is a people.
> — Jean-Jacques Rousseau

Remember the night of February 11, 2011. More than a million demonstrators had been occupying the Tahrir Square in downtown Cairo for eighteen long days when Hosni Mubarak, Egypt's longstanding president/dictator, finally gave in and stepped down. As the whole world was watching with intrigue, the Egyptian people enacted a revolution at a time and place that was perhaps least expected. The popular protest had begun a couple of weeks before Mubarak's resignation, first in Tunisia, then in Egypt, spreading like wildfire and catching everyone by surprise. Those who spontaneously populated the Tahrir Square were ordinary men and women from all walks of life. They were nonviolent but full of indignation, fed up with decades of dictatorship, with police brutality and emergency laws, with poverty, unemployment, electoral fraud, and political corruption. The protesters voiced two clear demands from the outset: immediate resignation of the president/dictator and establishment of a democratic regime.

Although it took less than three weeks to end Mubarak's thirty-year reign, the transition to democracy proved to be much harder. Perhaps this was not surprising in and of itself, but things went especially wrong in the process of constitution-making. Partisan imposition prevailed over collective deliberation, leading to new waves of strikes and protests, which eventually triggered a military coup. A politics of restoration is currently underway, and no one quite knows what it will take to set the country back on the track of democratization or how long this process will take. In the current situation and with the benefit of hindsight, it is not a moot speculation to say that things could have been drastically different if the constitution-making process had unfolded the right way. However, it did not, and the revolution was not succeeded by what Hannah Arendt called *constitutio libertatis,* the foundation of political freedom, or at least by a constitutional beginning which carries the promise thereof.[1]

Questions abound. How does democracy get off the ground? How can the revolutionary "event" transform itself into a constitutional "form" without degenerating into dictatorship or into the turmoil of permanent revolution? What does it mean to begin the experiment of self-government in the right way? Is it possible, for instance, to begin democratically where there was no democracy before? What sort of constitution-making process would promote widespread legitimacy at moments of foundation? Such questions bring home to us the central problem addressed in this book: the problem of democratic founding.

The Importance of Founding Moments

This book is about the importance of founding moments for the project of constitutional democracy. Its basic thesis is quite simple: *how* constitutions are made (or their pedigree) is morally and politically as significant as *what* they are made of (or their content).[2] In making this claim, I take my point of departure from a twofold observation. On the one hand, all democratic constitutions feature "the people" as their author and ultimate source of legitimacy. The principle of popular sovereignty has been indispensable to the normative self-understanding of constitutional democratic regimes since the American and French Revolutions. There is no constitutional democracy without popular sovereignty, and we do not recognize a source of authority superior to the people. On the other hand, however, we live in a world characterized by an ever growing awareness of difference and plurality—a world where the notion of a sovereign people acting on one will and speaking in one voice is inevitably met with suspicion. According to its critics, more specifically, the idea of a unified people is implicated in a hegemonic vision of political community, a vision which is almost always imposed on a diverse population through less than salutary means.[3]

Such imposition was unmistakably at work in the Egyptian process of constitution-making. The Muslim Brotherhood took the majority vote as the single and authoritative voice of the people, thereby adopting a winner-take-all approach. But sweeping statements in the name of the people are inherently difference-blind. They tend to ignore diversity and heterogeneity, while at the same time fostering partial interests, particular conceptions of the good and dominant ways of life under the guise of cherished democratic ideals. What this means is that the "people themselves" are never "the people." Lacking a single authoritative voice, they speak in a plurality of voices, and everyone wants to be heard, rightfully, in her own voice.

This leaves us with a pressing question: if the will of the people is the deep source of democratic legitimacy, but if the people speak only in a plurality of voices, then what do we make of constitutional claims of popular sovereignty? Again, every democratic constitution claims to embody the political form that citizens are in some sense supposed to have chosen for themselves. But in what sense, exactly? What is the sense in which the constitution is the expression or the embodiment of the people's will? Or to put it the other way around, how can citizens regard themselves as the authors of the higher law which claims to speak on their behalf? When does a constitution really or genuinely speak for the people? And how does it come to live up to the principle of popular sovereignty in a plausibly nonfictive way? Such questions are no doubt among the fundamental questions of constitutional and democratic theory, but they are especially pertinent to our present condition where the voice of the people turns out to be irrevocably fragmented.

This book has grown from the hunch that founding moments bear a particular significance under the circumstances that I have just described. There is a longstanding tradition in modern political theory—a tradition extending from Thomas Hobbes to John Rawls—that subscribes to a "hypothetical" account of popular sovereignty in one way or another. In this view, popular sovereignty is meant to convey the basic normative insight that political power should be justified in terms of those general principles that everyone—in their collective capacity as "the people"—*would* consent to, had they been acting on good will and right reason. But if the voice of the people is fragmented, if everyone wants to speak and to be heard in her or his own voice, then no such abstract or pre-political agreement can be justifiably stipulated in advance, and constitutional claims of popular sovereignty can no longer exclusively or even primarily rest on this type of "hypothetical" argument. That is to say, conversely, a democratic constitution must have a strong foothold in what actual citizens have to say in their own voices about the form and principles of their own political organization. Hence the central thesis of this book: the process of constitution-making (*how* a constitution is made) is morally and politically as significant as the content of the constitution (or *what* it is made of). In other words, I argue that a democratic constitution is not only supposed to set up the institutions of self-government, but it is also supposed to be formed, as much as possible, democratically. Constitutional claims of popular sovereignty would lay claim to democratic legitimacy to the extent that citizens themselves take part in the process of constitution-making, thereby underwriting their constitution in a nonfictive sense.[4]

For reasons that will become clear in due course, I hold that deliberative democratic theory offers the most developed paradigm for exploring the complex nexus between constitutional claims of popular sovereignty and the practice of constitution-making in our pluralistic age.[5] This being said, my argument moves away from a certain trend in deliberative democratic theory, a trend which dissolves actual political participants into an allegedly "subjectless" flow of communication. In a well-known statement of this position, for instance, Jürgen Habermas writes: "The 'self' of the self-organizing legal community disappears in the subjectless forms of communication that regulate the flow of discursive opinion- and will-formation in such a way that their fallible results enjoy the presumption of being reasonable. This is not to denounce the intuition connected with the idea of popular sovereignty but to interpret it intersubjectively."[6] While I agree that models of popular sovereignty subscribing to the notion of the people as a counterfactual macrosubject are no longer tenable, I doubt that a model centered around "subjectless forms of communication" is the sole or even the most plausible alternative. Rather, this book defends a deliberative politics of founding in which concrete forms of political agency play a pivotal role, and the constitution comes to have a toehold in the site of shared democratic experience created thereby. This is essential not only to the democratic legitimacy of a new constitution, I further argue, but also to the *experiential sources* of democratic peoplehood, of which some preliminary remarks are now in order.

The People in the Making

Throughout this book peoplehood comes into focus, primarily, in view of its relation to the normative foundations of constitutional democracy. But the issue of "the people" is prior to and broader than that.[7] Take, for instance, Robert Dahl's well placed question: "When does a collection of persons constitute an entity—'a people'—entitled to govern itself democratically?"[8] In view of the principle of popular sovereignty, a question of this sort indicates a limit condition. Although popular sovereignty presupposes the presence of the people as a "bounded community," it cannot be brought to bear on its composition. After all, how could it be? When the controversy is about the boundaries of the relevant constituency, there indeed seems to be no coherent way of appealing to the people to resolve it. As Bernard Yack puts it: "Who belongs to 'the people' in 1848 Venice, 1955 Algeria, or 1999 Quebec? Inhabitants of Venice, Algeria, or Québec or all of the Austrians and Italians, Frenchmen and Arabs, Anglophones and Francophones who share the boundaries of larger states to which they belonged at the time? . . . You cannot answer such questions without, in effect, taking sides in the issue that you want to put before 'the people.'"[9]

In one sense, of course, there is nothing surprising here. The *normative principle* that all legitimate power comes from the people does not—and more importantly, is not meant to—specify which *concrete group* of human beings should count as a distinct people entitled to self-government. Nonetheless, what determines the composition of the people as a bounded community is hardly irrelevant to the kind of normative claims characterizing the modern doctrine of popular sovereignty, given the fact that the doctrine affirms a voluntarist vision of political community, one that depends on choice and consent.[10] This reveals a problem residing at the heart of the democratic state. While democracy requires a bounded community of sorts, a *demos*, which distinguishes between insiders and outsiders, the moral scope of a voluntarist conception of legitimacy extends to all human beings in principle, making room for the claims of non-citizens, and thereby inscribing an element of radical openness into the concept of the people.[11]

The boundary problem involves a variety of issues (such as state-building, territorial borders, and immigration policies, to name a few) that it is not my purpose to explore here. Nonetheless, it is an important reminder of the fact that claims of peoplehood are contestable at every level of analysis. Hegel certainly did not overstate the point in 1821, when he remarked that "the people" is a "garbled notion."[12] Notice that, alongside the boundary problem, "the people" of constitutional democracy is subject to a further and perhaps philosophically more salient ambiguity. It seems to indicate, as Margaret Canovan aptly observes, "two quite different things" at once: "On the one hand it refers to something collective, abstract, dignified and mysterious: an entity—'the British people' or 'We, the people of the United States'—that has a continuous existence and history, transcending and outliving its individual members. On the other hand it also means those individual members themselves, a collection of ordinary, ever-changing people with their separate lives, interests and views."[13] This ambiguity brings home to us a fundamental (or, if you like, an ontological) question: what is a people? Is it an aggregate of individuals? Or should we rather think of it as a single whole, something like a corporate body? Or, perplexing as it may sound, both at once?

Arguably, much of the best scholarship in contemporary democratic theory would reject the static terms in which this question is posed. According to a variety of theorists working in different traditions, "the people" is neither a counterfactual macro-subject nor an amorphous multitude of individuals, but rather a practice, a doing, a political dynamic of sorts. In the second volume of his influential work, *We the People*, for instance, Bruce Ackerman writes that "for me, 'the People' is not the name of a superhuman being, but the name of an extended process of interaction between political elites and ordinary citizens."[14] From a quite different perspective (drawing on the work of Jacques Rancière), Jason Frank notes that "the people are a political claim, an act of political subjectification, not a pre-given, unified, or naturally bounded empirical entity."[15] In a somewhat similar fashion, Paulina Ochoa Espejo holds that "a people is always in the making and unmaking" because it is a "process, a series of events, rather than a collection of individuals."[16] In all these statements, despite the otherwise important differences among their authors, one finds an *agency-centric* conception of democratic peoplehood.[17]

This book adopts a similar approach. On the view to be defended here, what binds different people into "the people" is collective action, that is, the political experience of constructing life together. I intend to bring this basic insight to bear on the politics of constitution-making. Given the fundamental role that constitutions play—symbolically as well as institutionally, performatively as well as normatively—in the self-definition and self-understanding of the political community as a certain kind of "we," I argue that the politics of constitution-making is at the same time a politics of people-making. Founding moments or constitutional episodes are crucial junctures where the fundamental questions of politics are brought back in for everyone to see and to discuss. In these "extraordinary"[18] moments, the basic terms of the political association come to be (re)negotiated, and the given patterns of collective self-definition are publicly thematized, contested, and rearticulated. These are the stuff that claims of peoplehood are made of.

Alongside normative reasons about the democratic legitimacy of a new constitution, therefore, this book also highlights the importance of founding moments as experiments in democratic peoplehood. To be sure, this is not to say that claims of peoplehood can be decisively settled at any instance or that citizens should, once and for all, bind themselves into "the people" through an episodic act of constitution-making. Insofar as democratic politics is inherently open-ended, both the normative content of the constitution and the identity of the people are bound to remain contested.[19] The point of the matter is rather that what occurs in the process of constitution-making would make a great deal of difference not only in terms of our relation to the constitution or its meaning to us as citizens, but also in terms of our self-understanding as a people in the making. Founding moments leave their imprint in the "stories of peoplehood"[20] we tell about ourselves.

The Paradox of Democratic Founding

Up to this point, I have outlined a twofold argument. It highlights the significance of founding moments, first, in terms of the *democratic legitimacy* of a new constitution, and secondly, in terms of the *experiential sources* of democratic peoplehood. Both claims are basically about why democratic theory should take an interest in the politics of founding. Yet, any attempt to defend the notion of democratic founding (and this is precisely what this book is meant to do) must address itself to a further question: how is it possible—or is it ever possible—to begin democratically, especially when there is no democracy before? In other words, can we bring democracy, paradoxical as it may seem, to bear on the making of the democratic constitution itself? Questions of this sort drive home to us a highly vexing problem, which has been recently flagged as "one of the most intractable issues in political theory,"[21] namely, the paradox of democratic founding.

There is a sense in which, ever since Plato's "noble lie," the tradition of political philosophy has been aware of the fact that acts of foundation are inherently paradoxical. In the *Republic*, so as to introduce the psychological and cultural matrix of the "city in speech," Plato resorts to a rhetorical device, a noble lie or a founding myth, because he realizes that the creation of an optimally just and rational city is subject to a vicious circle: such a city can only be brought about by certain kind of men and women, whose breeding and education, however, is the very task of the same city.[22] In *The Social Contract*, Rousseau brings the same paradox to bear on the core democratic idea of self-legislation for the first time. For the people to act in their constituent capacity, i.e., as the collective author and creator of the constitution, they must be able to take a broader standpoint than the counsels of sheer self-interest and must place the common good at the center of their political considerations. And yet, Rousseau keenly observes, a collective capacity of this sort would only flourish in an *already existing* well-ordered society. It is by virtue of good laws that citizens are educated to take a principled standpoint and to attach themselves to the common good. Hence the outstanding question: how can the people carry out the first act of self-legislation, in fact the most important act of self-legislation, namely the making of the republican constitution, if the kind of moral and political capacities required to perform this act are to develop under an already functioning republican regime? For the people to underwrite their constitution "the effect would have to become the cause . . . and men would have to be prior to laws what they ought to become by means of them."[23]

To escape this vicious circle, Rousseau appeals to a "great lawgiver," who is supposed to educate the people into the ethos of self-legislation. Yet, this means that the achievement of political autonomy remains contingent upon a heteronomous intervention in the Rousseauian republic. A rift seems to open up between the *political origins* of the republic and its *normative foundations*, between the way in which political community gets off the ground and the principles on which it is meant to rest. While the act of foundation, carried out through the heteronomous agency of the great lawgiver, invokes certain normative principles and creates the suitable conditions for their realization, it cannot be justified, strictly speaking, from the standpoint of those very principles.

Needless to say, Rousseau's vision of political community integrated through a thick and substantive ethical consensus has considerably lost its normative purchase today. But the paradox of democratic founding is still with us—in two main forms, I think. For one, democratic constitution-making under conditions of diversity and plurality is itself a matter of ethos, though not in the same way envisioned by Rousseau. Citizens do not need to cohere around a particular conception of the good rooted in a single regime of republican ethos. Yet, if they are to construct "we the people" without erasing difference, they must still engage with one another in such a way as to build mutual trust and seek resolutions that are acceptable to all. This, in turn, requires a political culture of deliberation as well as certain forms of civic competence which are unlikely to have developed in societies where democracy is not already in practice. The kind of circularity that Rousseau so acutely diagnosed in *The Social Contract* is hard to miss in such transitional cases. South Africa had to face it in 1994, Egypt in 2012, but with tremendously different results.[24]

Democratic constitution-making appears to be paradoxical in yet another way: law and democracy presuppose one another. Notice that a constitution is an instrument or medium of self-organization. Its task is to set up the enabling conditions of democratic will-formation such as laws, procedures, and institutions by means of which a multitude of citizens would come to make collective decisions as a people. But if this is so, then, how is it possible for the people to underwrite their constitution, given the fact that the enabling conditions of democratic will-formation are to be set up by the constitution itself? While the constitution rests on the people for its democratic legitimacy, the people—in a perfectly circular fashion—rest on the constitution for their democratic agency. Again, it seems that every act of foundation with a democratic claim is inevitably caught up in a vicious circle.

In both of these versions, the paradox of democratic founding is a recurrent theme in contemporary political theory. It has been stated and analyzed by a variety of theorists working in different traditions.[25] Despite the rich variety of interpretations, however, what runs like a red thread through these contemporary treatments is a skeptical gesture, according to which the idea of democratic founding is at best self-contradictory and hence theoretically unsustainable, and at worst a hegemonic fiction that conceals the arbitrary origins of political power.[26] Edmund Burke once commented that "there is a sacred veil to be drawn over the beginnings of all governments."[27] Contemporary theorists prying into the paradox of democratic founding claim to draw aside this veil. Since the people themselves are never "the people" and hence unable to underwrite their constitution, we are told, the establishment of democratic autonomy is necessarily implicated in a heteronomous intervention, a moment of speaking in the name of a people that does not yet exist. As such, these theorists want to have us acknowledge the ways in which the making of the democratic constitution performatively contradicts the basic principles that it seeks to foster, and hence bring to our attention the crucial discrepancies between the normative foundations of constitutional democracy and its political origins.

A central agenda of this book is to engage in a critical dialogue with this "agonistic" line of interpretation. In doing so, my intention is not to dismiss the wide range of important issues that it brings to our attention. Viewed from an agonistic point of view, the paradox of founding is a potent motif that keeps us alert about the ways in which appeals to "the people" are inherently contestable, law may remain alien to its alleged authors, and the politics of founding may turn out to be a hegemonic enterprise which covers its own tracks. Without dismissing its merits, however, I argue that this line of interpretation is also prone to *hypostatize* the problem. What I mean by "hypostatization" is basically a strategy of problem statement, which directly transposes the formal or logical structure of the paradox onto the realm of political action.[28] An essentially political issue is thereby turned into a logical puzzle, an insurmountable aporia or impasse, which rules out the notion of democratic founding at its core.

Once the problem is hypostatized in this way, the paradox of democratic founding leaves us with a discomforting dichotomy between the "two bodies" of the people. On the one hand, we have the picture of an "amorphous multitude" incapable of any positive or constituent action whatsoever; on the other hand, we have the opposite picture of "the people" as a constitutionally organized corporate body capable of acting only in and through the institutional edifice of the state. This strikes me as a false dichotomy. There is a whole gray area extending between its poles, and the politics of democratic founding actually takes place in that gray area. If we are to reorient ourselves in this uncertain territory, we need to think about the people differently: neither as an amorphous multitude nor as a corporate body, but as a community of action in the making. And to do so, we also need a different vantage point, a different interpretive angle, from which to approach the paradox of democratic founding.

In this book, I propose to take the paradox under consideration as a *heuristic problem*. By "heuristic," I mean two things at once, both of which are related to discovery and problem solving, though from different points of view. From the observer point of view (i.e., the perspective of the political theorist), a heuristic approach stands in opposition to an aporetic one. On this register, the basic idea I want to defend is that the paradox of democratic founding does not necessarily lead us into an impasse, but opens up to us a gray area, in which the conditions of democratic peoplehood are in the making. The heuristic task of the theorist is to discover and navigate this gray area.[29] From the participant point of view (i.e., the perspective of political actors), I suggest that the quest for democratic founding is best understood as a process of problem solving. Take for instance the question of how to remain under the law while at the same time making the higher law. Citizens and framers typically grapple with such questions at moments of foundation.

Even if logically irresolvable, questions of this sort can be politically negotiated, and *how* they are negotiated would make all the difference in the world. To recapitulate, then, viewed as a heuristic problem, the paradox of founding does not rule out the possibility of a democratic act of foundation but rather invites us to investigate, doggedly and seriously, how to make sense of it.

Overview of the Chapters

In what follows, our inquiry begins with an observation about two central tenets of modern constitutionalism: first, the constitution is the product of a deliberate founding act, and second, it features the people as its author and ultimate source of legitimacy. Chapter 1 examines how these two motifs relate to each other. In contrast to a longstanding and influential tradition in modern and contemporary political thought, I argue that democratic theory can no longer heavily draw on the abstract notion of "the people," which informs hypothetical conceptions of popular sovereignty. What this means is that constitutional claims of popular sovereignty cannot be clearly severed from the modus operandi of the founding act, and citizens themselves must be included in the process of constitution-making.

In Chapter 2, I take up the vexing question of whether a democratic act of constitution-making is conceptually possible. The chapter offers a survey of canonical and contemporary takes on the paradox of founding, beginning with Rousseau's *The Social Contract* as well as the classical texts of the American and French Revolutions, and extending to the works of Jacques Derrida, William Connolly, Bonnie Honig, and Frank Michelman. But it also has a critical agenda, particularly with regard to the ways the paradox of founding is hypostatized in contemporary political theory. In contrast, I propose to take the paradox under consideration as a heuristic problem, one which allows us to think of the people neither as an amorphous multitude nor a corporate body, but as a community of action in the making.

The next two chapters are intended to pursue this possibility in the company of Rousseau and Arendt. In Chapter 3, I look at the complicated but often poorly analyzed relationship between the people and the lawgiver in Rousseau's work. Inspired by his reflections on Corsica, I argue that it is not the lawgiver who calls forth the people but the other way around. That is to say, it is the collective agency of a people in the making that prepares the suitable conditions for legislation. Chapter 4 offers a close reading of Arendt's

Jewish writings, most of which were penned during the turbulent 1940s. Attending to the role of collective action in transforming and redefining "who we are," these essays contain a rich reflection on the formation of the people in and through the shared experience of action, and especially the kind of world-building action oriented toward the creation of a "homeland." Taken together, thus, these chapters are meant to move us beyond the dichotomy between the "two bodies" of the people and to reorient our thinking about the possibility of democratic founding.

Chapters 5 and 6 focus on the problem of legitimacy. The central question that I aim to address in these chapters is the following: if the people themselves are not and can never be "the people" in whose name democratic constitutions claim to speak, then, are we not supposed to conclude that there is an unavoidable moment of "performative force," a moment of "original violence," which impugns every act of foundation with a democratic intent? My short answer is: it depends. Acts of foundation with a democratic claim may indeed turn out to be hegemonic enterprises, concealing their own groundlessness. But there is no conceptual necessity here, and the process of constitution-making itself can become a legitimacy-generating praxis.

More specifically, engaging with Arendt's *On Revolution* in Chapter 5, I suggest that the classical doctrine of constituent power, developed by Abbé Sieyès and later selectively appropriated by Carl Schmitt, cannot avoid the charge of foundational illegitimacy. This is why, at least in part, Arendt does not trace the legitimacy of a new constitution back to the allegedly united will of "the people" understood as a counterfactual macro-subject, but to the way and spirit in which the act of foundation is carried out. Based on a reconstructive reading of *On Revolution*, I argue that Arendt thereby points toward an account of constitution-making in which the question of "how" enjoys the place of pride, and that this is her most essential contribution to a theory of democratic founding.

Chapter 6 moves on to negotiate the problem of legitimacy from the standpoint of deliberative democratic theory in general, and in dialogue with Habermas in particular. A central tenet of deliberative democratic theory is that law and democracy belong together, or that they presuppose one another at a fundamental conceptual level. But is it possible to retain the interdependence of law and democracy at moments of foundation? How to exercise popular sovereignty in such a way as to create a new constitution while at the same time remaining "under the law"? I argue that deliberative democratic theory offers a fruitful paradigm to negotiate this question. More specifically,

I will try to show that it is possible to envision the reciprocal establishment of legal authority and democratic legitimacy, step by step, in a series of back and forth movements—so that the interdependence of law and democracy are performatively retained and realized in the course of building a constitutional democratic regime.

In the Conclusion, I draw together the various strands of argument thus far made, and bring them to bear on broader issues at play in contemporary democratic theory. At the same time, however, these concluding reflections are meant to highlight the basic insight that has stimulated this book in the first place: the founding act of the people is not a fantasy of democratic idealism, but it is a living and action-orienting idea in transformation.

Chapter 1

Origins and Foundations

Two Features of the Modern Constitution

The concept of founding is closely related to a certain way of thinking about political community, one which has a longstanding pedigree in modern political theory. In this way of thinking, political association is first and foremost a human artifact, something deliberately made or created "from reflection and choice."[1] Accordingly, in contrast to "ancient constitutionalism," the constitution of the polity is not seen as an inheritance, a felicitous gift of time and tradition, but as a founding charter.[2] It is the work of a "constituent power," and claims to express the deliberate will of the people. While this idea is familiar, it is by no means unambiguous. It points in two directions at once, referring us both to the *origins* of the political community and to the *foundations* it claims to rest on.

The term "origin" has an unmistakable temporal meaning which designates a starting point in time. It is about how the story begins and where we come from. From the vantage point of modern constitutionalism, founding in this sense amounts to the historically decisive act that creates a new constitution. Of course, this is not to say that political communities begin ex nihilo. The idea is rather that there are ruptures and new beginnings, which bring about new forms of political association and hence come to be marked as founding moments.[3] Unlike the temporal meaning of "origin," the term "foundation" conveys a primarily normative meaning, which is in turn colored by spatial metaphors: a place to stand on, a firm ground on which something else is built, a layer that lies beneath as a substratum. If origins are about where we come from as a community, foundations are about what makes us a certain kind of "we," what our political association rests on, or what we take to be its ground. In the tradition of modern constitutionalism, this foundation or ground is typically understood in voluntarist terms, according to which political community depends on the will of citizens in their collective capacity as "the people." Hence the foundational principle of popular sovereignty.

On the one hand, then, we have the temporal motif of a new beginning crystallized in the act of constitution-making. On the other hand, we have the normative motif of "the people" whose united will is claimed to be the matrix of the constitution. While both are characteristic features of modern constitutionalism, their relation to one another is nonetheless far from clear. According to an influential tradition in modern political theory, beginning with Hobbes and extending to the present day in various ways, these two motifs must be kept apart at a fundamental conceptual level. We are told that there is no substantial or theoretically demonstrable relationship between "origins" and "foundations," between the way in which a constitution happens to be framed and its capacity to speak for the people. On this view, constitutional claims of popular sovereignty are to be vindicated not in terms of the pedigree of a constitution but in terms of its content. To quote a contemporary restatement: "Popular sovereignty is a *feature* of political regimes rather than something actually exercised *prior* to the establishment of political regimes. The question is not whether it was the people that created the state for itself by some original act but what the practice of authorization is like in the state, once it has been established."[4] In the present chapter, I challenge this view.

My contention is that such a neat distinction between origins and foundations turns out to be less and less tenable in the contemporary world as the counterfactual picture of a unified people speaking in one voice and acting on one will has become increasingly problematic. Accordingly, I argue that the foundational principles of a democratic constitution—including, most notably, popular sovereignty—must be performatively manifest in its origins, and that citizens themselves must be included in the making of the democratic constitution that claims to speak for them. On the view defended here, citizen consultation and participation in the constitution-making process is important both for *normative* reasons regarding the democratic legitimacy of a new constitution and for *experiential* reasons regarding the formation of democratic peoplehood. In what follows, to put these claims in some perspective, I begin with a detour in the history of political thought, visiting some early objections to the consent theory of political legitimacy and Kant's attempt to counter those objections by means of a "hypothetical" account of popular sovereignty. A discussion on the limits and problems of hypothetical popular sovereignty will then bring us back to the central claim introduced above, allowing us to elaborate on it.

Popular Sovereignty in Question: Two Early Objections

A crucial problem that came up with full force in the context of the struggle between Royalists and Parliamentarians in the seventeenth-century England was the meaning of the term "people." Did the term primarily refer to an empirical entity, an aggregate of flesh-and-blood individuals, or something more abstract, a single whole which was to be conceived along the model of a corporate body? Robert Filmer, the arduous proponent of the doctrine of the divine rights of kings, picked up on the former interpretation of the term, and suggested that it was impossible to rely on the people and their consent as the source of political legitimacy because the people were nothing but an ever-changing multitude. In a famous passage, he wrote: "For the people, to speak truly and properly, is a thing or body in continual alteration and change. It never continues one minute the same, being composed of a multitude of parts whereof divers continually decay and perish, and others renew and succeed in their places. They which are the people this minute, are not the people the next minute."[5] With a twist of argument which is not rare in the history of political thought, however, what seemed to Filmer as the fatal weakness of an appeal to the people turned out to be a stepping-stone for its proponents. According to the Parliamentarians, it was precisely because the people themselves were never and could never be *present* as such that they stood in need of *representation*, and this was what the Parliament was basically all about. The idea was that the people were present as a corporate body in and through the Parliament and therefore the consent of the latter counted as the consent of the former.[6]

In Filmer's view, however, a move of this sort was far from satisfactory. He thought that such an argument undermined the rationale of invoking the people in the first place and hence attested to the inner contradictions of a consent theory of political legitimacy. So, he pushed the point: "If it be answered, that it is impossible to stand so strictly as to have the consent of the whole people, and therefore that which cannot be must be supposed to be the act of the whole people; this is a strange answer, first to affirm a necessity of having the people's consent, then to confess an impossibility of having it."[7]

Once the people is taken to be a corporate body rather than an aggregate of flesh-and-blood individuals, Filmer rightly observes, consent itself turns out to be hypothetical. Nor is this the sole problem. Filmer continues: "If but once that liberty [i.e., the right to consent]—which is esteemed so sacred—be broken or taken away but from one of the meanest or basest of all the people, a wide gap is thereby opened for any multitude whatsoever that is able to call themselves (or whomsoever they please) the people."[8] On the one hand, urging his opponents that they are on a slippery slope, Filmer's rhetoric is meant to play on the gentlemen's fear of the multitude. On the other hand, and beyond this rhetorical move, he perceptively points out a permanent problem of all democratic politics. If the actual consent of each and every individual is impossible to achieve, then, who is entitled to speak in the name of "the people"? And how do we—or can we ever—adjudicate between competing claims of representation?

Although we cannot further pursue here the historical unfolding of the argumentative battle between Royalists and Parliamentarians, it is important to note that, regardless of the rival claims about the proper locus of representation, a crucial effect of the entire debate was to entrench the notion of "the people" as designating an abstract and corporate entity alongside the concrete and natural body of an ever-changing multitude.[9] As we will see in a moment, this has been crucial for the development of philosophically more sophisticated accounts of popular sovereignty such as Kant's. If the people is envisioned as a corporate body rather than an atomistic aggregate of individuals, then it makes sense to speak of it as the matrix of common or generalizable interests that are putatively shared by everyone no matter what their differences might be in other respects. Before turning to Kant, however, it is worth taking a moment to consider a different kind of challenge to the consent theory of political legitimacy.

This other challenge came from David Hume. Unlike Filmer, Hume did not attack the idea of consent in the name of the divine rights of kings. He admits that "consent is one just foundation of government where it has place," and "it is surely the best and most sacred of any"—the problem is rather that "it has very seldom had place in any degree, and never almost in its full extent."[10] States are ordinarily established by force and violence, Hume observes, not through consent or voluntary association. "Almost all the governments, which exist at present, or of which there remains any record in story, have been founded originally, either on usurpation or conquest, or both, without any pretence of a fair consent, or voluntary subjection of the people."[11] While in an already established state, "in a settled constitution," people's inclinations are occasionally taken into consideration, Hume further observes, "were one to choose a period of time, when the people's consent was the least regarded in public transactions, it would be precisely on the establishment of a new government"—that is to say, it is precisely in founding moments, "during the fury of revolutions, conquests, and public convulsions," that consent is systematically disregarded and "military force or political craft usually decides the controversy."[12]

These may seem as merely descriptive claims about the historical origins of political order. Yet Hume's point is more subtle than it seems at first sight. He intends to suggest that *historical origins* of political order should not be viewed as irrelevant to the ways we make sense of its *moral foundations*. Political legitimacy (on the part of government) and political obligation (on the part of the people) do not actually rest on consent. The fact that states have originated in violence and attained legitimacy over time points toward a ground other than popular consent or voluntary agreement. According to Hume, to grasp this other source of legitimacy, one needs to inquire into habit and utility, into "the general interests and necessities of society," into how "time and custom give authority to all forms of government" and how "power, which at first was founded only on injustice and violence, becomes in time legal and obligatory."[13]

In drawing our attention to the gradual growth, via custom and utility, of a sense of legitimacy from a violent origin, Hume also touches on the retrospective justification of unjust beginnings in the imagination of present generations, thereby bringing up, at least by implication, the issue of the obliteration of founding violence. Consider the following passage: "Tho' the accession of the Prince of Orange to the throne might at first give occasion to many disputes, and his title be contested, it ought not now to appear doubtful, but must have acquir'd a sufficient authority from those three princes, who have succeeded him upon the same title. Nothing is more usual, tho' nothing may, at first sight, appear more unreasonable, than this way of thinking. Princes often seem to acquire a right from their successors, as well as from their ancestors."[14] The strange condition mentioned by Hume—that of a prince acquiring a title from his successors—is by no means peculiar to monarchy but applies to every founding act, including those with a democratic claim. In this respect, his remark about the Prince of Orange intriguingly resonates with Jacques Derrida's reflections on the retrospective justification of revolutionary violence: "All revolutionary situations . . . justify the recourse to violence by alleging the founding, in progress or to come, of a new law. As this law to come will in return legitimate, retrospectively, the violence that may offend the sense of justice, its future anterior already justifies it."[15] Derrida makes this point in the context of a discussion about the paradox of founding, which we will explore at length in Chapter 2.

The Founding Act of the People as an "Idea of Reason": Kant

One way to counter Filmer's and Hume's objections to the consent theory of political legitimacy is to offer a "hypothetical" account of popular sovereignty. In this kind of argument, the stress is not on the actual consent of the people but on what the people *would* consent to if they were to act on good will and right reason.[16] In other words, "the people," understood as a corporate body acting on a unanimous will and speaking in a single voice, is not an empirical reality and does not need to be. Rather, it is a vision of political legitimacy, a normative idea, according to which all political power comes from the united will of citizens and therefore ought to be structured in terms of the equal freedom and generalizable interests of everyone. This hypothetical conception of popular sovereignty is most systematically developed by Kant.

Speaking from within the contractarian tradition, Kant presents the founding act of the people as the "original contract," while at the same time urging that this contract should not be taken as a historical event: "as a fact it is indeed not possible," he notes, "it is instead only an idea of reason."[17] Or as he puts it elsewhere in a more systematic fashion: "The act by which a people forms itself into a state is the original contract. Properly speaking, the original contract is only the idea of this act, in terms of which alone we can think of the legitimacy of a state. In accordance with the original contract, everyone (*omnes et singuli*) within a people gives up his external freedom in order to take it up again immediately as a member of a commonwealth, that is, of a people considered as a state (*universi*)."[18] Kant's point is that the normative structure of the state, as a public order in which coercive power ought to be compatible with and justifiable in terms of individual freedom, makes sense only in light of the notion of self-determination—that is, the idea of a sovereign people placing themselves under a self-legislated law. This does not mean that citizens ought to be the actual authors of their constitution, but that actual legislators and constitution makers (whoever they happen to be) ought to give their laws "in such a way that they *could have arisen* from the united will of a whole people and to regard each subject, insofar as he wants to be a citizen, as if he has joined in voting for such a will."[19] Hence the main point of Kant's claim: the founding act of the people is an "idea of reason."

By presenting the original contract in this way, Kant aims at two things at once: to disentangle the concept of popular sovereignty from the troublesome problem of demonstrating actual consent, and to counter what he takes to be the historicist misunderstanding of the social contract theory such as Hume's claim that states are ordinarily founded through force and violence, and not through consent or voluntary agreement. Kant admits the historical unreality of a consensual act of foundation, but does not regard this as a refutation of contractarian arguments. He can easily afford to do so because the original contract is an "idea of reason," which has nothing to do with actual consent and the kind of historical contingencies that Hume is keen to highlight. What makes this solution work, however, needs to be spelled out more clearly.

Kant draws a clear distinction between the actual origins of the state and the normative foundations according to which its legitimacy is to be understood. In a sense, this distinction was already established by Hobbes in the *Leviathan*. According to Hobbes, even though "there is scarce a commonwealth in the world whose beginnings can in conscience be justified," there nevertheless exists no de jure difference between a "commonwealth by institution" and a "commonwealth by acquisition."[20] That is to say, political authority may have been established as well through force and conquest ("acquisition") as through contract ("institution") because "the rights and consequences of sovereignty are the same in both."[21] Kant follows Hobbes on this score. "Whether a state began with an actual contract of submission (*pactum subjectionis civilis*) as a fact, or whether power came first and law arrived only afterward, or even whether they should have followed in this order," he maintains emphatically, "for a people already subject to civil law these subtle reasonings are altogether pointless."[22] The basic idea is that there is a sharp distinction to be drawn between "origins" and "foundations," between the way in which a political community happens to be established and the normative principles that it is supposed to rest on. While the former is a "question of fact" regarding historical contingencies which may unfold in all sorts of ways, the latter is a "question of right" regarding principles—and no matter what, the two should not be conflated.

With regards to the "question of right" under consideration, however, Kant substantively disagrees with Hobbes, and takes issue with what we might call the private will model of the social contract theory. That political authority rests on our consent and that we are obliged to abide by it on account of our own will has been *the* point of contractarian arguments from Hobbes onward. Kant thinks that there is something deeply unsatisfactory in this idea: how can the consent of *private* individuals, each of whom after all acts on his own particular will, produce a *public* authority? The issue at stake is not simply a matter of enforcement as Hobbes would want to have us believe when, for example, he famously maintains that "covenants without the sword are but words."[23] For Kant, there is a deeper issue at stake, and it is one of *perspective*.

The fundamental distinction between private will and public authority is that while the former indicates a partial (or unilateral) point of view, the latter is by definition bound to proceed from an impartial (or omnilateral) one.[24] A contractarian theory representing the state as the product of an agreement between private wills is defective as a way of understanding the normative structure of the state because a coalition of partial perspectives, no matter how inclusive and voluntary such coalition might be, does not in itself add up to impartiality. This is precisely why Kant argues—strictly following Rousseau on this point—that public authority could only be based on the united will of "everyone (*omnes et singuli*) within a people." A united will of this sort, in its turn, requires each person (*singuli*) to take the perspective of the whole (*omnes*) and thereby to adopt an impartial point of view. Thus, in the Kantian framework, the original contract does not so much stand for a hypothetical act of promise making. Rather, it is first and foremost a hypothetical act of *perspective taking*. It is meant to articulate what everyone would consistently agree to if each of them were to take the standpoint of the whole.

On this view, then, to express it in the language of consent, public authority is legitimate and compatible with freedom not because we give our consent to it whether explicitly or tacitly, but because it is *worthy of our consent* on account of the impartial perspective from which it is structured.[25] Accordingly, constitutional claims of popular sovereignty do not rest on the people themselves. They are anchored in the hypothetical voice of the people, which speaks in terms of generalizable interests alone, thereby setting the rational principle of public law as such. In this way, Kant claims to have countered the aforementioned objections made by Filmer and Hume.

What Is the Problem with Hypothetical Popular Sovereignty?

This hypothetical conception of popular sovereignty has nonetheless become deeply problematic in the contemporary world. To give an overview of the problem, I want to distinguish between three ways in which it comes in for criticism. Let me call them "philosophical," "deliberative," and "pluralist" objections, respectively. The philosophical objection has to do with the metaphysical background against which hypothetical arguments are justified. In the Kantian scheme, the impartial perspective from which a "civil constitution" ought to be framed is not something we achieve ourselves in the real world through opinion exchange and political debate, through contestation, deliberation, and persuasion. Rather, it is *already there*, objectively and universally, set by practical reason alone in an a priori fashion. It is claimed to be accessible to all rational beings in the same way.

This means that the "original contract" designates a criterion of legitimacy which transcends all time and place. In Kant's telling formulation, it is a "Platonic ideal (*respublica noumenon*), which is not an empty figment of the imagination, but the eternal norm for all civil constitutions whatsoever."[26] A claim of this sort, however, is of course notoriously resistant to proof like all arguments about "first principles," "natural law" or "self-evident truths." Insofar as they appeal to an independent order of verification, which is beyond and above our temporal reality, such arguments are met with profound skepticism today. This is why prominent neo-Kantians such as Rawls and Habermas opt for, in their own ways, a philosophical program of intersubjective validation instead of a metaphysics of practical reason.

Hypothetical accounts of popular sovereignty come in for further criticism from a deliberative point of view. Notice that, for Kant, the legitimacy of public law is not related to what real citizens actually have to say on the subject of their constitution, on the forms and principles of their own political organization. Legitimacy is detached from the deliberative agency of citizens at a fundamental conceptual level, and tied instead to a formal test of consistency: "if it is only possible that a people could agree to it," Kant writes, "it is a duty to consider the law just, even if the people is at present in such a situation or frame of mind that, if consulted about it, it would probably refuse its consent."[27] While the hypothetical voice of the people, speaking in terms of generalizable interests alone, sets the rational principle of public law as such, the actual voices of the people are stripped of their constituent capacity.

It is important to realize that this problem applies to *all* models of hypothetical agreement whether or not they rest on metaphysical assumptions. Rawls's "original position" is a case in point.[28] Unlike the Kantian "original contract," the Rawlsian model does not involve any transcendental grounding. However, it leads to a similar deficit insofar as rational agreement is not the outcome of actual deliberation but a function of the theoretical design of the original position. This is one of the central challenges posed by Habermas in his critical encounter with Rawls. Consider the following remark:

> From the perspective of the theory of justice, the act of founding the democratic constitution cannot be repeated under the institutional conditions of an already constituted just society, and the process of realizing the system of basic rights cannot be assured on an ongoing basis. It is not possible for the citizens to experience this process as open and incomplete, as the shifting historical circumstances nonetheless demand. They cannot reignite the radical democratic embers of the original position in the civic life of their society, for from their perspective all of the essential discourses of legitimation have already taken place within the theory; and they find the results of the theory already sedimented in the constitution.[29]

At a fundamental conceptual level, Habermas's criticism turns on the meaning of political autonomy. "Citizens are politically autonomous only if they can view themselves as the joint authors of the laws to which they are subject as individual addressees."[30] By severing constitutional essentials from actual processes of political will-formation, however, Rawls's hypothetical model brings a substantive limitation to the quest for political autonomy. Consequently, as the Rawlsian "veil of ignorance" is raised step by step, citizens "find themselves subject to principles and norms that have been anticipated in theory and have already become institutionalized beyond their control."[31] There is a sense in which models of hypothetical agreement are inherently prone to compromise the promise of political autonomy.

Finally, in the contemporary world, hypothetical conceptions of popular sovereignty face the further challenge of pluralism. In an age of cultural diversity and struggles for recognition, the counterfactual picture of "the people" speaking in a single voice has increasingly come in for criticism as a hegemonic vision of political community, one which is imposed on a diverse population. Accordingly, statements in the name of "we the people" are claimed to be inherently difference-blind, to ignore diversity and heterogeneity, while at the same time fostering partial interests, particular conceptions of the good and dominant ways of life under the guise of cherished democratic ideals. Of course, this is not to say that the people don't speak. The point of the matter is rather that they speak in a plurality of voices—and crucially, everyone wants to be heard in her own voice.

This poses a pressing problem for contemporary democratic theory. If there is no "we the people" speaking in a unified voice, or if the voice of the people is more like a cacophony than a symphony, then what do we make of constitutional claims of popular sovereignty? Or, to put it differently, how can we account for the democratic legitimacy of a new constitution if there is no privileged and uncontestable vantage point from which to discern the supposedly "real voice" of the people? Simone Chambers sums up the problem succinctly: "on the one hand, we need a 'people' to be able to speak as one to fulfill the voluntarist aspirations of modern constitutionalism; on the other hand, creating a 'people' through assimilation and verbal fiat now appears to violate the very same democratic or voluntarist aspirations."[32]

The Normative and Experiential Significance of Founding Moments

Thus far, using Kant's argument about the "original contract" as the foil of discussion, I have looked at some contemporary objections to the hypothetical conception of popular sovereignty. It is now time to ask what follows from these objections. One important conclusion I want to draw is that the inclusion of the "people themselves"—that is, the people in their diversity and plurality, as well as in their embodiment and their empirical singularity—in the constitution-making process is essential to the *democratic legitimacy* of a new constitution. We live in a world where the abstract picture of a united people speaking in one voice has been irrevocably fragmented, where arguments about what everyone would agree to if they were rational and acting on good will turn out to be deeply controversial, and where democratic legitimacy can no longer be categorically severed from actual democratic agency. This point has a further corollary, which is of particular importance for our present purposes: the distinction between "origins" and "foundations" cannot remain intact under such circumstances. We can no longer draw a sharp line between the *pedigree* of a democratic constitution and its substantive *content*, between the way a political community happens to be established and the principles that it claims to rest on. To redeem their democratic credentials, in other words, constitutional claims of popular sovereignty must have a strong foothold in what the people themselves actually have to say in their own voices on the forms and principles of their own political organization.

To avoid misunderstanding, nothing I say here is meant to suggest that inclusion or participation is a magic stick in and of itself. The quest for a genuinely democratic act of constitution-making—in the sense of an inclusive and participatory exercise of popular sovereignty—is subject to conceptual paradoxes and practical limitations, as we will see in the following chapters. Nor do I suggest that the authorship of the constitution is or must be taken as the sole criterion that determines its legitimacy. Obviously, such an approach to the question of constitutional legitimacy, stressing the importance of pedigree and authorship, is inherently ill-equipped to account for what makes the constitution binding over time or what makes it binding for future generations.[33] At the moment, I just intend to highlight one single point: given the problems of a hypothetical account of popular sovereignty, and given the significant changes that have taken place in our notions of what it means for the people to speak, the "how" of constitution-making must be regarded as equal in importance to the "what" of the constitution itself. Or to put it in slightly different terms, the guiding principles of the democratic constitution must be performatively manifest in its making. This offers us one kind of reason, a *normative* reason, regarding the importance of founding moments for democratic theory.

Arguably, the stress that I have been placing on founding moments may seem to stand in tension with the dynamic and open-ended character of a democratic constitution. A constitutional settlement is always provisional and fallible in principle, and hence open to contestation, interpretation and revision. One might therefore suggest that we need to think of democratic self-determination not so much along the model of an episodic founding act taking place at one crucial *moment*, but rather in terms of an ongoing *process* that extends over time.[34] This dynamic or process-based approach to constitutional democracy, one might further argue, requires a corresponding shift in our conception of political legitimacy. In a recent article, Christopher Zurn presents an argument precisely to this effect. "A governmental system is legitimate," he claims, "to the degree to which its political processes, institutions, and laws provide good evidence that it has instantiated and will continue to instantiate the project of constitutional democracy in a dynamic, self-correcting, and thus progressive manner."[35] On this view, according to Zurn, "the origins of a polity are irrelevant in a significant sense: legitimacy is not a matter that can be settled by looking at the pedigree of a political system."[36] What matters is not how the project of constitutional democracy gets off the ground but rather how it moves on: whether it keeps going in such a way as to progressively realize its own guiding aspirations. "Judgments of legitimacy are thereby constitutively severed from the *who* and the *how* of a polity's founding—what matters is *what* was thereby put into motion."[37]

I do agree that it is important to view constitutional democracy as a work in progress, a dynamic and open-ended enterprise, which moves on through practices of deliberation and contestation, trial and error, self-correction and piecemeal transformation. In my view, however, a process-based approach along these lines neither requires us to drop the question of founding nor rules out its significance. After all, how plausible is it to divorce judgments of legitimacy, completely and severely, from considerations of authorship, especially in the case of a *new* constitutional order?

Zurn seems to think that in assessing the legitimacy of a new constitution we must exclusively focus on its content and we must do so in a specifically prospective or forward-looking fashion, say, by looking at "how likely its political processes, institutions and laws are to lead to achieving and reflexively developing the project of the realization of constitutional democratic ideals."[38] However, just as hypothetical arguments about what everyone *would* agree to if they were rational cannot replace actual deliberation, conjectural judgments about how *likely* it is that the structural features of a new constitution would enable a democratic process in the future cannot substitute for the kind of legitimacy stemming from practices of opinion- and will-formation at present. It is important to emphasize the open-ended nature of constitutional democracy as a work in progress not because authorship does not matter, but because no author, including the people themselves, can claim to achieve a once and for all constitutional settlement at a single point in time.

Apart from the issue of original legitimation, there is yet another reason why founding moments matter: how the project of constitutional democracy gets off the ground would make a good deal of difference with regards to its future prospects. To get a better grasp of this point, it helps to consider what actually makes constitutional democracy an *open-ended* project in the first place. In my view, a dynamic constitution is not simply a revisable or amendable constitution. Beyond and above this rather formal requirement, a dynamic constitution is supposed to set in motion a democratic process, while at the same time standing in relation to it in a responsive manner—so that new interpretations, new meanings, and new stories of citizenship would be grafted on to the constitution as the political community keeps changing. For this to happen, however, the constitution must take root in *political culture*. That is to say, it must belong to citizens not only in a formal sense (say, as the law of the land), but also and more importantly in an *experiential* sense (say, as their own law).

The pedigree of a constitution, I want to stress now, matters a great deal in terms of what the constitution means to citizens in this experiential sense. After all, supposing that we are talking about the founding generation and not later generations, when does a new constitution become our own? How do we come to claim a joint ownership in it in our capacity as citizens? Especially at moments of foundation, when new constitutional orders are in the making, this is not only a matter of content, but as much depends on whether or to what extent the process of framing the constitution itself is *experienced* as a joint enterprise. To put it the other way, so long as citizens themselves are not included in the practice of constitution-making in the right way—or worse, if they are not consulted at all—one can hardly expect them to recognize themselves in the outcome and take it as an expression of their own will in some stepped-up, amplified sense. Getting all the "right stuff" in the text of the constitution would make little difference in this respect, which is not to say that content does not matter for other important reasons. The point is rather that the "how" of a constitutional founding shapes our relation to the constitution—and our self-understanding as a political community at large—in ways that cannot be reduced to or fully compensated by considerations about the "what." Alongside normative reasons regarding the original legitimation of a new constitution, then, there are also *experiential* reasons as to why founding moments should matter for democratic theory. The kind of political experience that marks the making of a new constitution is important because it makes a difference in its meaning to us and in its prospects of taking root in political culture over time.

Democratic Regimes with Undemocratic Beginnings

I have been arguing that, from the standpoint of democratic theory, *how* constitutions are made (their pedigree) is as important as *what* they are made of (their content). Before concluding this chapter, let me address a forceful objection to this claim—an objection based on the case of successful democracies that have obviously undemocratic constitutional beginnings. Christopher Zurn poses the challenge in a clear way: "Consider, as examples, the Allies' virtual imposition of the German Basic Law and the Japanese Constitution after the end of World War II. Arguably both constitutions have both the requisite conceptual content to count as legitimate constitutional democracies and the historical record of having sustained constitutionally successful and democratically decent political practices and institutions for some sixty years. Might even such successful constitutional democracies be illegitimate in light of their nondemocratic origins?"[39]

Admittedly, the short answer—my short answer—to such a question is "no." A constitution which was not made democratically in the first place may indeed come to be embraced and regarded as democratically legitimate over time. The German Basic Law and the Constitution of Japan are good cases in point. Today, they can be said to bear democratic legitimacy precisely because generations of citizens have gradually appropriated these documents and made them their own constitutions in and through a long process of application, interpretation and reinterpretation (hence the "historical record" of "some sixty years"). However, notice that we can make a legitimacy judgment of this sort only in *retrospect*. What is the extent to which (and the ground on which) one can *prospectively* make such a judgment? After all, there is a difference—one would say a crucial difference—between looking backward and looking forward, between saying that an undemocratically adopted constitution *has already become* legitimate over time (a retrospective judgment) and *would perhaps become* legitimate in the future (a prospective judgment).

This difference is already reflected in the fact that, acting prospectively in 1949, the framers of the German Basic Law named it a "basic law" (*Grundgesetz*) and not a "constitution" (*Verfassung*) in the proper sense. As Donald Kommers rightly observes, they "did not want to bestow the dignified term 'constitution' on a document drafted to govern a part of Germany for a transitional period."[40] The Basic Law was considered "transitional" in two major ways. First, as Germany was divided at the time, the framers thought that a proper constitution would have to be adopted upon unification. Secondly (and for our discussion more importantly), the Basic Law was framed and enacted under the circumstances of postwar occupation, and hence lacked the kind of democratic legitimacy that the exercise of popular sovereignty alone could have bestowed on a new constitution. "The framers were looking forward to a time when Germany would be whole, not only in the physical sense of being unified, but in the moral/political sense of being a fully democratic society."[41]

Indeed, the framers clearly expressed in the Preamble both of these concerns by stating that the Basic Law was meant to "give a new order to political life for a transitional period," while at the same time calling upon "the entire German people . . . to accomplish, by free self-determination, the unity and freedom of Germany." Even more emphatically, the text ended with the famous Article 146, which read: "This Basic Law shall become invalid on the day when a constitution adopted in a free decision by the German people comes into force." Of course, when the prospect of a unified Germany ceased to be a remote hope and suddenly became a real possibility in 1989, the once transitional Basic Law had already grown into a real constitution and already assumed the "character of a document framed to last in perpetuity."[42] Thanks to several decades of democratic experiment, the Basic Law was now firmly rooted in the political culture of Western Germany and widely regarded as a legitimate constitution, notwithstanding its undemocratic beginnings.[43]

As I see it, there are two basic lessons to be drawn from the German case. First, an undemocratically enacted constitution may come to acquire democratic legitimacy over time. Secondly, as the framers of the Basic Law were keenly aware, this does not change the fact that there *was* a legitimation deficit at the beginning. Based on these two premises, I think, we can plausibly conclude that how democracy gets off the ground should be a matter of concern for democratic theory *even if* the deficit of original legitimation is not in principle irreparable and constitutions may *also* gain democratic legitimacy in retrospect. Let me deploy an analogy here. We all know that children can overcome bad starting points in life; but none of us would therefore think that, just because it is possible for them to *overcome* bad starting points in life, what has happened in their childhood is irrelevant or does not matter. Much better, naturally, if they had had supportive and flourishing childhoods. In line with that analogy, I therefore argue that democratic theory would be well-advised to attend to the "how" of constitution-making (the genesis or "childhood" of nations) *in addition to* the "what" of the constitution itself.

Finally, we also need to consider that the failures of democratic constitution-making can produce lingering problems as well. The Canadian Constitution Act of 1982, which was brought to pass without Québec's consent, would serve as a good example here. Strictly speaking, it was not an act of making a new constitution from scratch because most of the 1867 constitution was retained intact. Nevertheless, it was a founding act of sorts since it created, symbolically and legally, a new constitutional order: first, by patriating the existing constitution; and second, by supplementing it with a charter of rights and freedoms.[44] As such, the act was meant to entrench the pan-Canadian vision of an independent nation built on the equality of citizens and provinces. All this, however, was done despite Québec's grievances. "The government of Québec," James Tully tells us, "argued that the Charter constituted an imperial yoke over Québec's distinctive French-language and civil-law culture, forged through centuries of interaction with English-language Canada, and that it needed to be amended to recognize Québec's cultural distinctiveness."[45] But no such amendment took place, and the Constitution Act was brought to pass without getting on board the second largest province in the country—and this in spite of the fact that the constitution itself stipulated unanimous consent among provinces for any major or structural amendment in the future.

Now, let us reconsider the issues of "who," "how" and "what" in light of this example. What was put into motion by the Canadian Constitution Act of 1982? How was it put into motion? And by whom? Basically, the act endorsed a constitutional democratic system with a strong emphasis on individual rights and the political equality of the provinces. As such, there was no plausible evidence against the generic or abstract presumption that it was meant to carry on—to use Zurn's wording—"the project of constitutional democracy in a dynamic, self-correcting, and thus progressive manner." And yet, this did not suffice to make it legitimate or worthy of consent for many citizens of Québec. They perceived it as a *specific interpretation* of the constitutional democratic project, one that is deeply individualistic and pan-Canadian in spirit, and hence unresponsive to Québec's claims for cultural recognition.[46] Québec already had a problem with the proposed content of the Constitution Act, but the way it was brought to pass (i.e., the dimension of "how") added conspicuous insult to possible injury. Instead of seeking a resolution that was acceptable to all parties, the federal government decided to move without Québec's support—a decision that brought about deep resentment in the province and fueled separatist feelings.[47] Excluded from the table, many citizens of Québec were not in a position to view themselves among the possible owners of the constitutional project and become attached to it as their own constitution. As a result, the constitution was not only grafted onto a fragmented "who," but the way in which it was grafted led to deeper fragmentation.

* * *

This chapter opened with a simple observation about two characteristic features of the modern constitution: that it is the product of a deliberate founding act, and that it claims to rest on "the people." While the former refers us to the "origins" of the political association, the latter brings to our attention its "foundations." My contention is that, from the standpoint of democratic theory, these two motifs can no longer remain isolated from each other. The normative foundations of the democratic constitution must be performatively manifest in its origins. In other words, the people themselves must be included in the making of the constitution which claims to speak for them.

In the view presented here, this is important for two main reasons. The first one is a *normative* reason regarding the legitimacy of a new constitution. Under contemporary conditions, hypothetical arguments bypassing the actual voices of citizens inevitably lead to a democratic deficit. As our notions of what it means for "the people" to speak have undergone a significant transformation toward a pluralist and deliberative direction, the "who" and the "how" of a constitutional founding have increasingly become important markers of democratic legitimacy. The second reason might be called *experiential* in that it emphasizes how the experience of constitutional founding shapes our relation to the constitution, its meaning to us as citizens, and, by extension, the very meaning of citizenship itself. On this register, "origin" is a matter of concern because the way a constitution gets off the ground affects its capacity to become an object of identification, to take root in political culture, and to stand in a productive relation to the people as they keep changing. A constitution can open itself up to the future as a living project to the extent that it belongs to "us" in this experiential sense.

Thus far, then, our argument has spotted the idea of democratic founding and made a preliminary case as to why it matters. However, we have not yet said anything about how the people could actually get to underwrite their constitution. For example, are we to think of democratic constitution-making along the model of a full, actual, communicated consensus among literally all citizens? And if the answer is no, for practical limitations that should be obvious enough, then how are we supposed to make sense of it? This is a question to which we will keep returning throughout the following chapters, and the answer will emerge step by step. But there is also the related and logically prior question of whether a genuinely democratic act of constitution-making—in the sense of an inclusive and participatory exercise of popular sovereignty—is *conceptually* possible in the first place. Here, the worry is that the very idea of democratic founding is packed with a colossal paradox. I take up this paradox and its implications in the next chapter.

Chapter 2

The Paradox of Democratic Founding

Canonical Statements and Contemporary Perspectives

It is today a commonplace that a constitution is not simply a mechanism for restraining the power of government and securing the rights of citizens. From a democratic point of view, a constitution is at the same time an instrument or better yet a *medium* of self-determination. It is meant to set up the enabling conditions by means of which citizens would come to form and express something like a common will, consider themselves as the joint author of the laws, and steer the course of their political destiny. However, this enabling function of the constitution brings home to us a taxing problem, one which is peculiar to democratic theory: how can the citizens, in their collective capacity as "the people," underwrite their constitution, namely the law of making laws, if the conditions of democratic will-formation, necessary to carry out such an act, are to be established by the constitution itself? It seems that the idea of constitutional founding *by* the people presupposes what it sets out to accomplish in the first place, thereby sending us into a dizzying circularity. This is the paradox of democratic founding in a nutshell. The present chapter aims to explore it in detail.

Depending on how one conceives the fundamental conditions of democratic will-formation, the paradox of founding can be stated in two different ways: *substantively* (as a matter of ethos) and *procedurally* (as a matter of institutional forms). While the former version goes back to Rousseau's *The Social Contract*, the latter finds its expression in the classical texts of the American and French Revolutions, most notably in *The Federalist* No. 40 by James

Madison and "What Is the Third Estate?" by Emmanuel Sieyès. In what follows, as a first step in the analysis of the paradox of democratic founding, I begin with these canonical statements.

We will then consider two contrasting interpretations. For some, the paradox under consideration is after all a trivial issue. It arises from a category mistake regarding the meaning of the term "people," and more specifically from a misguided application of the principle of popular sovereignty. Hegel defended such a view, and its versions are held today by some prominent theorists of constitutional democracy. Others, by contrast, see the paradox of founding as a fundamental aporia, an insurmountable impasse, one that impugns all democratic politics and tangles it up in ever self-repeating vicious circles. In order to examine this latter view, we will engage with a diverse group of theorists, including Jacques Derrida, William Connolly, Bonnie Honig, and Frank Michelman.

For reasons that will become clear, I take issue with both these positions. While the former dismisses the paradox of founding without seriously taking into account its implications for democratic theory, the latter turns the problem into a "chicken-and-egg" kind of puzzle and hence forecloses its negotiation. In contrast to both approaches, the present chapter concludes with an alternative proposal. We would be well-advised to take the paradox of democratic founding neither as a category mistake nor as an insurmountable impasse, but as a *heuristic problem*, one which leads us into the gray area where the conditions of democratic peoplehood are in the making.

Ethos and Procedure: Two Canonical Versions of the Paradox

In Book II, Chapter 7 of *The Social Contract*—namely, the famous section on the lawgiver—Rousseau articulates the paradox of founding: "For a nascent people to be capable of appreciating sound maxims of politics and of following the fundamental rules of reason of state, the effect would have to become the cause, the *social spirit* which is to be the work of the institution would have to preside over the institution itself, and men would have to be prior to laws what they ought to become by means of them."[1]

The key notion in the passage is the "social spirit." Basically, it indicates a sort of civic ethos, or a shared orientation toward the common good. For Rousseau, such an orientation is essential to the functioning of a self-legislating political community, in which law arises from the general will of the people. The formation and exercise of the general will, in turn, are based upon the capacity of citizens to take a broader standpoint than the counsels of self-interest. Instead of sticking to the narrow perspective of their particular interests, citizens must be able to place the common good at the center of their political considerations. Notice that this capacity has both a cognitive and a motivational side. That is to say, citizens must both *see* the common good and actively *will* it. According to Rousseau, the right kind of ethos, the "social spirit," is of crucial significance precisely because it brings together these two aspects—insight and volition, reason and will—thereby providing the citizens with an embedded understanding of the common good. Penetrating deep into their dispositions, habits, and emotions, such an embedded understanding of the common good is the lifeblood of a self-legislating political community.

This is where the paradox of democratic founding comes in. If a "nascent people" are to organize themselves into a self-legislating political community, the social spirit must have been somehow operational beforehand. For the people to make the right kind of laws, expressive of the general will, the right kind of ethos must be already in place. And yet, Rousseau observes, an ethos of this sort would only flourish in an already existing and functioning republican society. It is by virtue of good laws that citizens are educated to take a principled standpoint and habituated to attach themselves to the common good, while at the same time learning how to confine and accommodate their private interests within its boundaries. This leads to the question of whether the people can carry out the first—in fact, the most important—act of self-legislation, namely, the making of the republican constitution, if the kind of ethical dispositions required to perform this act are to develop under republican laws and institutions. It seems that for the people to underwrite their own constitution, as Rousseau puts it, "the effect would have to become the cause," and the morals to be shaped by the constitution would have to precede its making.

According to Rousseau, there is but one escape from the paradox of founding. Only the formative and educative efforts of a "great lawgiver" can save the people from the vicious circle of democratic will-formation: "How will a blind multitude, which often does not know what it wills because it rarely knows what is good for it, carry out an undertaking as great, as difficult as a system of legislation? By itself the people always wills the good, but by itself it does not always see it. . . . Hence arises the necessity of a Lawgiver."[2]

Acting as a political educator and attending to the morals of the people, the lawgiver sows the seeds of civic virtue and sets in motion a moral transformation so that citizens would in the future become capable of exercising the general will on their own.[3]

No doubt, Rousseau's recourse to an enigmatic lawgiver in the midst of a theoretical inquiry aiming to map out the normative grounds of a self-legislating political community has sparked much debate and criticism. For some, the lawgiver indicates a democratic deficit in his thought. In this view, "Rousseau could not conceive of a self-fashioning people and so he invents, literally, a *deus ex machina*," a somewhat implausible conceptual device, designed to bridge the gap between will and reason, consent and wisdom, democratic legitimacy and the common good.[4] According to another line of interpretation, Rousseau's appeal to the lawgiver models how the achievement of democratic autonomy is contingent on a heteronomous intervention at a fundamental conceptual level, inviting us thereby to reflect on the limits of normative ideals and their problematic construction.[5] We will look at some of these interpretations more closely in due course, especially in discussing the contemporary restatements of the paradox of founding below.

In "What Is the Third Estate?" Sieyès encounters the paradox of founding from a different angle. Unlike Rousseau's formulation, this version of the paradox turns on the institutional and procedural presuppositions of democratic will-formation rather than its ethico-cultural conditions. The central question that frames Sieyès's argument is the following: "what should be understood by the political *constitution* of a society and how to identify its just relationship to the *nation* itself?"[6] In response, he writes:

> It is impossible to create a body for an end without giving it the organization, forms and laws it needs in order to fulfil the functions for which it has been established. This is what is meant by the constitution of that body. It is obvious that it could not exist without one. . . . Thus the body of representatives entrusted with the legislative power, or the exercise of the common will, exists only by way of the mode of being which the nation decided to give it. It is nothing without its constitutive forms; it acts, proceeds, or commands only by way of those forms.[7]

Notice that in defining the constitution this way, Sieyès puts the emphasis on its *enabling* rather than *restraining* functions. Even though constitutional laws do and must bring certain limits on the exercise of power, they always do so by establishing the institutional and procedural forms in and through which the exercise of power becomes possible in the first place. In this respect, to borrow John Searle's distinction, constitutional laws function not only or even primarily like "regulative rules," which govern practices that exist regardless of the rule (e.g., parking is prohibited), but also, and more important, like "constitutive rules," which make a certain kind of practice possible in the first place (e.g., the queen can move in all directions).[8]

Having thus clarified "what should be understood by the political constitution of a society," Sieyès then turns to the second half of the question: "how to identify its just relationship to the nation itself?"[9] In response to this question, he introduces the well-known distinction between "constituent" and "constituted" powers. The power of the government—or the power to rule in accordance with and as prescribed by the law—is a constituted power in that it is subject to the fixed forms articulated in the constitution. However, the power to articulate these forms, namely, the power to make the constitution itself, is by definition of a different order. "In each of its parts a constitution is not the work of a constituted power but a constituent power."[10] This power belongs only and exclusively to the people, who can use it at will and give the constitution whatever form it wants. "It would be ridiculous," Sieyès argues emphatically, "to suppose that the nation itself was bound by the formalities or the constitution to which it had subjected its mandatories."[11] In its capacity as the constituent power, thus, the people is claimed to be beyond and above all institutional forms.

The paradox of democratic will-formation asserts itself precisely here. On the one hand, Sieyès has a point. If the people are to be taken as the locus of constituent power and the ultimate source of legitimacy on which the constitution rests, then their will must in some sense precede and underpin the constitution. On the other hand, as Sieyès acknowledges in his own definition of the constitution, a collective body can hardly act in a purposive way without the "internal forms" or the "constitutive rules" that enable it to do so. This makes it hard to understand how the people can exercise their constituent power. "There is no reason to be afraid of repeating the fact that a nation is independent of all forms," Sieyès wants to reassure his readers, "however it may will, it is enough for its will to be made known."[12] But this is not a solution to the problem; if anything, this is a restatement of the problem. After all, how is it possible for the people to form and express their will outside all procedural and institutional forms, the establishment of which is of course the task of the constitution itself?

Sieyès seems to think that the solution resides in the concept and practice of representation. "Since a great nation cannot in real terms assemble every time that extraordinary circumstances may require," he says, "it has, on such occasions, to entrust the necessary powers to extraordinary representatives."[13] But notice that the problem at hand does not primarily turn on the *practical* impossibility of convening the people together. It is first and foremost a *conceptual* problem, and the call for "extraordinary representatives" would only highlight its persistence. How can the people—abstracted from all positive forms whatsoever, including by definition the electoral laws and regulations as well—elect these extraordinary representatives, that is, the members of the constituent assembly, and give them a coherent mandate?[14] It seems that beyond and above all established procedures, the people are not only incapable of exercising constituent power on their own, but they cannot even delegate or entrust it to a constituent assembly, except on pain of circularity.

In 1788 (just a year before the publication of "What Is the Third Estate?"), Madison addressed the same issue in the context of the American constitutional debates. Unlike Sieyès, however, he acknowledged the vexing nature of the problem from the outset. In response to the charge that the Philadelphia Convention of 1787 transgressed its mandate by framing a new constitution, he writes: "in all great changes of established governments, forms ought to give way to substance ... since it is impossible for the people spontaneously and universally, to move in concert toward their object; and it is therefore essential, that such changes be instituted by some *informal and unauthorised propositions*, made by some patriotic and respectable citizen or number of citizens."[15] Madison squarely admits that an "unauthorised" move is necessary to break the vicious circle in which every act of foundation with a democratic intent is caught up. Those who get together to frame a new constitution in an assembly speak in the name of a people who could not have duly authorized them or given them a coherent mandate. In this respect, there is a sense in which constituent assemblies play a formally similar role to Rousseau's lawgiver. In both cases, "the people" seems to emerge as a democratic agent capable of self-determination only after the fact, that is to say, only when somebody else lays down the enabling conditions of democratic will-formation, whether these conditions are construed in terms of a civic ethos or a set of procedures and institutional forms.[16]

Does the Paradox of Founding Involve a Category Mistake?

What do we make of the paradox of democratic founding? The foregoing exposition is meant to give the conceptual contours of the problem; yet, it does not tell us how we are supposed to make sense of it. The problem is clear in its two basic versions, but what does it really signify? For some, to put it in a straightforward manner, it does not signify anything important or consequential. This, for instance, is Hegel's view on the topic. He thinks that the paradox in question designates a trivial issue, which hardly merits serious treatment. More specifically, he takes it as yet another example of "those confused thoughts" arising from the "garbled notion of the people"—or, which comes down to the same thing, as a category mistake regarding the meaning of popular sovereignty and its proper sphere of application.

Hegel puts the point in a compelling way in the *Philosophy of Right*, first published in 1821, when the memory of the French Revolution was still fresh everywhere in Europe. The passage is worth quoting at length:

> the usual sense in which the term "popular sovereignty" has begun to be used in recent times is to denote *the opposite of that sovereignty which exists in the monarch*. In this oppositional sense, popular sovereignty is one of those confused thoughts which are based on a *garbled* notion of the people. *Without* its monarch and that *articulation* of the whole which is necessarily and immediately associated with monarchy, *the* people is a formless mass. The latter is no longer a state, and *none* of those determinations which are encountered only in an *internally organized* whole (such as sovereignty, government, courts of law, public authorities, estates, etc.) is applicable to it. It is only when moments such as these which refer to an organization, to political life, emerge in a people that it ceases to be that indeterminate abstraction which the purely general idea of the *people* denotes.[17]

To be sure, Hegel's defense of constitutional monarchy as the sole form of the rational state has been long outdated (in fact, it was hardly tenable even in his own time[18]). Yet his complaint about "the people" has a much broader purchase.

Hegel does not take issue with the basic normative insights underpinning the doctrine of popular sovereignty. On the contrary, his philosophical account of the modern state is structured around the idea of freedom as self-determination and its realization through an institutionally mediated web of interactions among equal citizens.[19] His point is rather that popular sovereignty is exercised *in and through* the institutional edifice of the state, and hence does not apply to the founding of this edifice. Without the constitutional state as an "internally organized whole," the people is either a "formless mass" or an "indeterminate abstraction," that is unable to carry out any positive or constituent action.[20] In other words, popular sovereignty makes sense only in the context of an established political order by virtue of which the people already exists as an organized community. This is a view that widely resurfaces, albeit in different ways and with different twists, in contemporary treatments of constitutional democracy.

According to János Kis, for example, as we already quoted in the previous chapter: "Popular sovereignty is a *feature* of political regimes rather than something actually exercised *prior* to the establishment of political regimes. The question is not whether it was the people that created the state for itself by some original act but what the practice of authorization is like in the state, once it has been established."[21] Stephen Holmes makes a similar point when he insists that we can meaningfully speak of popular sovereignty as a democratic principle only within the framework of constitutional restraints that establish procedures of decision-making and enable the practice of self-determination. Echoing Hegel's complaint about the "garbled notion of the people," Holmes writes: "A collectivity cannot have coherent purposes apart from all decision-making procedures. The people cannot act as an amorphous blob."[22] Working through the difficulties of the concept of constituent power, Ulrich Preuss likewise comes to the conclusion that it is not the people who make the constitution but the other way around. Since "constitutions are instruments of collective self-organization," Preuss maintains, "the idea of a constituent power which creates a new order ex nihilo is a (perhaps necessary) fiction"—that is to say, "the constitution gives birth to the people in the sense in which this notion has been developed for the concept of democracy."[23]

Whatever its merits may be in other respects, this line of argumentation does not squarely face up to the paradox of founding. Arguments locating popular sovereignty within the constitutional democratic state and taking it in relation to the *structure* of the regime rather than its *pedigree* do not make the paradox disappear or save us from the vexing issues involved in it. What they do instead is to shift the emphasis from the primacy of the people to that of the constitution. However, such a move raises more questions than it actually answers. Several issues come to mind immediately. If it is the constitution that makes the people, then, who makes the constitution? How are we to understand the making of the democratic constitution anyway? If the people themselves cannot act in a constituent capacity and exercise popular sovereignty prior to the making of the democratic constitution itself, who speaks in the name of the people and with what title? At any rate, how do we know (or can we ever know) whether a constitution actually and authentically stands for the people? I do not think that democratic theory can afford to ignore such questions. Even when one concedes that the people cannot underwrite their political organization through an original exercise of popular sovereignty—as Kis, Holmes, and Preuss seem to suggest in their own ways—what *this* would signify for the concept of democracy in general and for the formation of a democratic political community in particular is still far from self-evident and stands in need of elucidation.

All in all, there is something deeply unsatisfactory in dismissing the paradox of democratic founding as a category mistake about the proper application of popular sovereignty. Such an approach leaves the issue of founding simply intact. Hegel is again illustrative here. At one point in *The Philosophy of Right*, he takes up the question of constitution-making, but only to dismiss it immediately: "It is at any rate utterly essential that the constitution should *not* be regarded as *something made*, even if it does have an origin in time. On the contrary, it is quite simply that which has being in and for itself, and should therefore be regarded as divine and enduring, and exalted above the sphere of all manufactured things."[24] One cannot help but infer that Hegel's ultimate response to the question of constitutional founding is that one ought not to ask that question![25]

Despite Hegel's best efforts to efface it, the question has proved to be persistent. The paradox of democratic founding is a recurring theme in contemporary political theory, and theorists working in different traditions have picked up on it from a variety of angles, unpacking its implications in their own ways. In what follows, we will look at these contemporary restatements more closely in three consecutive steps: our first stop is Jacques Derrida's reformulation of the paradox of founding through the lens of speech act theory; next, we turn to recent interpretations of Rousseau's paradox, particularly those offered by William Connolly and Bonnie Honig; and finally, via Frank Michelman's writings, we will focus on the procedural version of the problem and explore the ways in which it is brought to bear on the deliberative conception of constitutional democracy. Before moving on, a final reminder is in order: these three sections are primarily intended to be expositional. The reader will find a critical discussion at the end of the chapter.

Founding Acts and Speech Acts: Jacques Derrida

Beginning with a short but provocative essay on the American Declaration of Independence, the paradox of founding comes in focus in Jacques Derrida's work via linguistic means of analysis derived from speech act theory. At the center of Derrida's reading of the Declaration is the seemingly neat distinction between "constative" and "performative" utterances, developed (and later abandoned) by J. L. Austin in *How to Do Things with Words*. According to Austin, a constative is a verifiable utterance, the paradigm of which is the traditional proposition. It is meant to state some fact or to describe some state of affairs, and it must do so either truly or falsely. A performative is also an utterance, but of a very different kind. It does not describe a state of affairs, it *brings about* one. When I say "I promise," I do not describe myself as promising, I perform the act of promising. Austin rightly observes that such utterances are not subject to verification in the same way as constative ones because actions cannot be "true" or "false." Nonetheless, there is success or failure in the performance of an action, which prompts Austin to suggest that a performative utterance can be "felicitous" or "infelicitous" depending on whether it succeeds or not in doing what it says.[26]

Reading the American Declaration of Independence through Austin's distinction, Derrida asks a basic question: does the Declaration make a constative utterance or a performative one? "Is it that the good people have already freed themselves in fact and are only stating the fact of this emancipation in the Declaration? Or is it rather that they free themselves at the instant of and by the signature of this Declaration?"[27] One cannot say for sure, Derrida observes, whether independence is "stated" (as in a constative utterance) or "produced" (as in a performative one). This "undecidability" is due to the circular relationship of the text to its signer, namely "the people," or the "we" of the Declaration. On the one hand, it seems, it is the signature of the people that authorizes the Declaration—in which case the Declaration would consist in a constative utterance by an already independent people stating its independence. On the other hand, however, "this people does not exist," Derrida argues, "*before* this declaration, not *as such*"[28]—in which case it would be the

Declaration itself that brings about independence by a performative utterance, thereby creating the people as an authoritative subject capable of underwriting the Declaration. Thus, at one and the same time, the Declaration both presupposes and constitutes its signer. The paradox of founding is at play.

Much of this may look like a case of old wine in new bottles.[29] But there is actually more to Derrida's argument than a simple restatement of the paradox of founding via linguistic analysis. Derrida attempts to reshape our understanding of the problem at a fundamental conceptual level by presenting the act of foundation itself as a speech act. If he is right in this claim, then it means that speech act theory is not simply applied to the problem of founding as though from without, and that the problems of speech act theory are also the problems of the politics of founding and vice versa. To get a better grasp of this point along with its wide-ranging implications, we need to get back to Austin's theory of performative utterance and see Derrida's critique of it.

According to Austin, the efficacy of a performative is ultimately a matter of *convention*. Take for instance the words "the class is dismissed." They mark the end of the lecture and effectively dismiss the class only when they are uttered by the lecturer in the classroom. This is because there are certain conventions in place, some formal and some informal, that determine how lectures are to be conducted, thereby enabling the efficacy of the performative. "There must exist an accepted conventional procedure having a certain conventional effect"—this is Austin's famous Rule A.1, the first rule of performative felicity.[30] But now consider the same sentence, "the class is dismissed," as being uttered by a student who thereby reports to another student what has just happened. Although the utterance is linguistically the same, not only do the student's words lack the power to dismiss the class (a matter of convention), but their meaning is also different. This is because the *context* has changed. In terms of a distinction that Austin developed later in the text, the same "locution"—the same sentence taken as an isolated linguistic unit—would have quite different "illocutionary" meanings depending on the context.

The underlying idea is that in order to give an account of language as a way of doing things in the world one must consider the interaction between linguistic utterance and social practice, which in turn involves issues of context and conventionality. Derrida applauds Austin for this move. However, in Derrida's view, something has also gone wrong in Austin's project from the outset. While Austin acknowledges that no sentence can be self-identifying and that its meaning depends on the context, he proceeds with the assumption of a stable and static context that serves as the guarantor of meaning. Just as a free-standing sentence cannot identify its own meaning, Derrida objects, a context cannot be fully transparent either. "This is my starting point," he announces: "no meaning can be determined out of context, but no context permits saturation."[31] Contexts are unsaturated, conventions are dynamic, and both are essentially exposed to indeterminacy. Austin comes to acknowledge this, but only in passing, when he admits that "it is difficult to say where conventions begin and end."[32]

We may begin to see here the big picture regarding the profound affinity between the problems of speech act theory and the problems of the politics of founding. It is indeed difficult to say "where conventions begin and end," and this is particularly so in revolutionary situations. When the American colonists declared independence in 1776, or when the delegates of the French Third Estate adopted the title "National Assembly" in 1789, they did not rest on "an accepted conventional procedure having a certain conventional effect" (Austin's Rule A.1). Rather, it was the other way around. In both cases—and many others since then—the performative speech of the dissenters challenged existing conventions, while at the same time creating new ones. Revolutionary acts of foundation turn Austin's Rule A.1 upside down. Instead of performatives depending on conventions, conventions are brought to depend on performatives.[33]

What follows from this reversal, according to Derrida, is that every act of foundation is by definition groundless and violent in a certain sense. In the "Force of Law," he puts the point emphatically:

> The very emergence of justice and law, the founding and justifying moment that institutes law implies a performative force. . . . Its very moment of foundation or institution (which in any case is never a moment inscribed in the homogeneous tissue of a history, since it is ripped apart with one decision), the operation that amounts to founding, inaugurating, justifying law (*droit*), making law, would consist of a *coup de force*. . . . Here the discourse comes up against its limit: in itself, in its performative power itself. It is what I here propose to call the mystical. Here a silence is walled up in the violent structure of the founding act.[34]

That every act of foundation is groundless and that law is anchored in a moment outside the law are not bad news for Derrida. Rather, they are suggestive of the fact that no institution can completely close on itself and fully colonize performative speech. The groundless beginning of the political community involves the seeds of its own destabilization and hence the very possibility of politics.[35]

In Derrida's view the danger resides elsewhere: acts of foundation are prone to cover their own tracks. The retroactive production of authority, by way of an extraordinary performative creating the conditions of its own felicity, draws a mantle over the groundless beginning of the political community, thereby keeping out of sight the foundational deficit of legitimacy. One is tempted to recall Edmund Burke here. "There is a sacred veil to be drawn over the beginnings of all governments," he suggested once, "time, in the origin of most governments, has thrown this mysterious veil over them; prudence and discretion make it necessary to throw something of the same drapery over more recent foundations."[36] The oscillation between constative and performative modes of speech, which structures the Declaration of Independence in Derrida's reading, is a symptom of this hiding operation. Speaking as if "the people" are already present as a sovereign entity, the Declaration helps disguise the fact that independence is produced performatively and that "the people" arrives only after the fact.[37]

Rethinking Rousseau's Paradox: William Connolly and Bonnie Honig

Among contemporary political theorists, William Connolly is arguably the most persistent and meticulous reader of Rousseau's paradox of founding.[38] He has repeatedly revisited this version of the paradox with a view to unpacking its implications for democratic theory, and offered a prolific interpretation that has been developed and fleshed out in various directions by others. On the one hand, Connolly celebrates Rousseau for identifying and articulating the paradox of founding; on the other hand, he observes that "Rousseau then conceals the legacy of this paradox in the operation of the general will after it has been founded by the creative intervention of a wise legislator."[39] Like Derrida, Connolly too thinks that there is a hiding operation going on. What sort of "legacy" is at stake here and how is it concealed?

According to Connolly, the paradox of founding is never truly resolved. Despite Rousseau's artful efforts to imagine the lawgiver as a non-authoritarian authority who would not jeopardize the future autonomy of the people, what lurks behind the figure of the lawgiver is in the end an "element of arbitrariness that cannot be eliminated from political life."[40] This element of arbitrariness has both a conceptual and a historical side. Conceptually, the invocation of the lawgiver designates an unavoidable "impurity" inherent to the ideals of general will and popular sovereignty. There is no self-sufficient practice of political autonomy that is not inhabited by its own other, by some sort of heteronomous element that enables the exercise of popular sovereignty while remaining unaccountable in view of its normative aspirations. Hence, Connolly concludes that "the very structure of sovereignty compromises the integrity and coherence idealists of democratic sovereignty demand."[41] Historically, in real-world political foundings, this "impurity" refers us, among other things, to the less than salutary practices including the repression of certain voices, the formation of hegemonic political identities, and the use of techniques for ensuring allegiance without consensus—all of which Connolly treats under the rubric of founding violence.

Connolly's central claim is that, once the political community is established, the legacy of this founding violence has to be concealed for the general will to function as a regulative ideal. Rousseau conceals it through his imagery of the lawgiver. The office of the lawgiver has no place in the constitution; he can move the people without forcing them; he is most likely a foreigner who has no reason to stay in the republic once the task of foundation is accomplished, and so on.[42] Imagining the lawgiver this way, Rousseau wants to get his readers to infer that the heteronomous intervention of the lawgiver would not compromise the hoped-for autonomy of the people, and that the paradox of founding is to be overcome without leaving behind troubling traces. In actual polities, the legacy of founding violence is concealed by the hegemonic political identity which treats it as having no actual hold on the current operations of the general will, "as if, for instance . . . the systematic violence against indigenous inhabitants in the founding of the United States carries no continuing effects into the present"—the paradox of founding thereby dissolves into "the politics of forgetting."[43] Insofar as not only what we remember but also and perhaps more significantly what we forget is constitutive of who we are, the symbolic authority of founding moments originates as much from what is left to oblivion as from what is memorable.[44]

Following on from Connolly's work, Bonnie Honig also holds that Rousseau's paradox remains ultimately unresolved. And yet, in her view, "nor is it just concealed, as Connolly argues, by way of unacknowledged, foundational violence in Rousseau."[45] Rather, in every effort Rousseau makes to solve the paradox of founding, it moves on to another register and defies resolution. Rousseau introduces the figure of the lawgiver because the people are considered to be not yet enlightened enough. They are not yet capable of forming and exercising the general will on their own. Nevertheless, Honig draws attention to the fact that the lawgiver and the people are dependent on each other from the very beginning: for the lawgiver to accomplish the task of foundation properly, he must be recognized by the people as a "true lawgiver" in the first place. "The lawgiver may offer to found a people, he may even attempt to shape them, but in the end it is up to the people themselves to accept or reject his advances. They may be dependent on his good offices, but he is no less dependent on their good opinion."[46] Once this interdependence is acknowledged, however, the paradox moves on to a new register. Instead of asking how a people who is not yet shaped or educated by good laws can themselves make them, one would ask now (as Rousseau himself actually did) how a people who is not yet enlightened by the lawgiver can distinguish between a true lawgiver and an impersonator, a charlatan?[47]

On this reading, the main significance of the paradox of founding, which defies a definitive resolution and replays *ad infinitum*, does not only reside in its concealed or repressed repercussions. It merits our attention also because the paradox in focus illustrates a fundamental ambiguity, "the mutual inhabitation of general and particular will, people and blind multitude, lawgiver and charlatan, properly durable institutions and those stabilized by force."[48] Even though these can be analytically separated by way of normative philosophical inquiry, they are inextricably intertwined in the real world of politics where there is no sure way to distinguish them. Honig thus concludes that Rousseau's paradox of founding is not really a paradox of *founding*, which applies only to the beginning or inauguration of a regime. It spills over into political life at large and becomes "the paradox of politics."

Alan Keenan develops the same line of interpretation in a slightly different direction by reading Rousseau's lawgiver "as the figure for those elements and actions in democratic politics that prove necessary to the people's autonomy without being reducible to its logic."[49] What comes into foreground in Keenan's parsing of the problem is the form of agency and claim-making, personified in the figure of the lawgiver, which generates a new sense of peoplehood by acting and speaking in its name in advance—or to put it in Madison's memorable formulation, via "unauthorised propositions." Consider the following passage:

The paradoxical task of the legislator—or rather, of all democratic political actors—then, is to make an appeal that sets the conditions for its own proper reception: one must appeal to the political community in such a way that its members will accept the regulations that will make them into the kind of (general) people able to "hear" such an appeal. The work of (re)founding the people is thus never ending. If "the people" ever come into existence, it can only be in the form of *claims* made about them, on their behalf, or *in their name*.[50]

This in turn means that there is no politically neutral form of "generality" and no self-transparent sense of democratic peoplehood. Since one must "speak and act in the name of the people before receiving the people's own sanction," Keenan maintains, "one can never be certain of their identity or of whether one has successfully 'achieved' it."[51] The identity of the people as a democratic people is bound to remain in question.

Applying the Paradox to Deliberative Democracy: Frank Michelman

The procedural version of the paradox of founding that we previously explored—the version that preoccupied Madison and Sieyès in the context of the American and French Revolutions—is also a recurring theme in contemporary scholarship. Here I particularly focus on Frank Michelman's reflections on the topic. Michelman takes his point of departure from a problem which is arguably *the* big issue of constitutional theory: the tension-ridden relationship between constitutionalism and democracy.[52] As a political form, constitutional democracy is based on two premises: "the government of the people by the people and the government of the people by laws"—which means that "if we are sincerely and consistently committed both to ruling ourselves and to being ruled by laws, there must be some sense in which we think of self-rule and law-rule (if not exactly of 'people' and 'laws') as amounting to the same thing."[53]

In a sense, this is what the doctrine of popular sovereignty is meant to do. It claims to tie together "self-rule" and "law-rule" by presenting the people as the author of the constitution and its ultimate source of legitimacy. However, for Michelman, the promised reconciliation is not thereby achieved. While the project of democracy demands that we should be able to trace a country's fundamental laws back to the people's legislative will "in some nonfictively attributable sense,"[54] this demand is impossible to meet on account of the familiar problem of circularity. Law stands in a circular relationship with the legislative will of the people as both the prior condition and the outcome of the democratic practice, which turns the notion of "constituent power" into a self-contradictory idea. As Michelman puts it:

> Short of the miracle of actual, present, full, communicated consensus, the people in the raw, so to speak, are and must always remain strangers to the law . . . Only under constitutive legal provision already in force, defining what concatenations of institutional events will count legally as representations of the people's legislative will, can a "people" exist or conceivably legislate anything. The unorganized, unconstituted, prelegal populace-at-large cannot be a *pouvoir constituant*, authors of the very law that initially regiments them into a legislatively capable *pouvoir constitué*.[55]

In Michelman's view, the circularity of democratic will-formation not only renders the classical theory of constituent power unpersuasive but has a wider purchase. It applies to the radically proceduralist conception of "deep democracy" at a fundamental conceptual level. On this register, Michelman critically engages with Habermas's "discourse theory of law and democracy."

Recall that Habermas criticized Rawls (as we have seen in Chapter 1) for jeopardizing the radical meaning of political autonomy through the hypothetical device of an "original position." Once the "veil of ignorance" is lifted, he claimed, citizens "find themselves subject to principles and norms that have been anticipated in theory and have already become institutionalized beyond their control."[56] In contrast to a model of hypothetical agreement, Habermas maintains that the "democratic procedure for the production of law evidently forms the only postmetaphysical source of legitimacy."[57] It is at this point that Michelman picks up on Habermas. He begins with an affirmation of the enabling *and* legitimating role of procedures. "A truly democratic process is itself inescapably a legally conditioned and constituted process."[58] This implies that the outcome of democratic deliberation derives its legitimacy from the procedures according to which it is conditioned and carried out. Therefore, Michelman argues, "in order to confer legitimacy on a set of laws issuing from an actual set of discursive institutions and practices in a country, those institutions and practices would themselves have to be legally constituted in the right way."⁵⁹ This presupposition, however, takes us back directly to the question of constitutional authorship. Can we demonstrate, in proceduralist terms, the legitimacy of the rules and arrangements according to which the "higher law" itself is framed?

As Michelman argues emphatically: "If it takes a legally constituted democratic procedure to bring forth valid fundamental laws, then the (valid) laws that frame *this* lawmaking event must themselves be the product of a conceptually prior procedural event that was itself framed by (valid) laws that must, as such, have issued in their turn from a still prior (properly) legally constituted event. And so on, it would appear, without end."⁶⁰ Notice the shift in the logical formulation of the problem. Rather than the "vicious circle" of democratic founding, Michelman now frames it in terms of "infinite regress," familiar from the tradition of legal positivism. On this formulation, the question is not "Which comes first, the chicken or the egg?" but rather "Where does the buck stop?"⁶¹—and the troubling answer is that it just doesn't. "Infinite regress seems a most unwelcome result here, given the apparent difficulty of finding an institutional form to contain it."⁶²

According to Michelman, this places the proponents of "deep democracy," in the "unrestricted procedural sense of the term"⁶³—such as, arguably, Habermas—between a rock and a hard place. Either the buck doesn't stop at all or it indeed stops somewhere but only arbitrarily. In the former case, the democratic process cannot even get off the ground. If the presuppositions of procedural legitimacy lead to an infinite regress, then, the founding act could never be "anchored" in history and could never make the kind of beginning it claims to make.⁶⁴ In the latter case, the constitution gets enacted but only in a procedurally arbitrary way that cannot vouch for its own democratic credentials. Hence, there is no guarantee that the higher law enables a "truly democratic" process and delivers the kind of procedural legitimacy it is supposed to confer on subsequent legislation.⁶⁵

The Paradox of Founding Hypostatized: A Critical Assessment

Thus far, we have seen a number of contemporary perspectives on the paradox of democratic founding. A critical evaluation is now in order. Admittedly, there is something instructive—or to recall Richard Rorty's characterization, "edifying"—in the foregoing arguments. They move us away from the political mythology of constituent power resting on the general will and interrupt the illusion of a once-and-for-all constitutional settlement under the authority of "we the people." They keep us alert about the fact that appeals to "the people" are essentially contestable, law may remain alien to its alleged authors, and the politics of founding may turn out to be a hegemonic enterprise which covers its own tracks. By embracing paradox as an important element in political life, they attempt to redeem the possibility of a democratic advantage in its persistence. As such, they invite us to question—and can actually help us reorient—our relation to the ideals and promises of democratic politics in light of its ambiguities.

However, their merits notwithstanding, contemporary treatments of the paradox of founding involve a certain—and in my view crucial—risk as well. Many of the theorists emphasizing the persistence of the paradox are also prone to *hypostatize* it in one way or another. By this, I do not mean that the paradox of founding (or if you like, the paradox of politics) is unnecessarily overstated. Rather, what I mean by "hypostatization" is basically an interpretive strategy, or better yet a mode of problem statement. It directly transposes the *logical* structure of the paradox to the realm of *political* action, thereby turning a primarily political issue into a logical puzzle. What follows is a formalistic interpretation of the paradox of founding, which is framed along the model of questions such as "Where does the buck stop?" or "Which comes first, the chicken or the egg?" Admittedly, there is no clear-cut answer to questions of this sort. That is to say, the paradox of founding is irresolvable at a formal level of analysis. The people themselves are never "the people," and the constitution invariably stands in a circular relation to the latter. But to leave matters here would be to present only one side of the coin. A political paradox is not identical to its logical form. There are ways in which political action can *respond* to it. In other words, even though the paradox of founding is *logically irresolvable*, it can be *politically negotiated* in such a way as to relax and untighten its grip. My hunch is that this possibility is lost on the hypostatized restatements of the paradox.[66]

To get a better sense of what is at stake here, it would be helpful to look at some instances of hypostatization in the writings of the theorists discussed earlier. Consider the following passage by Michelman as a case in point: "If someone told you to write a book whose every chapter begins with the terminal sentence of an immediately preceding chapter, your problem wouldn't be an inability to complete the task, but rather an inability to begin it. The assignment would immobilize you; there would be nothing at all that you could do about it."⁶⁷ The analogy is certainly intriguing, and it is meant to illustrate the problem of infinite regress. Just as one cannot start writing a book whose every chapter begins with the terminal sentence of the previous chapter, one cannot start making the higher law in a procedurally valid way. The implication is that either we cannot get off the ground at all or the constitutional beginning is bound to be arbitrary (involving, to put it in Derrida's terms, a moment of "originary violence" or a "groundless performative force"). It is precisely this way of framing and stating the problem that I call "hypostatization." It leads us into a paralyzing dead end from which there appears no way out.

But is this a true dichotomy, to begin with? On what implicit assumptions does Michelman's analogy rest? And even more pointedly, what is lost or taken out of sight by way of such analogy? We cannot indeed start writing a book whose every chapter begins with the terminal sentence of the immediately preceding chapter—fair enough. Nonetheless, consider the following scenario: what if we are *already* engaged in the practice of writing when we are commissioned with the task of beginning every chapter *from now on* with the terminal sentence of the previous chapter? Although we cannot begin to write such a book from scratch, there is nothing that can possibly bar us from modifying an ongoing process of writing in accordance with the demand. What follows is that the task is impossible only in the case of an *absolute* new beginning—beginning from scratch or beginning *ex nihilo*. This is the implicit assumption that gives Michelman's analogy its peculiar bite.

Michelman loads the argument in advance in favor of a certain conception of what it means to begin, which then leads us into a dichotomy between infinite regress and performative fiat. At this point, however, we may want to know whether the idea of an absolute new beginning is appropriate in the political realm. And more important, should we think of a democratic founding along the model of an absolute new beginning? Hannah Arendt's reminder seems pertinent here: "A characteristic of human action is that it always begins something new, and this does not mean that it is ever permitted to start *ab ovo*, to create *ex nihilo*."⁶⁸ The basic point should be clear enough. There is a distinction to be drawn between "absolute" and "relative" new beginnings, between beginning from nothing and beginning anew, a distinction which seems to get lost on Michelman's hypostatizing analogy.⁶⁹

Let us consider another instance of hypostatization, this time from Bonnie Honig's argument about the persistence of the paradox. You will recall that, in her view, the paradox is not one of "founding" but of "politics" at large. She especially argues that presenting it as the paradox of founding is a strategy of displacement. "Recast as a paradox of founding, the paradox of politics is *thereby* resolved; that is to say it is rendered in principle soluble or at least escapable by way of its location in linear time."[70] Confining the paradox to the temporal context of founding makes us think that it applies only to the beginning of a regime and that it can be surmounted by time. But the promise turns out be false, Honig argues, because the "vicious circle of chicken-and-egg (which comes first—good people or good law?)" is insurmountable; it is a paradox that "cannot be resolved, transcended, managed, or even affirmed as an irreducible binary conflict."[71] The circle lingers indefinitely and applies to every moment of political life in a democratic polity.

If the paradox is permanent, however, isn't it plausible to assume that the possibility of responding to it is also permanent? This does not go unnoticed in Honig's argument. There are forms of political action, she admits, which "respond to the paradox of politics."[72] However, she promptly (perhaps too promptly) adds that "they may also cast us once again into that paradox, leaving us with no firm criteria or ground from which to distinguish with confidence the will of all and general will, multitude and people, because the perspective from which to do so and the identities at stake are themselves in question or in (re)formation."[73] Honig may be right in claiming that there is no escape from circularity, but then the question is perhaps how the circle works. Does it necessarily work in the same way as the vicious circle of chicken-and-egg, as she repeatedly claims? Or does it possibly have a different modus operandi, one that might be more or less similar to a "hermeneutic circle"?[74]

What is the difference? The difference is not that we are cast into the paradox in one case and we surely leave it behind in the other. In both cases we are bound by paradox, but not in the same way. The difference is that, to put it somewhat schematically, in the former case the circle repeats itself simply *as such* whereas in the latter case it moves along a *spiral* so that the horizon expands from within the participant's point of view. The hermeneutic circle does not "iron out" or "displace" the paradox of founding/politics; it does not provide us with a "firm criteria or ground from which to distinguish with confidence the will of all and general will." In short, the hermeneutic circle is not immune to aporia. Yet, it does not give in to the vicious circle of chicken-and-egg either. It accommodates the possibility of bootstrapping, of accumulating experience, of learning, self-correction, and self-transformation so that as we keep responding to the paradox and move along the spiral (and there is no end to it) we nonetheless see it (and ourselves) differently, expanding our horizon and building a biography of our (always incomplete) engagement with it. This option is on the table unless its pursuit is forestalled by hypostatizing the paradox of founding/politics along the model of a chicken-and-egg kind of vicious circle.

* * *

How can the people get to underwrite their constitution? How is a democratic founding possible? The present chapter has explored a vexing problem that seems to suggest that it isn't possible at all: since the people and the constitution presuppose one another, every act of foundation with a democratic intent is invariably implicated in a colossal paradox. We have seen that this is a problem with a history, thematized and rethematized in various ways from Rousseau to the constitutional revolutions of the eighteenth century and up to the present day. In contemporary political theory, it is stated in a particularly pointed fashion that discredits the idea of democratic founding in and of itself. We are repeatedly told that such an idea is at best illusory and self-contradictory, at worst inherently hegemonic, concealing its own arbitrariness. As I hope to have shown, however, these contemporary restatements are misguided in one crucial aspect. By approaching the paradox of founding exclusively through the lens of its formal structure, they hypostatize the problem, and turn a political question into a logical puzzle. As such, they make us lose sight of other options and possibilities open for pursuit. What this means is that we need a different vantage point, a different interpretive angle, from which to approach the paradox of democratic founding.

I want to argue that we should approach the paradox under consideration neither as a category mistake to be diagnosed and dismissed (in contrast to Hegel, for instance) nor as an insurmountable aporia that impugns every act of foundation and tangles it up in ever self-repeating vicious circles (in contrast to its recurrent interpretation in contemporary political theory). Instead of "displacement" and "hypostatization," my proposal is to regard the paradox of founding as a *heuristic problem*. I use the term "heuristic" in a twofold sense, both aspects of which are related to "discovery" and "problem solving" but from different perspectives. From the standpoint of political theory, the paradox of founding is a heuristic problem in the sense that it opens up to us the gray area extending between a "formless mass" and "we the people," that is, the gray area in which the politics of founding takes place and the conditions of democratic peoplehood are in the making. The heuristic task of the theorist is to discover and navigate this gray area with a view to theorizing the dynamics of becoming a people as well as the elements of democratic constitution-making. Basically, this is what I seek to do in the following chapters. In the meantime, however, I also argue that the quest for democratic founding has a heuristic side to it from the standpoint of political actors as well. What sort of constitution-making praxis would restrain the arbitrariness of beginning and generate widespread legitimacy? How to involve citizens in the process of constitution-making in the right way? How to remain under the law while at the same time making the higher law? Citizens and framers typically grapple with such questions at moments of foundation. Hence the reason why the process of democratic founding itself is best understood as a process of problem solving. This is a point that we will keep in mind and revisit in the rest of our inquiry.

Chapter 3

The People and the Lawgiver

Rousseau on the Possibility of Democratic Founding

Taking the paradox of founding as a heuristic problem and in order to navigate the gray area it opens up to us, this chapter turns to Rousseau. After all, if the paradox of democratic founding finds its first canonical expression in his work, it is worth asking whether Rousseau has also something to tell us about how to address that paradox. My claim is that he does. I argue that we are indebted to him not only for articulating the paradox in question, but also for reflecting on how to relax its grip, and more specifically how to make sense of the people neither as an "amorphous multitude" nor a constitutionally organized "corporate body," but as a community of action in the making. In what follows, to make a case for this claim, I closely attend to the complicated relationship between the people and the lawgiver in Rousseau's work.

All too often, readers of Rousseau provide us with the picture of a one-way relationship, in which the agency of the lawgiver stands out whereas that of the people goes unacknowledged and remains undertheorized. As a result, the figure of the people is seen as hardly more than raw material to be shaped and molded in the image of the lawgiver. Admittedly, Rousseau himself is responsible for this picture, at least in part, when for instance he notoriously portrays the people as a "blind multitude," or when he presents the lawgiver as an "architect" who designs the "national physiognomy" of the people. Without denying this current in Rousseau's thought, I nonetheless insist that his discussion of the lawgiver also has a democratic side, which reflects an awareness of and sensitivity to the bootstrapping efforts of the people themselves. In fact, I shall also argue, it is precisely such efforts that make possible and fundamentally condition the agency of the lawgiver in the first place.

In this chapter, by reading Rousseau against the grain this way, I aim to reconstruct an underappreciated strand in his thought, one that can enrich our conceptual resources in thinking through the possibility of democratic founding. However, this is not our sole purpose. Following the proposed reconstructive reading, we will also turn the tables on Rousseau to see what we can learn from the limits of his argument as well. That is to say, the chapter also develops a critical stance on Rousseau's conception of founding. On this register, my claim is that the way Rousseau theorizes the politics of founding is problematic not because the appeal to the lawgiver inevitably compromises its democratic credentials (and we will see why it does not), but because it involves a moment of strict closure, which turns the act of foundation into a frozen instant without a real future.

The Need for the Lawgiver: An Overview

What is the problem to which the lawgiver is the answer? Let us briefly cover the familiar territory first. In Rousseau's view, the creation of a self-legislating political community is ultimately a matter of generalizing the will, which requires a fundamental moral transformation on the part of citizens. Instead of sticking to the narrow perspective of their particular interests, they must be able to place the common good at the center of their political considerations. Notice that a requirement of this sort has both a cognitive and a motivational side; namely, citizens must both *see* the common good and actively *will* it. The problem is how to get them to do this, given the particularistic nature of human beings—and this is why, for Rousseau, "it would require gods to give men laws."[1] Of course, strictly speaking, who is supposed to give laws to men is not a divine but a human agent, the "great lawgiver," whose historical exemplars are figures such as Moses, Numa, and Lycurgus.[2] Rousseau's basic idea is that the desired unity of reason and will, insight and volition, is not given to us by nature, nor is it a felicitous outcome of an impersonal historical process spontaneously moving toward an ever more rational form of life (say, in a Hegelian fashion). Instead, it must be deliberately created by transforming self-interested human beings into public spirited citizens. This means that the lawgiver is above all a political educator. His ultimate task is to tune the inner operations of the will to the common good by shaping the morals of the people. Citizens must be habituated to take the perspective of the whole, and would thereby become capable of exercising the general will on their own.

This familiar overview of the lawgiver is nevertheless incomplete in one crucial aspect. It tells us nothing about why this benevolent political educator arrives in the figure of a political *founder* situated at the very specific temporal context of the beginning of a regime. In other words, why does Rousseau prefer to negotiate the problem of will-formation—the problem of how to generalize the will—in relation to the theme of *founding*? After all, it is possible to imagine the practice of political education in all sorts of different ways, including the "arts of government," to which Rousseau's political thinking was by no means unfamiliar. So, one cannot help but ask: why incorporate the task of political education into the act of foundation? What is it, if anything, in the idea and event of founding that proves important for effecting a normatively desirable transformation in the morals of the people?[3]

Contemporary readers of Rousseau seem to have their own responses to such questions. As we have seen in the previous chapter, according to William Connolly and Bonnie Honig, for example, Rousseau presents the lawgiver as a founding figure because he recasts the paradox of politics as the paradox of founding. In Connolly's words, "he located the paradox in time (perhaps to imagine another time when it could be resolved)."[4] Or as Honig explicates: "In so doing, Rousseau leads his readers to infer that they must just somehow get through the founding, whether by way of a lawgiver's impositional guidance or if necessary by way of a more explicit violence that can produce by force that which will later come by way of education and culture."[5] The crux of the argument is clear enough: the lawgiver appears at the temporal context of a founding moment because Rousseau wants to confine the paradox of politics to the beginning of a regime, as if it does not attach to political life more broadly and constantly impugn the practice of self-legislation in myriad ways. Viewed in this light, the lawgiver is primarily a *deus ex machina*, a strategic conceptual device designed to "conceal" or "displace" the paradoxical and irresolvable circularity of the law and the people.

Insightful as it is, a reading along these lines neglects and eventually obscures an alternative interpretive possibility. Here is what I have in mind in a nutshell. It may well be the case that Rousseau situates the lawgiver in the specific context of a founding moment because he attributes a genuine and fundamental importance to acts of foundation in the first place. In other words, my working hypothesis is that Rousseau sees in founding moments not only a paradoxical circularity, but also an extraordinary window of opportunity to negotiate this paradox and relax its grip. As we will see, should we take this possibility seriously, it opens up to us a whole new perspective on the complicated—but often poorly analyzed—relationship between the people and the lawgiver. In the reading that I propose and develop below, it is not simply the overwhelming agency or "impositional guidance" of the lawgiver that makes the people into the kind of people that they are supposed to be. Quite to the contrary, surprising as it may seem at first sight, it is the agency of a people already *in the making*—the bootstrapping endeavor of the people themselves—that creates the favorable conditions for the enterprise of the lawgiver. This democratic side to Rousseau's fable of the lawgiver goes often unnoticed in the relevant literature despite the fact that there is enough, albeit fragmented, textual evidence to support it.

The Concept of *Moeurs*

To set the scene for this reconstructive reading, we need to take a closer look at Rousseau's conception of *moeurs*. It is a term notoriously difficult to render in English, and Rousseau's not always strictly consistent usage makes things only more difficult. Depending on the context, *moeurs* could mean "morals," "manners," "customs," or "ways." Construed in view of their political relevance, all these terms, in turn, point toward the broad phenomenon that is often treated under the rubric of "political culture." To be sure, the latter is neither identical to nor less elusive than *moeurs*. Nonetheless, if Rousseau has a theory of political culture—and it would be quite counter-intuitive to argue that he does not—it is one in which the notion of *moeurs* is assigned the pride of place. In Rousseau's usage, *moeurs* bears a theoretical weight comparable to, say, Aristotle's *ethos*, Montesquieu's *esprit*, and Hegel's *Sittlichkeit*. Since both *moeurs* and political culture are "soft concepts"[6] resistant to a strict definition, it is perhaps best to begin with an overview of what Rousseau actually means by them.

Three features of *moeurs* are particularly recurrent in Rousseau's thought. First, *moeurs* belong to a community in distinctive ways. Revealed in social practices, habits, and everyday patterns of interaction, they indicate a shared and customary way of life. As such, they inform our notions about who we are as a particular human community, and set a point of reference for collective identity. Second, *moeurs* have a normative content, a moral core, which is best captured by the term "morals." They serve as the repository of morally significant evaluative standards such as what is right and wrong, what is to be honored and shamed, what is to be expected from whom and when. It is this moral core of the *moeurs* that provides the members of the community with an internalized action-orienting framework. Finally, *moeurs* constitute a deep-rooted motivational resource. They penetrate to the self-understanding of individuals, shape their emotions and dispositions, and have a strong hold on their volition. Thus, in addition to their action-orienting function, *moeurs* also have an action-generating power.

In Book II, Chapter 12 of *The Social Contract*, Rousseau presents *moeurs* as the "genuine constitution" of the state. It is a different kind of law, he argues, apart from the three kinds of positive law: political, civil, and criminal.

> To these three sorts of laws must be added a fourth, the most important of all; which is graven not in marble or bronze, but in the hearts of the Citizens; which is the State's genuine constitution; which daily gathers new force; which, when the other laws age or die out, revives or replaces them; and imperceptibly substitutes the force of habit for that of authority. I speak of morals [*moeurs*], customs, and above all of opinion; a part of the laws unknown to our politicians but on which the success of all the others depends: a part to which the great Lawgiver attends in secret, while he appears to restrict himself to particular regulations which are but the ribs of the arch of which morals [*moeurs*], slower to arise, in the end form the immovable Keystone.[7]

Rousseau's emphasis on the ultimate significance of *moeurs* has to do with his skepticism about the efficacy of reason, that is, about the extent to which reason can effectively generalize the will by counter-balancing the impulse of inclinations and the counsels of self-interest. Thus, he would certainly consider it unacceptable had he known Kant's (in)famous claim that "the problem of establishing a state, no matter how hard it may sound, is soluble even for a nation of devils (if only they have understanding)."[8]

On the one hand, Rousseau's skepticism toward the efficacy of reason leads him to underscore, ever more emphatically, the significance of *moeurs* as the repository of culturally embedded normative dispositions that cut deeper than reason. On the other hand, however, Rousseau also recognizes the persistence of the prevalent opinions and beliefs, habits and dispositions which constitute a people's distinctive way of life and inform its political culture. In other words, he is only too well aware of the fact that such deep-rooted structures, produced over a long period of time, do not easily lend themselves to being transformed and remolded as one wills. Hence, the following question inevitably comes to the foreground: how to render the *moeurs* ever more conducive to the normative demands of the general will? How is it possible to foster among the people the kind of dispositions, habits, and cultural meanings required for sustaining a self-legislating political community?

It is here that we can catch a first glimpse of why founding moments deeply matter to Rousseau. In such junctures he sees an actual and extraordinary opportunity to effect a substantial change in the *moeurs* of the people and to stimulate the development of normatively desirable structures of political culture. This is not to say that Rousseau does not consider the possibility of improving *moeurs* under the ordinary circumstances of an already established political community. He does. His reflections on the topic cover a broad territory, spanning from the micro politics of education to the macro political plane of constitutional reforms, from the administrative strategies of steering public opinion to the institutional arrangements that are meant to foster patriotism.[9] Nonetheless, his ultimate position remains pretty cautious about the extent to which *moeurs* practically admit of social engineering, political steering, and legal regulation in an already established political community. He concedes that the government has at most a limited leeway, but it cannot (and, as we will see, should not attempt to) stimulate a comprehensive transformation.

In this respect, political foundings constitute a sharp contrast to the limited prospects of an already established regime. They offer a unique and extraordinary possibility to give a new shape and direction to the patterns of political culture. This notion finds one of its most articulate expressions in a passage from the *Letter to d'Alembert*: "If the government can do much in morals [*moeurs*], it is only in its primitive institution; when once it has determined them, not only does it no longer have the power to change them without itself changing, it has great difficulty in maintaining them against the inevitable accidents which attack them and the natural inclination which corrupts them."[10] Rousseau makes a similar point in *The Social Contract* as well. "Peoples, like men, are docile only in their youth," he suggests; "once customs are established and prejudices rooted, it is a dangerous and futile undertaking to try to reform them."[11] How are we to make sense of these claims? Why is an attempt to transform and reconstruct *moeurs* more likely to succeed in the context of foundation, or in the "primitive institution" of the political community? And what actually does "youth" mean in relation to a human group, a people?

Transformations of Political Culture: Two Scenarios

Questions of this sort refer us to the temporal dimension of Rousseau's conception of *moeurs*. He seems to assume that the shared moral dispositions of a people are especially malleable under certain historical circumstances that do not last for long. Accordingly, attempts to stimulate the development of normatively desirable structures of political culture have a much better chance to succeed if they are undertaken in these extraordinary and temporary periods of openness.

I want to suggest that this assumption takes two different forms in Rousseau's work. That is, he explores two different conditions under which *moeurs* come to be malleable, lending themselves to the kind of comprehensive endeavors to be carried out by the lawgiver. One of these conditions is primarily "anthropological" in the sense that it concerns the developmental stages of human sociality. The other one is strictly "political," implicated in extraordinary historical experiences such as big crises and revolutions, which uproot the prevalent structures of *moeurs* and clear the ground for a substantial reorientation. Let us see Rousseau's take on each condition more closely.

In *The Social Contract*, after having introduced the figure of the lawgiver and explained the nature of his task, Rousseau turns to the issue of "the people" and raises the following question: "what people, then, is fit for legislation?" In response, he writes: "one which, while finding itself already bound together by some union of origin, interest, or convention, has not yet borne the true yoke of laws; one with neither deep-rooted customs nor deep-rooted superstitions."[12] To put it differently, if the people are to hear the call of the lawgiver and benefit from his constitutive endeavors, they must have some prior sense of commonality along with a nascent state of *moeurs*, which is yet to be stabilized in the medium of positive law. This notion strongly resonates with the conjectural history that Rousseau narrates in the *Discourse on Inequality*.[13] At a certain point in the development of human sociality, he assumes, there exists a temporary state of affairs, where human beings enjoy the benefits of living together without being exposed to the destructive forces of civilization. From the standpoint of the anthropological strain in his thought, it is only in such a state of affairs that the *moeurs* of the people can be properly organized into the cultural foundations of a self-legislating political community, provided that the people are fortunate enough to have a genuine lawgiver.

The pre-civilizational stage of social development, however, is not the only condition under which *moeurs* admit of substantial and comprehensive reconstruction. Apart from the anthropological account of the malleability of *moeurs*, Rousseau also mentions a strictly political possibility, drawing attention to periods of turmoil and moments of rupture that make a new beginning possible. After having argued that "once customs are established and prejudices rooted, it is a dangerous and futile undertaking to try to reform them," he immediately adds:

> This is not to say that . . . there may not also sometimes occur periods of violence in the lifetime of States when revolutions do to peoples what certain crises do to individuals, when horror of the past takes the place of forgetting, and when the State aflame with civil wars is so to speak reborn from its ashes and recovers the vigor of youth as it escapes death's embrace. Such was Sparta at the time of Lycurgus, such was Rome after the Tarquins; and such, among us, were Holland and Switzerland after the expulsion of the Tyrants.[14]

Rousseau's reference to Lycurgus is important. Lycurgus is for him one of the three exemplars of a genuine lawgiver, along with Moses and Numa.[15] Thus, one could take this reference as an indication of the idea that the lawgiver does not need to arrive, as if out of nowhere, in the course of a conjectural history, as the anthropological account would suggest. Rather, actual political foundings take place in the wake of decisive turmoils that uproot the entrenched structures of the political community and open the possibility for reconstruction. In times of turbulence, both the institutional arch of the political community and the culturally embedded moral dispositions that sustain it are shaken in such a way as to lose their hold on the people, leading to an extraordinary openness for the creation of new institutions and new politico-cultural resources.

To recapitulate, then, on the reading I propose here, Rousseau attaches an immense importance to founding moments because of their potential impact on political culture. Acts of foundation take place in those rare historical circumstances—whether such circumstances are construed anthropologically or politically—when the deep structures of *moeurs* lend themselves to reconstruction, which is unlikely to occur in ordinary times. Accordingly, what happens at these crucial junctures is likely to have a decisive influence. The effects of founding are woven, for better or for worse, into the very fabric of the political community and keep lingering not only in its institutions, but also in the patterns of collective self-understanding, in the sphere of symbolic meanings, in the soft flesh of habits, dispositions, and emotions. In light of the foregoing, let us turn now to the figure of the lawgiver and take a closer look at his complicated relationship to the people.

The Lawgiver: Architect or Interpreter?

Implicit in Rousseau's paradox of founding is a keen awareness of the difficulties of transition from a non-republican condition, along with the morals it has produced over time, to a politics of self-legislation, which requires the cultivation of a new kind of political culture. Consider the sometimes desperately painful transitions to democracy, particularly in societies where the politico-cultural resources required to sustain democratic deliberation and form of government are not readily given but need to be stimulated, as much as possible, in and through the process of transition. Rousseau's discussion of the lawgiver offers a way of theorizing how these resources are to be generated. More specifically, far from inventing a *deus ex machina*, Rousseau captures in the figure of the lawgiver an all too tangible aspect of transitional periods and the politics of founding they foster; namely, the significant role of the elite in stimulating the politico-cultural resources of a new regime.

It is often (and not without good reason) suggested that Rousseau's expectations of the elite in the course of political founding indicate a democratic deficit. One may even say that this is *the* standard interpretation of the lawgiver. Compromising Rousseau's vision of a self-legislating political community, the emphasis on the role of the elite, so the argument goes, reveals the "authoritarian strain" in his thought.[16] It is my contention that the way Rousseau conceives of founding moments can help us see the issue from a broader angle. The theme of the "great man" has no doubt a certain and well-documented attraction for him.[17] But so does the theme of "the people." Hence, the question is how exactly does the great man, the lawgiver, or the leading elite, relate to the people in the context of political founding? I think that Rousseau's reflections on the topic point in two directions at once, each of which suggests a different picture of the lawgiver. I want to call them the lawgiver as "architect" and the lawgiver as "interpreter," respectively.[18]

According to the image of the architect, the lawgiver designs the institutional arch of the political community and its "national physiognomy"[19] by creating the morals of the people more or less from scratch. On this reading, somewhat in line with Sheldon Wolin's claim that the lawgiver is a *deus ex machina*,[20] the people are hardly more than the raw material on which the formative endeavors of the lawgiver are imposed. Admittedly, Rousseau himself is responsible, at least in part, for this untenable notion of a Demiurge-like founder, as for instance his remarks on Moses would suggest. Moses, according to Rousseau, had the kind of genius that "creates and makes everything out of nothing."[21] He "formed and executed the astonishing enterprise of instituting as a national body a swarm of wretched fugitives who had no arts, no weapons, no talents, no virtues, no courage, and who, since they had not an inch of territory of their own, were a troop of strangers upon the face of the earth."[22]

In this picture, the *receptivity* of the people is either completely ignored in favor of the overwhelming *agency* of the lawgiver or, at best, treated as a function of the latter. Being equipped with both wisdom and charisma, the lawgiver makes his appeal in such a way as to establish the proper circumstances for his own reception. As we have already seen in Chapter 2, that is also the crux of Alan Keenan's take on the lawgiver: "One must appeal to the political community in such a way that its members will accept the regulations that will make them into the kind of (general) people able to 'hear' such an appeal. . . . If 'the people' ever come into existence, it can only be in the form of claims made about them, on their behalf, or in their name."[23]

This view is not wrong, but neither is it altogether right. Theorists approaching the lawgiver through the lens of the "architect" miss out something crucial, which comes to the foreground only when we turn to the image of the lawgiver as an "interpreter." The latter image offers us a quite different angle from which to approach the relationship between the people and the lawgiver. On this reading, the task of the lawgiver is first and foremost a hermeneutical one. In almost every occasion where he speaks of the lawgiver, Rousseau time and again argues that the main issue regarding legislation is not so much to find the best laws in themselves as to articulate them in view of their context of application. In a passage worth quoting here, he tellingly juxtaposes Plato and Solon, the philosopher and the lawgiver, to underscore this *interpretive* nature of legislation:

> Where is the least student of the law who cannot erect a moral code as pure as that of Plato's laws? But this is not the only issue. The problem is to adapt this code to the people for which it is made and to the things about which it decrees to such an extent that its execution follows from the very conjunction of these relations; it is to impose on the people, after the fashion of Solon, less the best laws in themselves than the best of which it admits in the *given situation*.[24]

This interpretive dimension of legislation already has a broad democratic relevance insofar as it is a reminder of the fact that there is no escape from the will of the people.[25] It is eventually up to the people themselves to accept or reject the law, not merely through an episodic act of consent, but more significantly through everyday practices extending over time. Law comes to belong to the people when it is reflected into their *moeurs*; and for this to happen, the very act of legislation must take its cue from the "given situation" of the people in the first place.

This is only half the story, though. We should also consider the fact that—and this is crucial for our present purposes—the "given situation" of the people is not simply "given" at all. It is often the product of the people's own collective action, and particularly so in revolutionary periods. In Rousseau's work, the relationship between the hermeneutic character of legislation and the collective action of the people appears most vividly in his *Plan for a Constitution for Corsica*.[26] "There is one country left in Europe capable of receiving legislation," he already declared in *The Social Contract*: "it is the island of Corsica."[27] But the receptivity of Corsicans was not just "given" as Rousseau himself had been well aware.[28] It was the result of their own shared efforts, sustained over a forty-year struggle for independence from the domination of Genoa. Rousseau followed the episodes of this struggle with great admiration. And tellingly enough, unlike his *Considerations on the Government of Poland*, which was addressed to the politically active Polish elite, the *Plan for a Constitution for Corsica* was addressed directly to the "brave Corsicans" themselves, in the second person plural.

Situated in the historical context of a popular struggle, the task of the lawgiver takes on a different form, one that is hard to capture from the vantage point of the "architect." The would-be lawgiver is now supposed to read the text of collective action and shared experience, hear its underlying meaning, and interpret the historically conditioned endeavors of the people in their true light.[29] He does not aspire to create new realities on his own, but channels the creative energies of the people, unleashed in revolutionary politics, into the institutional and cultural foundations of a self-legislating political community. Accordingly, his deliberate attempts to attend to the *moeurs* of the people are carried out not in the spirit of creating new citizens from scratch, but in the spirit of reorienting what is already *in the making* through the bootstrapping efforts of the people themselves. Under such circumstances, the lawgiver is able "to rally without violence and to persuade without convincing"[30] because (with reference to Josiah Ober's interpretation of what Cleisthenes did in the Athenian revolution) he "stands up before the people."[31] On this view, then, it is not so much the lawgiver's agency that frames the receptivity of the people but the other way around. It is the collective action of the people and the kind of receptivity generated in the course of such action that calls forth the lawgiver and sets the conditions for the enterprise of legislation.

My overall claim here is not that the notion of the lawgiver as "interpreter" captures Rousseau's own intentions better than that of the lawgiver as "architect." Nonetheless, I would suggest that the former is theoretically more fruitful and intriguing than the latter. In the end, however, both possibilities remain integral aspects of the way Rousseau conceives of the lawgiver. The point of the argument resides elsewhere. The interpretive dimension of legislation and its relation to the collective action of the people fades away once the paradox of founding is hypostatized and Rousseau's fable of the lawgiver is exclusively read as a strategy of concealing or displacing it. Thus, in contrast to hypostatized restatements of the paradox, I want to emphasize that there is *also* a democratic side to Rousseau's fable of the lawgiver, one which invites us to attune ourselves to the endeavors of a people in the making.

Rousseau's Trouble with Time

Now I want to turn the tables on Rousseau in order to see what we can learn from the limits of his argument as well. As I hope to have shown thus far, Rousseau attributes an immense significance to founding moments primarily because of their impact on political culture. However, his conception of political culture—or of *moeurs*, for that matter—is itself deeply problematic. I have in mind not only Rousseau's emphasis on ethical homogeneity, which culminates in a regime of republican *moeurs* entrenched by civic religion, but also the "temporal" aspect of his argument about the transformations of political culture. By this, I mean that Rousseau exclusively confines the prospect of normatively desirable change to the extraordinary moment of founding, while at the same time precluding the possibility of piecemeal and incremental transformation over time.

Why would this be a problem? Here is my short answer: the "ways" that define the political community as a certain kind of "we"—that is, the *moeurs* of the people, the "genuine constitution" of the republic—are constantly challenged, interpreted and redeployed in the fluctuating course of political life, particularly so in the political life of a democratic community. Those "ways" exist in time and they change by time. At its most basic, Rousseau considers this level of complexity as a threat to the republic. Once the foundations of the regime are settled—but can they be settled once and for all?—it seems that all that remains is a single-minded politics of preservation, whose ultimate gesture is to withstand the passing of time. Still, Rousseau worries that there is no ultimate escape from corruption and doom. "If Sparta and Rome perished, what State can hope to last forever," he asks; "the body politic, just like the body of a man, begins to die as soon as it is born and carries within itself the causes of its destruction."[32] As William Connolly puts it nicely, Rousseau's response to the prospect of inevitable doom is to slow down the tempo of political life, that is to say, to "imagine a regime where time crawls slowly, so that a homogeneous ethos of sovereignty can persist across generations."[33]

One can easily read here a sort of tragic sensibility, inherited from the tradition of Roman republicanism, to a large extent via Machiavelli. On this outlook, political freedom is not the norm but the exception in the human condition. Gained through heroic efforts and great sacrifices, it is utterly fragile and lost all too easily once the counsels of self-interest make their way into the souls of citizens. The twin dangers of tyranny and anarchy are always on the horizon, generating a sense of inescapable and ever impending doom. This sensibility is further intermingled in Rousseau's thought with the depth of a social theory, according to which human sociality is perverted in self-destructive directions through the very process of historical development. As the first arduous critic of the modern notion of progress, Rousseau rejects the view that the formation of a republican political culture would be conceived as the outcome of long-range trends and impersonal processes over which no one has strict control. He is committed to *deep voluntarism*, not only in the normative sense that the morality of the law must be rooted in the "causality of the will," but also in the sense that only deliberate human action, working against the forces of nature and history, is capable of creating—with great difficulty and only for a limited time—the conditions of political freedom.

Where do these remarks lead us with respect to Rousseau's conception of founding? One point needs to be highlighted: his perspective sets in motion a hyperbolic vacillation between the hope for novelty and the commitment to permanence, between a radical politics of beginning anew and a conservative politics of withstanding change. On the one hand, the act of foundation responds to the endeavor of a people in the making; on the other hand, it is inhabited by a moment of closure, a commitment to settlement, which is meant to stabilize the "genuine constitution" of the state, the *moeurs* of the people, and eventually the people themselves, leaving them incapable of opening themselves up to the future. There is a sense in which the act of foundation is at once both the beginning and the end of genuine politics in Rousseau.

In fact, this dangerous drive to closure is an essential reason why the paradox of founding has become a recurring theme in contemporary political theory. Theorists who constantly turn to the paradox, by bringing it to the fore and arguing for its persistence, want to demonstrate thereby something utterly important: no law, no institution, or no "people" for that matter, can completely close in on itself. Recall Derrida, for example. As we saw in the previous chapter, the problem for him is not that acts of foundation are paradoxical; on the contrary, the problem is rather that they pretend to be unparadoxical. Every act of foundation tends to gloss over its groundlessness and to cover its own tracks. In the paradox of founding, accordingly, Derrida sees a chance to interrupt this move, a chance to challenge the claims of settlement and hence to force open the limits on the future. On this interpretive strategy, the paradox of founding is a potent conceptual resource that can be turned into a democratic advantage vis-à-vis the forces of closure.

From the standpoint of this study, the concern about closure and the desire to resist the colonization of future are absolutely important. Yet, how are we supposed to address them in a helpful way? I doubt that a strategy premised on the paradox of founding can get us far enough in the right direction. Such a strategy seems to me problematic for reasons already discussed under the rubric of "hypostatization" in Chapter 2. In its stead, we would be well advised to consider a different option, and to seek the possibility of keeping the future open from within the *experience* of a people who can claim joint ownership in their constitution. Within the confines of the present chapter, however, I cannot make a full case to support this claim (for which we will have to turn to the work of Hannah Arendt and Jürgen Habermas in Chapters 5 and 6). It would be nonetheless helpful here to juxtapose Rousseau's insistence on founding with Kant's forward-looking politics.

Of Gods and Devils: Kant's Critique of Rousseau

When it comes to the issue of founding, nothing perhaps better illustrates the contrast between Rousseau and Kant than the fact that, while in Rousseau's view "it would require gods to give men laws," in Kant's view "the problem of establishing a state, no matter how hard it may sound, is soluble even for a nation of devils."[34] Such a contrast is particularly intriguing given that both Rousseau and Kant take the united will of the people as the normative ground of a republican constitution. How are we to understand this talk of gods and devils, then? On what assumptions does it rest? And what does it tell us with regard to the relationship between time and founding?

From the vantage point of Kant's practical philosophy, we don't need the educative authority of a Moses or a Lycurgus to open up to us a broader perspective than that of our particular interests. Rather, we are always already aware of the claims of "ought," as a "fact of reason," demanding that we not make exception "just this once" for our own case but instead weigh all cases from an impartial point of view. With regard to our external actions affecting others, this impartial point of view finds its expression in the "principle of right." Accordingly, in sharp contrast to Rousseau, the political problem for Kant is not how to generalize the inner operations of the will or to stimulate a moral transformation of self-interested individuals into public-spirited citizens. The political problem is rather how to ensure that rational but particularistic creatures such as ourselves comply with the demands of "right" in their external actions. This, in turn, allows Kant to articulate a different conception of founding.

In the Kantian scheme, the act of foundation amounts to nothing more nor less than the replacement of the state of nature with a civil or rightful condition.[35] Kant's understanding of the state of nature is purely juridical. It refers to any condition in which a multitude of human beings who cannot avoid affecting one another are not subject to a system of coercive public laws regulating their interaction. Everyone in such a condition is for Kant under a moral obligation to abandon it and enter with others into a civil condition. And yet the state of nature does not by definition admit of an established and valid procedure for this transition. How then do we proceed from the state of nature to a state of right?

Kant has a straight answer: "each may impel the other by force to leave this state and enter into a rightful condition."[36] Or as he puts it elsewhere, emphasizing the necessity of founding violence: "the only beginning of the rightful condition to be counted upon is that by power, on the coercion of which public right is afterward based."[37] In recognizing the necessity of founding violence, Kant does not appeal to historical evidence as, for instance, Hume does. For Kant, by contrast, it is not experience that shows us why the political order has its origin in founding violence. Rather, one can a priori deduce from the concept of the state of nature that force is the only conceivable way of inaugurating a state of right, if for no other reason than that in the state of nature there is no valid and established procedure to replace it with a rightful condition.

Kant does not say anything farther about the modus operandi of this constituent force or founding violence that inaugurates the political order. In a sense, this is no surprise since the nature of the topic does not lend itself to a priori analysis. It seems that any course of action would do, so long as it *effectively* abandons the juridical state of nature and enacts a state of right to replace it. However, he notes the following remark in passing: "since we can scarcely allow for a moral disposition of the legislator [*der Gesetzgeber*] such that, after the disorderly multitude has been united into a people, he will now leave the people to bring about a rightful constitution by its common will, it can be anticipated that in actual experience there will be great deviations from that idea (of theory)."[38]

We find here an image of the lawgiver, one fundamentally different from Rousseau's. While the task of Rousseau's lawgiver is to attend to the morals of the people in such a way as to transform the *inner* operations of the will, the sole task of Kant's lawgiver is to set up a legal condition, in which the *external* actions of individuals are brought under the force of law. Furthermore, Kant has no visionary expectations regarding the moral assets and personality of the lawgiver. In contrast to the "great soul" of Rousseau's *législateur*—which is the "true miracle which must prove his mission"[39]—Kant's *Gesetzgeber* does not need to be a good man at all, or a "foreigner" for that matter, who would leave the people on their own once the transition from the state of nature to a rightful condition is accomplished. This, Kant notes with a touch of sober realism, we cannot assume.

The difference between the two images of the lawgiver parallels the substantial difference in Rousseau's and Kant's respective approaches to founding moments. Rousseau deeply cares about the way in which political community begins because the prospects for gradual reform are in his view too bleak to count on. By contrast, in Kant's view, any beginning would do insofar as the juridical state of nature is abandoned and "the disorderly mass has been united into a people" through coercive laws. What ultimately matters is not how the state is originally constituted, but the rationalization and republicanization of state power over time through piecemeal and gradual reform. Consider the following passage, where Kant's reformist outlook is aptly captured:

> The spirit of the original contract (*anima pacti originarii*) involves an obligation on the part of the constituting authority to make the kind of government suited to the idea of the original contract. Accordingly, even if this cannot be done all at once, it is under obligation to change the kind of government gradually and continually so that it harmonizes in its effect with the only constitution that accords with right, that of a pure republic, in such a way that the old (empirical) statutory forms, which served merely to bring about the submission of the people, are replaced by the original (rational) form, the only form which makes freedom the principle and indeed the condition for any exercise of coercion, as is required by a rightful constitution of a state in the strict sense of the word.[40]

One is tempted to pitch the contrast between Rousseau and Kant in a particularly pointed fashion: for Rousseau, founding is everything because gradual reform is nothing (or almost nothing); for Kant, on the other hand, founding is nothing (or almost nothing) because gradual reform is everything.

Yet, there is actually something more to Kant's disenchanted view of founding moments. The origins of political community have no real significance for him for the related and crucial reason that Kant (unlike Rousseau) puts his trust in progress. The above passage already gives us a glimpse of the sense in which political progress is transcendentally anchored in the "original contract." As we have seen in Chapter 1 in some detail, Kant takes the original contract as an "idea of reason," which nonetheless has "its undoubted practical reality" in such a way as to "bind every legislator" to give his laws in a certain way.[41] As such, it serves as the a priori ground of (and the normative point of reference for) constant gradual reform. Furthermore, this transcendentally anchored prospect for progress is politically fostered in and through the public use of reason, on which constitutional reform feeds. The result is a forward-looking politics, i.e., a politics of taming the state power in the medium of law over time, no matter how this medium itself happens to be originally established.

What follows from this comparison of Kant and Rousseau for our discussion? Kant's future-oriented outlook has a certain appeal, one which is crucially missing in the politics of the Rousseauean republic committed to the preservation of its settled foundations. Contra Rousseau, many of us would readily acknowledge today that for a more or less democratic community, it is hard work to live up to its own normative aspirations, and that it requires a commitment to sustain an ongoing conversation and contestation on matters of constitutional significance. In other words, translating Kant's forward-looking perspective into our own parlance, we might want to say that democracy is ultimately a matter of constant democratization. All these stand in sharp contrast to Rousseau's insistence on founding. He wants to set up the republic on the right foundations from the beginning, and then to preserve those foundations, as much as possible, by withstanding the passing of time and the corruption that comes along with it.

Nonetheless, can we actually follow Kant in his claim that any beginning would do, that the moment of founding has no real significance whatsoever apart from its juridical meaning, and that the problem is soluble even for a "nation of devils"? This aspect of Kant's argument makes sense—if it makes sense at all—in a world where the prospect of progressive reform is firmly anchored in the reassuring "facts of reason." In the postmetaphysical world, however, this backdrop is gone along with the metaphysics of practical reason, and we are left to our own *historically conditioned* resources. Under such circumstances, it is hard to ignore the importance of founding moments in opening up or precluding different future prospects, in shaping the kind of "we" that we deem ourselves to be, and in setting the paths of constitutional reform.

In all these respects, properly construed, Rousseau is still our contemporary. One does not need to share Rousseau's tragic outlook on history or his limited view on the transformations of political culture, or his vision of republican virtue for that matter. The formation of a more or less democratic community, we may plausibly hold against him, is an open-ended work in process. Nevertheless, in a world devoid of transcendental guarantees and yardsticks, the way in which this process is set in motion (and occasionally punctuated in constitutional moments) is all the more likely to bear weight in and of itself, to shape our relation to the project of constitutional democracy as citizens, and to produce lingering effects on the later course of its development. Rousseau's insistence on founding can make sense to us from within our own horizon. This does not mean that "it would require gods to give men laws," but all the same, no democracy can arise on the shoulders of devils either.

* * *

This chapter has offered a new account of the relationship between the people and the lawgiver in Rousseau. Inspired by Rousseau's reflections on Corsica, this account proposes to view the lawgiver as an "interpreter" responding to the collective action of a people in the making. In contrast to the widely held view that the lawgiver is a deus ex machina of sorts (or worse, an impositional figure compromising the very possibility of democratic founding), I argue that it is not the lawgiver who calls forth the people but the other way around. The collective action of the people creates the suitable conditions for legislation and calls forth the lawgiver, whose task is to interpret the underlying meaning of this experience and to inscribe it into the foundations of the new republic.

This alternative story is meant to illustrate—in the context of Rousseau's work—what interpretive possibilities would open up to us if we approach the paradox of democratic founding as a heuristic problem rather than an insurmountable logical aporia. More specifically, the reading that I propose here urges a critical distance from the rigid dichotomy between the "two bodies" of the people. To put it with Margaret Canovan, "either the people are simply an aggregate of individuals with no capacity for collective sovereignty, or else they form a corporate body that can exist and act as other corporate bodies do."[42] In reading Rousseau against the grain, however, we have seen that it is possible—and I would add, desirable—to move beyond such a dichotomy, and to think of the people neither as an "amorphous multitude" nor a constitutionally organized "corporate body," but instead as a community of action in the making.

To be sure, a reading of this sort does not simply discard or intend to discard the paradox of founding in and of itself. Nor does it claim to explain with any precision how the people get to underwrite their constitution. Nonetheless, it takes a first step in thematizing the sense in which the emergence of a new constitutional form is after all made possible by and fundamentally related to the bootstrapping efforts of the people themselves, no matter how inchoate or even perhaps episodic those efforts might be. To recapitulate, then, once we approach the paradox of democratic founding as a heuristic problem, it brings home to us the importance of collective action or a shared experience of agency in *becoming* a people. The next chapter continues to explore this motif in the work of Hannah Arendt.

Chapter 4

Building a Homeland

Founding and Identity in Hannah Arendt's Jewish Writings

There is a sense in which Hannah Arendt's significance for our study is self-evident. After all, among the major political thinkers of the twentieth century, no one has been more interested in the question of founding than she was. This is far from surprising given the fact that Arendt witnessed the drastic unmaking of the public world under the onslaught of totalitarianism, and eventually placed the problem of its making anew at the center of her theoretical preoccupations. From her early writings on the "Jewish question" to *On Revolution* and all the way to the very last pages she wrote (namely, "The abyss of freedom and the *novus ordo seclorum*," the final chapter of the incomplete and posthumously published *The Life of the Mind*), the question of founding remained close to the nerve of her guiding concerns.

As she described herself once, Arendt was a "sort of phenomenologist."[1] In order to account for the meaning of an experience, phenomenological analysis thematizes the structures in which that experience becomes possible. Throughout her work, Arendt applied this mode of analysis to various political phenomena as well as to politics itself as a distinctive human endeavor. Her reflections on the politics of founding are no exception. At a fundamental conceptual level, they are oriented toward the "field of experience" in which a new political community emerges and remains anchored. As such, Arendt is arguably the first thinker who theorized the politics of founding from within the postmetaphysical world—a world where philosophical foundationalism has lost its longstanding grip on political theory, where there is no viable way of appealing to "first principles," "self-evident truths," or "facts of reason," and where the people do not have "two bodies," one real and located in time, the other ideal and beyond our temporal reality. In this respect, there is a certain affinity between her work and the central thesis of this book: that the normative "foundations" of the democratic constitution must be performatively manifest in its "origins," and that how the process of constitution-making is *experienced* matters as much as the outcome of that process. The basic reason we turn to Arendt now is to gain insight into this experiential dimension of democratic founding.

Students of Arendt's political thought often take *On Revolution* as the primary text where her theory of founding is stated. In that book, Arendt inquires into the meaning of revolution as a new beginning, and grapples with the thorny question of how the "event" of revolution could stabilize itself and give rise to a constitutional "form" housing the experience of public freedom. To this end, the book involves a sustained critique of the classical theory of constituent power, and offers in its stead an alternative, post-sovereign account of constitution-making. As I see it, this is a crucial contribution to a theory of democratic founding, and we will explore it in the next chapter. In the present chapter, however, our discussion begins elsewhere. I take my point of departure from Arendt's early essays on Jewish identity and politics, most of which were written during the 1940s and are now available in a single volume, *The Jewish Writings*.[2] In those essays, by focusing on the meaning and future of the Jewish settlement in Palestine, Arendt offers a vivid reflection on the problem of founding, which is almost systematically neglected in the relevant literature.

Let me introduce two thematic angles from which the politics of founding comes in for discussion in *The Jewish Writings*. The first has to do with the question of *identity* in the sense that this term applies to the self-understanding of a people as a certain kind of "we." In deliberate acts of foundation expressive of a political will to live together, Arendt sees an alternative to essentialist notions of peoplehood that take ethnic belonging or some form of cultural homogeneity as the substratum of the political association. On this register, largely inspired by the republican tradition, her thinking proceeds from the familiar contrast between "ethnic" and "civic" conceptions of peoplehood, and clearly favors the latter. Second, in theorizing the phenomenon of founding, Arendt takes her cue from the distinction between nature and human artifice, and emphasizes the significance of an *artificial space* in and through which human beings make themselves at home in the world. In contrast to our natural environment, "home" in this sense refers to a human-made reality, an artifact created through collective endeavors that find their political manifestation in the emergence of public spaces, the founding of cities and republics, and the making of constitutions.

These two perspectives on founding are tied together in *The Jewish Writings*. In the political mobilization of a stateless people to set up a "homeland" for themselves, Arendt sought the possibility of cultivating a civic identity, which was to be anchored in the experience of building a common world and based on voluntary commitment rather than ethnic belonging. In other words, attending to the role of world-building action in transforming and redefining who "we" are, *The Jewish Writings* contains a rich reflection on the field of political experience in which claims of peoplehood are in the making. I flesh this point out in the rest of the chapter.

In Search of a Jewish Politics: The Pitfalls of Humanism and Nationalism

An apparent tension runs like a red thread throughout Arendt's voluminous essays on the "Jewish question." On the one hand, she emphatically called her fellow Jews to assume political responsibility for their own future. It was her considered opinion that to be a Jew had become a political fact in the twentieth century and that Jews were supposed to act accordingly. That is to say, they had to take collective action as a people vis-à-vis the events endangering their very existence, and organize themselves into a political community. On the other hand, contradictory as it may seem, she adopted a highly critical attitude toward Zionism, which was, after all, the "only political answer Jews have ever found to antisemitism," as Arendt herself admitted.[3] She took issue with mainstream Zionist politics for its single-minded focus on the prospect of the Jewish nation-state, and for having succumbed to what she deemed to be a crude nationalist creed. Let us take a closer look at her position.

Arendt critically observes that the Jewish people persistently evaded political action to their own detriment throughout the long period of diaspora. This withdrawal from politics resulted in a dangerous exposure to the whims of contingent forces in history, and an ever growing dependence on the powers that be. At the beginning of "Antisemitism," the first volume of *The Origins of Totalitarianism*, she writes:

> Jewish history offers the extraordinary spectacle of a people, unique in this respect, which began its history with a well-defined concept of history and an almost conscious resolution to achieve a well-circumscribed plan on earth and then, without giving up this concept, avoided all political action for two thousand years. The result was that the political history of the Jewish people became even more dependent upon unforeseen, accidental factors than the history of other nations, so that the Jews stumbled from one role to the other and accepted responsibility for none.[4]

Arendt traces the modern forms of this escapism not only to nineteenth-century Jewry's hope for complete assimilation into respectable society, of which she was bitterly critical as the prospect of the "parvenu," but also to the eighteenth-century Jewish reception of Enlightenment humanism, for which she had a good deal of respect.

In an address occasioned by her acceptance of the Lessing Prize in 1959, speaking with the benefit of hindsight, Arendt refers to Lessing's play *Nathan the Wise* to highlight what she takes to be problematic in the unqualified humanism inherited from the Enlightenment: "the statement with which Nathan the Wise (in effect, though not in actual wording) countered the command: 'Step closer, Jew'—the statement: I am a man—I would have considered as nothing but a grotesque and dangerous evasion of reality."[5] The problem with the statement "I am a man" does not reside in the appeal to a notion of common humanity beneath the multiplicity of races, religions, and nations. Rather, the problem is that this appeal seeks a refuge from the political reality of persecution that confronts Jews qua Jews and not simply as human beings. Hence its failure to realize that "one can resist only in terms of the identity that is under attack."[6] Or, as she puts it elsewhere, "from the 'disgrace' of being a Jew there is but one escape—to fight for the honor of the Jewish people as a whole."[7]

Shortly after her arrival in the United States in 1941, Arendt started to write in *Aufbau*, a German-language Jewish weekly published in New York, where she advocated the establishment of a Jewish army to fight in World War II. The demand for a Jewish army had already been raised by the American Zionist Organization and received considerable popular support. If the Jews were to have any real say about their own fate after the war, Arendt argued, they should join the fight against the Nazis, not as nationals of other countries, but "as Jews, in Jewish battle formations under a Jewish flag."[8] She was hoping that this could be the beginning of a genuine Jewish politics, in which the entrenched habits of dependence on great powers would be broken and the "politics of petition practiced by our notables"⁹ would finally be replaced by a politics of popular mobilization. The Jewish Agency in Palestine, however, did not succeed in making a principled case for the formation of such an army, leading to one of Arendt's many disappointments with the Zionist leadership of the time.¹⁰

Despite her acknowledgment of the fact that the Zionist movement was the only "truly political organization"¹¹ of the Jewish people, Arendt's disagreement with its political vision and day-to-day politics became ever deeper in the years following 1942. In this period, when she explicitly distanced herself from mainstream Zionist politics, her attention also turned more emphatically to the twin problems in Palestine: the question of Jewish-Arab relations in the region and the question of the political form the Palestinian Jewry should give itself—both of which, of course, were to become the central issues in the founding of the state of Israel. This was also the period in which Arendt published almost all her major essays on Jewish politics. To understand her take on the founding of Israel, it is necessary to take into account the critique of mainstream Zionism developed in these essays.¹²

In Arendt's view, the decisive limitations of Zionist thinking and practice in the 1940s were closely tied to the political vision of its founding father, Theodor Herzl. She applauds Herzl for turning to politics as the sole medium of a real solution to the problems confronting the Jews in the modern world. "Herzl's lasting greatness lay in his very desire to do something about the Jewish question, his desire to act and to solve the problem in political terms."¹³ This celebration of Herzl's recovery of political action, however, hardly extends to his politics. Arendt does not hide her dislike for Herzl's elitist and top-down modus operandi that tends to infantilize the common people.¹⁴ Beneath this modus operandi is the conviction that high diplomacy is the primary form of politics, which led to Herzl's eventually unsuccessful attempts at behind-the-scenes negotiations with great powers to secure a Jewish territory in Palestine. Arendt contrasts this approach to French Zionist Bernard Lazare's call for popular action, self-organization, and solidarity with other oppressed groups in contemporary Europe.¹⁵

More significantly, Herzl's political thinking comes in for sharp criticism on account of its theoretical postulates concerning the nature of antisemitism and the organic unity of the Jewish people. For Herzl, the hatred that had chased Jewish communities since the destruction of the Temple consisted primarily in the hostile reaction of one people against another because of the somewhat "natural" differences between them. In this view, antisemitism displays a disturbing consistency over time, and constitutes a permanent, unchanging, and most likely unchangeable reality confronting the Jewish people. Arendt labels this conception as the "doctrine of eternal antisemitism."[16] According to her, an understanding of this sort renders irrelevant from the outset any serious analysis of modern antisemitism as an outcome of historically conditioned political institutions and social practices that can be resisted and transformed through conscious political action precisely because they are *not* natural forces. Her ultimate response to Herzl on this point is the first volume of *The Origins of Totalitarianism*, subtitled "Antisemitism."

In that volume, Arendt traces the structural elements of modern antisemitism back to the inner contradictions of the nation-state and the ways the discontents of bourgeois society spilled over into the relations between Jews and gentiles throughout the nineteenth century. In Arendt's view, failing to analyze the political grounds and social dynamics underpinning the persecution of the Jews in modern Europe, the doctrine of eternal antisemitism seeks the solution to the Jewish question in a politics of exodus. If antisemitism is rooted in the permanent features of the human condition, as Herzl would have us believe, then Jews would be safe from hatred and persecution only in isolation from other nations. The inevitable conclusion was that "a people without a country would have to escape to a country without a people."[17]

The doctrine of eternal antisemitism, however, is not the only source of isolationist tendencies inherent in Herzl's thought. For Arendt, an equally decisive factor is the influence of nineteenth-century German nationalism with its conception of the people as an organic entity whose unique spirit can unfold only if it follows the path of its natural growth without being hampered by other peoples. In this respect, Arendt takes her point of reference from the familiar distinction between civic and ethnic conceptions of peoplehood, associated with the French and German streams of nationalism respectively. "Herzl thought in terms of nationalism inspired from German sources," she writes, "as opposed to the French variety, which could never quite repudiate its original relationship to the political ideas of the French Revolution."[18]

The problem with the ethnic notion of peoplehood inherent in Herzl's thought is twofold. First, it turns pre-political categories of kinship and ethnicity, which emphasize *homogeneity* by their very nature, into the constitutive principles of the political community. As such, it leads to a structural distortion of the political realm because politics depends on opinion and deliberate action, both of which, by their own nature, point in the direction of *plurality* rather than homogeneity. Once pre-political qualities become the organizing principles of the political community, Arendt concludes, "the grand French idea of the sovereignty of the people is perverted into the nationalist claims to autarchical existence."[19] This, in turn, indicates the second problem with the notion of the people as an organic body, naturally isolated from other such bodies by virtue of its pre-political essence. It can neither relate itself to humanity in a meaningful way nor endorse a principle of justice among different peoples.

Redefining Who "We" Are in Action

We appear to have come full circle. On the one hand, Arendt argues that if Jews are to take matters into their own hands and determine their own fate, they must engage in collective action as a *people*. The unqualified humanism of Nathan the Wise—"I am a man"—is a red herring that fails to acknowledge the real issue at stake, which is the "admission of Jews *as Jews* to the ranks of humanity."[20] On the other hand, she criticizes mainstream Zionism, the "only political answer Jews have ever found to antisemitism," for its appropriation of a crude nationalist creed that lacks a constructive openness to the idea of common *humanity*. As Ronald Beiner puts it succinctly, "Arendt wanted Jewish politics but not Jewish nationalism."[21]

In fact, this position fits with the broader conclusions Arendt drew from the catastrophic events of the 1930s and 1940s in Europe. The fate of European Jewry made it clear for her that a political community providing its members with legal status and a place in the world was a fundamental human good, something that had to be deliberately built and cared for. It was in the light of this insight that she defended a Jewish politics of peoplehood. Vis-à-vis the horrors of totalitarianism and its unprecedented assault on human dignity, however, Arendt also highlighted the importance of an organized humanity. In her view, the calamities of the twentieth century demanded with unmistakable urgency the establishment of a global framework of responsibility beyond and above sovereign nations. In the 1950 preface to *The Origins of Totalitarianism*, she thus wrote: "human dignity needs a new guarantee which can be found only in a new political principle, in a new law on earth, whose validity this time must comprehend the whole of humanity."[22]

It seems that Arendt's thinking was guided by a double commitment. Its gist is beautifully expressed in the closing statement of her seminal essay, "The Jew as Pariah": "only within the framework of a people can a man live as a man among men, without exhausting himself. And only when a people lives and functions in consort with other peoples can it contribute to the establishment on earth of a commonly conditioned and commonly controlled humanity."[23] However, a double commitment of this sort, turning around the notions of "peoplehood" and "humanity," presents Arendt (and her readers) with a difficult question. Is it possible to have it both ways, after all? How to intertwine the politics of peoplehood with the idea of common humanity? How can a people act on the basis of—and even for the sake of—a shared identity, while at the same time endorsing an openness to humanity at large and avoiding the moral dangers of nationalist closure?

It is precisely this question, I want to suggest, that frames Arendt's reflections on the issue of founding in her early writings. In search of a politics of peoplehood—which would affirm the historical identity of the Jewish people, on one hand, and which would reconstruct it in such a way as to reject nationalist closure, on the other—Arendt turns to the idea of a republican act of foundation expressive of a political will to live together. Her guiding insight is that a politically constituted people, whose self-understanding refers back to a deliberate founding act and whose self-organization depends on voluntary commitment, is capable of relating itself to humanity in ways that are foreclosed or even categorically denied by essentialist models of peoplehood resting on ethnic belonging and cultural homogeneity. In deliberate acts of foundation expressive of a political will to live together, moreover, she sees not only a viable alternative to the pernicious politics of nationalism, but also a historical possibility to reconstruct the inherited Jewish identity—"the identity that is under attack"—around the commitment to build a "homeland" and to care for it.

This insight resides at the very heart of Arendt's reflections on the Jewish politics of founding in Palestine. In May 1948, immediately following the proclamation of the state of Israel and the outbreak of the Jewish-Arab war, she published an essay with the title "To Save the Jewish Homeland." The essay was motivated by an overwhelming concern about how the outcome of the war would affect Jewish life and the Jewish self-understanding at large. "Palestine and the building of a Jewish homeland constitute today the great hope and the great pride of Jews all over the world. What would happen to Jews, individually and collectively, if this hope and this pride were to be extinguished in another catastrophe is almost beyond imagining."[24] Intriguingly enough, however, Arendt's fears did not exclusively focus on the catastrophic prospect of defeat but also extended to what would happen in the case of victory as well. She quite accurately anticipated the long-term moral and political costs of sustaining the sovereignty of a tiny Jewish state, which is surrounded by hostile Arab neighbors, on one hand, and oppressing the Arab minority in its midst, on the other. Under such circumstances, she warned with distress, the new Jewish country "would be something quite other than the dream of world Jewry, Zionist and non-Zionist."[25] For Arendt, the name of this dream was the "Jewish homeland" and she was firmly convinced it ought not to be sacrificed on the altar of a "Jewish nation-state."

How are we to make sense of such a distinction? What would a homeland politically mean other than a nation-state in the political landscape of the 1940s? What, if anything, does the plea for a homeland have to offer in terms of the Jewish demand for survival with dignity in the aftermath of the Holocaust? What kind of polity could fulfil this undeniably urgent demand in the context of a global system of sovereign nations? And why would the establishment of a nation-state turn out to be detrimental to the Jewish homeland in the long run? These are serious questions and Arendt faced them as such. It seems to me that her answer can be best understood, for both its merits and shortcomings, by viewing it as composed of two different trains of thought intertwined with one another. The first is the phenomenological interpretation of the Jewish settlement in Palestine as a *human artifact* that gives the term "homeland" its distinctive meaning in Arendt's account; the second is her political and normative defense of the founding of a *federal republic*, as opposed to a nation-state, on the basis of a discursively achieved agreement between Jews and Arabs.

Founding a Homeland: The *Yishuv* as a Human Artifact

When Arendt maintained that "even if the Jews were to win the war, its end would find the unique possibilities and the unique achievements of Zionism in Palestine destroyed," one of her main concerns was the fate and significance of the *yishuv*.[26] Literally meaning "settlement" in Hebrew, the term *yishuv* refers to the Jewish community in Palestine prior to the state of Israel. While its achievements have been widely considered "artificial" in a derogatory sense, Arendt celebrates them precisely on this score. From the cultivation of the land to the experiment of the kibbutzim, from the establishment of health centers and the Hebrew University to the foundation of local political institutions, all major Jewish achievements in Palestine were "artificial" in the sense of having been initiated by the deliberate political will to institute a homeland for a stateless people. However, as Arendt observes critically: "A generation brought up in the blind faith in necessity—of history or economy or society or nature—found it difficult to understand that precisely this artificiality gave the Jewish achievements in Palestine their human significance. The trouble was that Zionists as well as anti-Zionists thought that the artificial character of the enterprise was to be reproached rather than praised."[27] We can read in Arendt's interpretation of the *yishuv* a guiding trope of her later political and philosophical thought, namely the utmost importance that she attributes to the human-made space that provides human beings with a "home" as distinguished from their natural environment.

In her 1946 essay "What Is Existenz Philosophy?" for example, she notes the "modern will to create a human world which can be a home within a world which is no longer a home."[28] In *The Human Condition*, she brilliantly explores the meaning of an artificial world, consisting of tangible objects as well as deliberately created institutions and organizations, in terms of the "temporality" and "plurality" of human existence.[29] As for temporality, the idea is that the human-made world outlasts the life of each individual, thereby ensuring a certain stability along with the prospect of permanence. And as for plurality, this human-made world sets the background against which each of us becomes visible as a unique individual. As such, in other words, it constitutes the medium in and through which an individual life unfolds and acquires a unique meaning among the lives of others.

Thus, when Arendt spoke of the "homelessness" of the Jewish people (of which "statelessness" was the specific political form), what she primarily had in mind was that the Jews were deprived of an artificial space where one's life, one's story, one's actions and opinions would matter.[30] In her view, therefore, it was above all the founding of such a space—and not the consolidation of an ethnic community—that gave the Jewish achievements in Palestine their human and political significance. The great importance that she attributes to acts of foundation, beginning with her reflections on the *yishuv* and going all the way to *On Revolution*, stems in part from this notion of the human world as an artifact. Through acts of foundation human beings create an artificial world and transform the territory that they inhabit into a political space, thereby building a home for themselves and their posterity.

In the creation of the Jewish settlement in Palestine, Arendt also saw an affirmation and expression of the human capacity to make a new beginning. "The Palestinian experiment," she wrote, "has not been in the nature of things, not according to the ways of the world"—rather, it was "initiated by a spirit of enterprise which paid no heed to calculations of profit and loss."[31] She was hoping that, had the Jews themselves understood its meaning and importance properly, this positively artificial character of the *yishuv* could become the matrix of a new political identity among Palestinian Jewry and prevent them from following in the footsteps of a pernicious nationalism. A people who had to engage in political action precisely because of their ethnic identity—"the identity that is under attack"—would nonetheless, Arendt believed, cultivate a different sense of peoplehood in the course of political action devoted to building a homeland.

Her approach is remarkable not simply in that she rejects the nationalist vision of political community based on ethnic belonging, and defends instead a republican vision emphasizing the political will to live together. Equally important is her attempt to associate the normative idea of a political will to live together with the collective experience of building a shared world. In this view, what holds Palestinian Jewry together as a "people" and defines them as a particular kind of "we" is neither simply their inherited identity nor an abstract idea such as consent. Rather, it is the artificial space which opens up in-between them as a result of their own agency, a space which provides them with a "world," a context of meaning, belonging, and solidarity.

To get a better sense of Arendt's originality on this point, it would be helpful to recall Bernard Yack's challenge to the clear cut distinction between "civic" and "ethnic" identities: "it all seems a little too good to be true, a little too close to what we would like to believe about the world."[32] What especially comes in for criticism in Yack's argument is the portrayal of civic identity as a mode of rational attachment, a freely chosen allegiance to a set of normative principles, while ethnic identity is then conveniently associated with the emotional celebration of inherited culture, a celebration of something primordial that makes a claim on us despite our will. Yack does not deny that it is possible and plausible to contrast "nations whose distinctive cultural inheritance centers on political symbols and political stories with nations whose cultural inheritance centers on language and stories about ethnic origins."[33] His point is rather that a civic identity is no less an inherited cultural phenomenon than an ethnic one, and that this *particular* cultural baggage matters. "No matter how much residents of the United States might sympathize with political principles favored by most French or Canadian citizens," Yack rightly observes, "it would not occur to them to think of themselves as French or Canadian."[34] Each of these political identities is bound up with its own peculiar history and developmental contingencies that make up the cultural background against which it makes sense, and against which it bears weight. I don't think that Arendt would disagree with the gist of this argument. Like Yack, she also seems to think that civic identity is not simply a matter of rational attachment to a set of abstract principles, and that there is a strong cultural dimension to it. Unlike Yack, however, Arendt takes a further step and offers us an account of the kind of political experience—the experience of constructing life together, of shared agency—which would underlie the development of a civic identity as opposed to an ethnic one.

Founding a Federal Republic: The Politics of Enlarged Mentality

Arendt's interpretation of the *yishuv* brilliantly outlines a humanist understanding of homeland. The political counterpart of this humanism was her conviction that Jews and Arabs must constitute a federal republic, an artificial world of legal and political institutions in which they were to partake of citizenship on equal terms. In supporting a federal solution to the Jewish-Arab conflict, Arendt was self-consciously following in the footsteps of what she called the "nonnationalist tradition."[35] Among the milestones of this tradition were Ahad Haam's defense of cultural Zionism in the 1890s, the Brit Shalom movement in the 1920s, and Judah Magnes's initiative against partition in the 1940s.

Arendt was opposed to the prospect of a nation-state in Palestine, whether a Jewish or an Arab one, for both normative and political reasons. Normatively, her objections take their cue from the critique of nationalism that we have already seen. Resting the legitimacy of the state on an essentialist understanding of the people seemed to Arendt unacceptable as a vision of political community. Politically, she thought that the nation-state had been an exhausted political form, which could "no longer either guarantee true sovereignty of the people within or establish a just relationship among different peoples beyond the national borders."[36] Although her normative criticism was compelling, today we can say with the benefit of hindsight that she was too hasty in announcing the fall of the nation-state as such. At any rate, it was her considered opinion that federation was the only realistic and normatively desirable alternative to the nation-state, primarily on account of its capacity for decoupling the institutional edifice of the state from essentialist models of peoplehood.[37]

In Arendt's view, a federal republic in Palestine "would have to rest on Jewish-Arab community councils, which would mean that the conflict between two peoples would be resolved on the lowest and most promising level of proximity and neighborliness."[38] She was hoping that Jews and Arabs could thereby set an example and "show the world that there are no differences between two peoples that cannot be bridged," an example serving in the end as a model of "how to counteract the dangerous tendencies of formerly oppressed peoples to shut themselves off from the rest of the world and develop nationalist superiority complexes of their own."[39] Furthermore, a Jewish-Arab modus vivendi of this sort would have long-term stabilizing effects in the region and become the "stepping-stone for any later, greater federated structure in the Near East and the Mediterranean area."[40] In her last major essay on Jewish politics, "Peace or Armistice in the Near East," she presented a regional federation, beginning with Jewish-Arab cooperation in Palestine and gradually extending to other peoples in the region, as "the only alternative to balkanization" in the long run.[41]

Whether these were viable political options at the time is of course a highly controversial question. In this respect, some of Arendt's expectations in 1948 seem "historically moot" even to her sympathetic readers.[42] Nonetheless, Arendt herself was aware of the immense difficulties standing in the way of such a modus vivendi between Jewish and Arab communities. In her view, the most decisive difficulty was the refusal of both communities to think beyond the closed framework of their own histories. She knew very well that the Jews judged the situation in Palestine not simply in terms of the present realities but in light of a very distant past, going back to the destruction of the Temple and charged with messianic yearnings. They went into battle "with the 'spirit of Masadah,' inspired by the slogan 'or else we shall go down,' determined to refuse all compromise even at the price of national suicide."[43] Hence, in the eventual military victories over Arab troops they saw a "historical momentum" and a "final verdict" of history. Just as the Jews were determined to regard the outcome as final, Arendt observes, Arabs were determined to view it as an interlude. "Arab policy in this respect is very simple and consists mainly in a diplomacy which discounts defeats and states and restates with undisturbed stubbornness the old claim to ownership of the country."[44] In Arendt's view the predominant Jewish and Arab attitudes were in the end marred by the same failures, which seemed to her confirming her insights into the moral and political dangers of nationalism: the failure to engage with the concrete factors of the situation in a pragmatic spirit, the failure to take each other's claims seriously and to seek a fair compromise, the failure to exercise enlarged mentality and to adopt a moral point of view beyond the narrow mindset of nationalist aspirations.

According to Arendt, the conflict between Jews and Arabs was neither natural, simply stemming from the hostility of one people toward another (as opposed to Herzl's doctrine of "eternal antisemitism") nor a necessary and inevitable consequence of the circumstances in Palestine (as, for example, Ben-Gurion's "realist" approach held it to be). Rather, it was the outcome of *political responses* to the historical circumstances in which Jews and Arabs had found themselves. Thus, at a fundamental level, Arendt puts the emphasis on the primacy of human agency and responsibility. This is why she could maintain even after the outbreak of war in 1948 that "the idea of Arab-Jewish cooperation, though never realized on any scale and today seemingly farther off than ever, is not an idealistic daydream."[45] Its realization, however, was contingent on a mutual willingness, or at least some sort of readiness, to step out of the closed framework of one's own people and history. A sustainable form of cohabitation, whose terms were equally acceptable to both parties, could "only be the result of negotiations, of mutual compromise and eventual agreement between Jews and Arabs."[46]

Arendt's defense of a federal republic in Palestine is remarkable in that it thematizes the politics of founding in terms of a discursively achieved agreement in contrast to force, imposition, and hegemonic fiat. Political founding in this sense designates the establishment of voluntary ties, in reference to which peoples coming from different histories and ethnic origins can see themselves as forming a single political community. However, in a sense, the plea for a discursively achieved agreement is not so much a solution to the problem as a restatement of it. What this means would be better understood if we recall Rousseau's paradox of founding, and bring it to bear on Arendt's argument. As we have already seen, Rousseau maintains that the kind of practical dispositions and ethical resources necessary for the people to carry out a republican act of foundation would only develop in an *already existing* republican polity, thereby sending us around a dizzying circle. One might argue that a similar circularity was at work in the historical context of Jewish-Arab politics in Palestine.

Moral and political assets such as mutual trust and understanding, willingness to adopt a moral point of view and to exercise enlarged mentality, which are—in Arendt's own account—essential to the founding of a federal Jewish-Arab republic, presuppose an already existing framework of cooperation between the two communities. To borrow Rousseau's formulation of the paradox of founding, for Jews and Arabs to be capable of instituting a federal state on the basis of a political will to live together, "the effect would have to become the cause," and the spirit of mutual trust and understanding would have to precede the establishment of the framework in which it would flourish. That is to say, the question is not only whether a federal republic would have to be based on mutual agreement or whether this would be something normatively desirable—it surely would, provided that one is not a staunch nationalist. The deeper question is how to generate the moral and political resources necessary to enable and sustain the process of reaching agreement between distrustful communities.

This point may seem to confirm contemporary arguments about the persistence of the paradox of founding (i.e., the arguments we previously examined and criticized in Chapter 2). In one sense, there is nothing wrong with such an impression. The paradox of founding is not an artificial problem made up by theorists; it designates a real issue. Nonetheless, restating it against the background of Jewish-Arab politics in Palestine has a further implication. Situated in such a historical context, the paradox of founding no longer confronts us as a formal or logical dilemma akin to the chicken-or-egg question. Rather, it points out a thoroughly *political* problem, and like all political problems it is embedded in a context consisting of the perceptions, choices and actions of agents who are both historically conditioned *and* capable of changing their own environment. This means that the context in which political actors encounter the paradox of founding is also inscribed by various possibilities of responding to the same paradox. In *The Jewish Writings*, we see Arendt perceptively picking up one such possibility: to reconstruct the "identity under attack" around the collective endeavor to build a homeland, instead of turning this homeland into a vehicle of nationalist consolidation.

* * *

In concluding this chapter, to underline what is important for our inquiry in *The Jewish Writings*, I want to engage with a remark made by Richard Bernstein. He critically observes that in much of her discussion of the "Jewish question," Arendt falls back on the factual existence of the Jewish people without actually clarifying either what makes Jews a distinct people or the grounds on which they may claim recognition as such.

> What is it that characterizes a people as a people? Specifically, what is it that characterizes the Jews as Jews? What is the *normative* basis for claiming political rights and recognition of the Jews as Jews? Sometimes it seems as if Arendt simply takes the existence of the Jewish people as a historical fact and then concerns herself with the social and political questions about the history, responsibility, and destiny of that people. But this is to avoid the question of Jewish identity, not to answer it. It is not satisfactory to fall back upon the "factual" existence of the Jewish people.[47]

Notice that Bernstein's remark turns on two different issues. One of them is about the *normative grounds* on which Jews—or any other group of human beings for that matter—may claim political recognition as a "people" entitled to self-determination. This point seems to me misplaced as a criticism because the answer to a question of this sort is that there is no normative answer to it. The principle of popular sovereignty cannot (and is not meant to) stipulate which *concrete* group of human beings should count as a "people" in distinction to others.[48] The other point made by Bernstein is about the *historical identity* of the Jewish people, and it requires closer attention.

On this register, he criticizes Arendt for her failure to give an account of what she took to be the epicenter of Jewish identity. "What is it that characterizes the Jews as Jews"—religion, culture, ethnicity? Bernstein is absolutely right that Arendt did not offer such an account. However, in my view, this was a deliberate choice on her part, and a great deal of what makes her reflections pertinent to our inquiry stems from that choice. Let me explain. As Bernstein observes, Arendt indeed proceeded from a "fact." Yet, this was not so much the "factual existence" of the Jewish people per se as the political fact of persecution. As we have already seen, Arendt herself emphatically claimed that to be a Jew had become a "political fact" in the twentieth century and that Jews had to act accordingly. This was what she had in mind when she argued that "one can resist only in terms of the identity that is under attack." So, it is not surprising at all that Arendt did not try to ground her call for Jewish politics in an account of a pre-political identity. She knew quite well that the only case to be made in that direction would be a nationalist one, and she systematically tried to avoid it. Instead, Arendt argued for a politics that was to transform the Jewish identity under attack into a project of peoplehood, one which could at the same time enable a constructive relation to other peoples and humanity at large.

In search of such a politics, she increasingly focused on the formation of peoplehood in and through the shared experience of action, and especially the kind of action oriented toward the making of a common world. That is to say, Arendt did not look at the Jewish homeland from the vantage point of the historically embedded identity of a people; on the contrary, she looked at the political formation of Jewish peoplehood from the vantage point of what it means to build a homeland. These two are very different perspectives.[49] In the former case, identity precedes action. An already existing people is claimed to consolidate itself. In fact, this is a longstanding strategy in both political theory and practice. Collective identity is taken for granted, as something given and already embedded in history. The act of foundation is then imputed to this already existing "subject," claiming to give it political expression. The identity of the people is thereby projected back on to the past by way of narratives, civic mythologies and "stories of peoplehood."[50] Geoffrey Bennington puts it perceptively: "At the origin of the nation, we find a story of the nation's origin."[51] Regardless of their content, these stories are "essentialist" in the sense that they present the act of foundation as the expression of an already given identity, allegedly complete in itself. Throughout *The Jewish Writings*, Arendt confronts this essentialist strategy with an agency-centric approach. In this view, identity is not simply given or inherited but constructed in and through action. In other words, action is not the expression of a given identity, but rather constitutive of who "we" are in a fundamental sense—in the sense that we make and remake ourselves anew in the course of acting.[52] This is precisely why the way we act and the way we begin have a hold on who "we" shall turn out to be. To recapitulate, then, Arendt's ultimate answer to Bernstein's question—"What is it that characterizes a people as a people?"—is that it is the shared experience of world-building action.

Chapter 5

Revolution and Constitution
The Legitimacy of Beginning in Question

In the last two chapters, by engaging in a dialogue with Rousseau and Arendt respectively, we have thematized the politics of founding in terms of its relation to political culture and collective identity. Our reading of Rousseau has suggested that the formation of a republican *moeurs* conducive to the project of self-legislation is not merely or even primarily the work of a great lawgiver. Rather, it is anchored in the perhaps inchoate and inarticulate but still unmistakable agency of a people whose collective efforts create suitable conditions for legislation and call forth the lawgiver. In reading Arendt's *Jewish Writings*, we have also seen that identity does not simply precede action but accompanies it, and that the enterprise of building a homeland could be fundamentally transformative of who "we" are or who we take ourselves to be as a people. So far, thus, questioning the rigid dichotomy between the "two bodies" of the people, our discussion has navigated the gray area in which the people is neither an "amorphous multitude" nor a constitutionally organized "corporate body," but rather a community of action in the making. No matter what the merits of such an inquiry might be, however, the fact remains: the people themselves are never "the people" in whose name modern constitutions claim to speak. And this inevitably brings home to us the fundamental question of legitimacy, with which we have not yet come to grips.

A crucial implication of the paradox of founding is that every act of foundation with a democratic intent is by definition implicated in a colossal deficit of legitimacy. This point is forcefully argued by a diverse group of contemporary theorists, as we have seen at length in Chapter 2. Recall, for example, Derrida's deconstruction of the Declaration of Independence. Appeals to "the people" cannot deliver the kind of legitimacy they claim to deliver because "this people does not exist," as Derrida observes, "*before* this declaration, not *as such*."[1] It seems that a moment of speaking in the name of a people that does not yet exist, a moment of performative fiat or original violence, is unavoidable. In "Force of Law," Derrida puts the same point in even stronger terms. "Here the discourse comes up against its limit," he writes, "here a silence is walled up in the violent structure of the founding act."[2]

One finds an apparently similar insight in Hannah Arendt's work, most notably in her *On Revolution*. Like Derrida, she underscores the inherent contingency and groundlessness of the act of beginning. "It is in the very nature of a beginning to carry with itself a measure of complete arbitrariness."[3] Nonetheless, the similarity does not cut deep because the groundlessness of beginning is not for Arendt necessarily violent in the sense meant by Derrida.[4] In fact, it is precisely an assumption of this sort, equating violence and beginning, that Arendt sets out to discredit in *On Revolution*. As I see it, her guiding claim on this score is the following: "what saves the act of beginning from its own arbitrariness is that it carries its own principle within itself, or, to be more precise, that beginning and principle, *principium* and principle, are not only related to each other, but are coeval."[5] To be sure, it is by no means self-evident what this means. Arendt puts forward the notion of a beginning that contains its own "principle," a beginning that can somehow restrain its own arbitrariness and lay claim to legitimacy. What I aim to do in the present chapter, at its most basic level, is to spell out this notion and to explore whether (or to what extent) it can help us negotiate the question of legitimacy pertaining to the politics of founding. Since *On Revolution* will be at the center of our discussion, it would be appropriate to begin with some remarks on the argument of the book and its place in Arendt's political theory.

How to Read the Story of Two Revolutions?

Throughout *On Revolution*, Arendt grapples with the tension between novelty and permanence, between the creativity of revolutionary new beginnings and the stability of the world they help bring about. In fact, this is a tension that hovers over much of her political theory, and one can actually trace it back to *The Origins of Totalitarianism*. Of all the topics covered in that book, arguably, two issues played the most decisive role in setting the agenda of Arendt's later political thought, including her preoccupation with modern revolutions and constitutional foundings. The first of these issues has to do with the analysis of "total domination" that achieved its peak in concentration camps. The camps were designed in such a way as to eliminate the "infinite plurality and differentiation of human beings," and to destroy "spontaneity itself as an expression of human behavior."[6] Arendt's well-known theory of action, devoted to unpacking our experience of spontaneity and self-disclosure in the presence of one another, was her philosophical response to what she saw as the heart of total domination. The second issue was the rise of totalitarian movements against the background of a pervasive sense of homelessness and rootlessness, and their profound hostility to established institutions along with all sorts of boundaries, territorial as well as legal, that sustained a shared world in which common sense, responsibility, and basic assets of humanity would continue to function. "If homelessness, rootlessness, and the disintegration of political bodies and social classes do not directly produce totalitarianism," she acutely observes, "they at least produce almost all of the elements that eventually go into its formation."[7] It was in the light of this lesson that she came to attribute a central significance to elements of permanence in political life and to the stability of political bodies providing their members with a shared world, a home, a context of solidarity and responsibility.

These two issues—the human capacity for spontaneity and novelty, on the one hand, and the human need for permanence and stability, on the other—crystallize around the concepts of "action" and "world" in Arendt's later work.[8] Both *The Human Condition* and the essays collected in *Between Past and Future* turn on these concepts in various ways, and explore their complex relation to one another. According to Arendt, put in a nutshell, the relationship between action and world is at once both complementary and tension-ridden. Complementary because just as action stands in need of an institutionally structured public space for its performance and a shared interpretive repertoire for the identification of its meaning, both this space and this repertoire, which constitute our common world, reproduce themselves through the interaction between acting and speaking agents. And tension-ridden because while action is an open-ended business that inevitably sets off unpredictable processes and has "an inherent tendency to force open all limitations and cut across all boundaries,"[9] the primary function of laws and institutions is to ensure the continuity and stability of the world vis-à-vis the potential boundlessness of action. In both *The Human Condition* and *Between Past and Future*, this tension between action and world, novelty and permanence, comes in focus as a fundamental and unavoidable, but also productive and salutary feature of political life in general.[10] Yet it takes on a further and inevitably more compelling twist with Arendt's turn to the phenomenon of revolution.

It is not difficult to see why. The phenomenological account of action developed in *The Human Condition* takes for granted the existence of an already instituted public world, focusing on what comes to pass there and thus suspending the question of its foundation. The question of founding, however, returns in full force in Arendt's study of revolution, now entailing an expanded account of action not only in terms of its spontaneity and boundlessness, but also in terms of its world-building potential, namely, its capacity to give rise to laws and institutions. This, in turn, leads to the philosophically compelling problem of how to derive the elements of permanence and stability from a human activity whose distinctive features are contingency, unpredictability, and the potential for novelty. How can a revolutionary act of beginning stabilize itself and give rise to an institutional structure, an organized public sphere, in which the experience of freedom survives the event of revolution and becomes a permanent reality? This is the central question of *On Revolution*.

Arendt claims to have found an answer—or at least the crucial components of an answer—in the American revolutionary experience as opposed to the French one. She observes that while the revolution was followed by a successful act of constitution-making which laid down the foundations of a federal republic in America, it paved the way for a series of violent irruptions in France. In the tradition of Burke and Tocqueville, thus, *On Revolution* draws a sharp contrast between the two cases. The book was published in 1963, and has been severely criticized since then. The wide-ranging criticisms can be grouped around three main themes. The first has to do with the method and accuracy of Arendt's historiography, or the lack thereof.[11] The second turns on her controversial analysis of the "social question," according to which, put in a nutshell, the problem of abject poverty and the popular rage inspired by it overshadowed the cause of freedom in revolutionary France and led to escalating cycles of violence.[12] And finally, the third concerns Arendt's idealization of the American Revolution, which, critics claim, neglects its inherent violence and promotes a politics of origin worship imbued with conservative overtones.[13] All in all, generations of critics have made it sufficiently clear that Arendt's historiography is loose and inaccurate, her account of the "bad" French Revolution is untenable, and the quest for an alternative in the "good" American Revolution is equally misguided. One cannot help but ask: what is left, if anything, to be learned from *On Revolution*?

While much of the criticism is fair (and we will revisit some of it in more detail below), there is still merit to Arendt's guiding theoretical insights, if not exactly to her historiography. She claims that novelty and permanence, revolution and constitution (or if you like, "event" and "form"), are not irreconcilable or contradictory in and of themselves. "Perhaps the very fact that these two elements, the concern with stability and the spirit of the new, have become opposites in political thought and terminology," Arendt holds, "must be recognized to be among the symptoms of our loss."[14] Accordingly, in her attempt to redeem the "lost treasure" of modern revolutions, she inquires into the meaning of constitution-making in terms of its relation to the experience of collective action and public freedom. I want to suggest that, from the standpoint of democratic theory, Arendt's inquiry yields two important conclusions. First, Arendt levels a sustained critique against the classical doctrine of constituent power as developed by Abbé Sieyès and later selectively appropriated by Carl Schmitt. Second, she traces the legitimacy of a new constitution not back to the allegedly united will of "the people" understood as a counterfactual macro-subject, but to the way and spirit in which the act of foundation is carried out. As such, her argument points toward a "post-sovereign" understanding of constitution-making, which is perhaps *the* essential Arendtian contribution to a theory of democratic founding.

Constituent Power from Sieyès to Schmitt

Let me briefly outline the classical doctrine of constituent power before turning to Arendt's critique of it. At its most basic, the concept of constituent power is premised on the idea that there exists a fundamental distinction between the making of a constitution and the ordinary competencies of the government. The idea has a long and complicated history, but its classical statements are available in the revolutionary texts of the late eighteenth century.[15] According to Thomas Paine, for example, as he famously wrote in *The Rights of Man*: "A constitution is not the act of a government, but of a people constituting a government."[16] In "What Is the Third Estate?" Sieyès gave the same basic view a more systematic formulation: "In each of its parts a constitution is not the work of a constituted power but a constituent power."[17] That is to say, all the competencies of government, including legislation, are "constituted powers" in that their scope, institutional locus, and mode of exercise are framed by the higher law of the polity. The power to make this higher law, however, is of a different order and belongs exclusively to the people. While this much was common to both revolutions, it was the specific version advocated by Sieyès that gained eminence, and eventually came to be known as the classical doctrine of constituent power.

Sieyès's doctrine has three major components: a *moral* claim about the voluntarist ground of constitutional legitimacy; a *juridical* claim about the unbounded exercise of constituent power; and a *political* claim about the central role of representation in constitution-making. With regard to the moral aspect of his argument, Sieyès was firmly in line with the social contract tradition. In a rhetorical question, he asks: "Is there any antecedent authority, able to have told a multitude of individuals, 'I have united you under this set of laws, and you will form a nation under the conditions which I have laid down'? Here we are not dealing with brigandage or domination but with a legitimate association, one that is voluntary and free."[18] His conception of a "legitimate association" was specifically indebted to Rousseau. Like him, Sieyès considered the "general will" as the true foundation of the social union. Thus, "the people" or "the nation" (which were interchangeable terms for him) was a corporate body with a common interest, the unity of which was the spring of constituent power.

Furthermore, according to Sieyès, constituent power resides in a juridical state of nature—in a condition *extra leges* or outside the law. The basic idea is that the power to create a new constitutional form cannot be subject to an already existing positive determination. In other words, the exercise of constituent power is by definition juridically unbounded. As Sieyès puts it emphatically: "There is no reason to be afraid of repeating the fact that a nation is independent of all forms and, however it may will, it is enough for its will to be made known for all positive law to fall silent in its presence, because it is the source and supreme master of all positive law."[19] Nonetheless, a juridical state of nature did not mean for him a complete normative vacuum. For one thing, Sieyès had an affirmative understanding of natural law as the right reason that should guide the exercise of constituent power.[20] For another, even though constituent power was juridically unbounded, it was to be circumscribed by the impartial perspective inherent to and stipulated by the general will.

Of course, the categorical distinction between constituent and constituted powers and the placement of the former into a juridical void present Sieyès with a pressing question: how can the people exercise their constituent power outside all positive forms? His simple answer is that they cannot, hence the need for representation. "Since a great nation cannot in real terms assemble every time that extraordinary circumstances may require, it has, on such occasions, to entrust the necessary powers to extraordinary representatives."[21] Sieyès carefully distinguishes between "ordinary" and "extraordinary" representation. While the former takes place under an existing constitution, the latter is meant to frame a new one. Ordinary representatives are endowed with legally structured or constituted powers; they "act for" the people in accordance with the regulations stipulated by the constitution. Extraordinary representatives bear the constituent power of the people as a sovereign body. As such, they "stand for" the people, and in a sense they *are* the people.[22] "Their common will has the same worth as that of the nation itself."[23] Even though it remains a mystery how the constituent power of the people is actually entrusted to extraordinary representatives outside all positive forms, Sieyès does not seem to be disturbed by it. "Here reality is everything and form nothing."[24] The result is a specific model of constitution-making: a constituent assembly, which represents the people as a unified whole in its independence from all positive forms, and which is convened together for the sole purpose of framing a new constitution.

The most influential reformulation of the classical doctrine of constituent power is that of Carl Schmitt. He systematically reconfigured Sieyès's argument while at the same time wiping out its normative elements. In Sieyès, for example, the concept of constituent power is meant to answer a question of *right*: who has the ultimate right to decide on the forms and principles of the political association? It is the people, and only the people, who have that right because (to requote his nice phrase) "here we are not dealing with brigandage or domination but with a legitimate association, one that is voluntary and free." In Schmitt, by contrast, the concept of constituent power is meant to answer a question of *fact*: who has the monopoly on decision? "The constituent power is the political will," he clearly stressed, "capable of making the concrete, comprehensive decision over the type and form of its own political existence."[25] So it is not surprising to find him talking about, say, "the constituent power of the monarch," which was, of course, nothing but an oxymoron from the standpoint of Sieyès's constitutional theory.[26]

What especially comes to the fore in Schmitt's analysis (and arguably what attracts him to Sieyès in the first place) is the extra-legal nature of the constituent power. With much greater clarity than Sieyès himself, Schmitt saw that the exercise of constituent power beyond and above all positive forms had a dictatorial character. "The distinctive position of a 'constituent' assembly, which convenes after a revolutionary elimination of the preexisting constitutional laws, is best designated a 'sovereign dictator.'"[27] According to Schmitt, such an assembly not only bears the power to make a new constitution, it also bears the plenitude of undifferentiated power, the separation of which into the constituted powers of the government is to become possible only with the new constitution. But since the new constitution is not yet in effect, the power of the assembly is absolute. "Consequently, it can undertake any measures that appear necessary in the present situation without any limitations other than those it imposes on itself. Such measures are part of the characteristic content of *dictatorship*."[28]

To recapitulate, then, all three aspects of the Sieyèsean doctrine of constituent power undergo a significant transformation in Schmitt's constitutional theory. The notion of will as the matrix of political freedom (which Sieyès inherited from Rousseau) is replaced by a decisionist notion of will as a sovereign command; the juridical void in which the constituent power is exercised turns into an absolute normative vacuum; and the assembly of extraordinary representatives becomes the locus of sovereign dictatorship. Thus, in the model of democratic founding offered by Schmitt, a sovereign "organ" is endowed with undivided and unlimited power following the dissolution of all constituted powers; it acts in the name of the people and frames a new constitution, which is then offered for a national referendum. The people's constituent will, in turn, "expresses itself only in a fundamental yes or no and thereby reaches the political decision that constitutes the content of the constitution."[29] This model comes in for withering criticism in Arendt's *On Revolution*.

Arendt's Critique of Constituent Power

On Revolution does not contain any specific reference to Schmitt's work.[30] Yet Arendt's interpretation of Sieyès (and to a lesser degree, of the French Revolution in general) parallels Schmitt's interpretation, while at the same time turning its evaluative standards upside down. Like Schmitt, Arendt sees the French conception of constituent power as intrinsically tied to the modern discourse of sovereignty and hence as an instance of political theology. Unlike Schmitt, however, for Arendt sovereignty is not the matrix of "the political" but rather its antithesis. She holds that "in the realm of human affairs sovereignty and tyranny are the same," and that the foundation of political freedom, the *constitutio libertatis*, required "the abolition of sovereignty within the body politic of the republic."³¹ Thus, there is a sense in which Arendt takes issue with the Sieyèsean doctrine of constituent power precisely for what makes it attractive to Schmitt in the first place. This is why, for instance, Andrew Arato and Jean Cohen suggest that *On Revolution* implicitly targets Schmitt, "whose textual stand-in is Sieyès interpreted in the same one-sided manner of Schmitt himself!"³² To be sure, there is a kernel of truth in this claim. In the end, however, my hunch is that little would have changed in Arendt's take on the classical doctrine of constituent power even if she had paid sufficient attention to the differences between Sieyès and Schmitt. Her criticism just cuts deeper than these otherwise important differences.

So, what is it that Arendt objects in the classical doctrine of constituent power? For one, she takes issue with the kind of voluntarism that Sieyès inherited from Rousseau and turned into the moral ground of his own constitutional theory. To recall briefly, departing from the traditional school of natural law, Rousseau rejected the notion of moral action as compliance with an externally given code, of which the moral subject is not the author but merely the observer. Instead, he tied the morality of action back to the immanent modus operandi of the agent's volition. The decisive result was the identification of freedom with self-determination in a nexus of what Kant was later to call "moral causality." In Arendt's seminal essay "What Is Freedom?" this turn to will as the primary paradigm of freedom comes in for sharp criticism from the standpoint of human plurality. She maintains that freedom is thereby transposed from the domain of human interaction unfolding between acting and speaking individuals to the inward domain of the will, and becomes the property of a mute and solitary subject.³³

According to Arendt, once this voluntarist and monological conception of freedom is projected back onto politics via the notions of general will and popular sovereignty, it obscures the very meaning of public freedom and distorts the qualities that characterize a talkative public space.³⁴ The plurality of acting and speaking agents, the diversity of their opinions and perspectives, and the communicative practices of deliberation, contestation, and persuasion—all of which are indispensable to the experience of public freedom in Arendt's view—pale under the weight of "the people," now conceived as a macro-subject with a united will of its own. Thus, one crucial reason why she takes issue with the classical doctrine of constituent power is that it is implicated in a nonpluralist and noncommunicative conception of popular sovereignty.

This point is closely related to another one. At a fundamental conceptual level, Arendt highlights the intersubjective texture of power and its relation to collective action. Unlike Max Weber, for instance, she does not see power merely as an instrumental capacity designating the "probability that one actor within a social relationship will be in a position to carry out his own will despite resistance."[35] For her, at its most basic, power is not a domination-concept but rather a cooperation-concept with strong normative dimensions. In *The Human Condition*, she writes: "Power is actualized only where word and deed have not parted company, where words are not empty and deeds not brutal, where words are not used to veil intentions but to disclose realities, and deeds are not used to violate and destroy but to establish relations and create new realities."[36] That is to say, power amounts to a shared capacity that springs up among acting and speaking individuals only when they relate to one another in a particular way, namely in the manner of noncoercive action and nonmanipulative speech.

Arendt holds that power in this sense authentically manifests itself in revolutionary junctures where practices of citizenship receive free play, where issues of common concern are discussed and opinions are exchanged, where relations are established and actions are coordinated. This view stands in sharp contrast to the classical conception of constituent power based upon the model of a sovereign subject with a united will of its own. For Arendt, the matrix of constituent power is not the allegedly united will of a sovereign subject, namely "the people" in the abstract, but the intersubjective praxis of the people themselves in the plural, who create their own public spaces by "acting in concert." Arendt therefore severely denounces the model of constitution-making in which a sovereign assembly claims to represent the people en masse and holds the plenitude of power. Although she is often read as a root-and-branch critic of representation, I think that her primary concern, at least in this context, does not so much have to do with representation as such but with "organ sovereignty", that is, the concentration of constituent power in the hands of a single assembly.[37] In such a model, the process of constitution-making is cut adrift from what citizens themselves have to say on the forms and principles of their own political organization. Her basic insight is that if the revolution is to culminate in the foundation of political freedom, if it is to establish an organized public space with a view to "housing" the public freedom of citizens and their shared capacity to act, the exercise of constituent power must remain faithful to the intersubjective experience that brings about such power in the first place.

Finally, besides her reasons concerning public freedom and the intersubjective texture of power, there is a further and equally important issue that stimulates Arendt's criticism: the positioning of the constituent power in a juridical void as a "*potestas legibus soluta*, power absolved from the laws."[38] She finds this kind of power deeply troublesome not only because it is antithetical to the experience of collective action and public freedom but also because a sovereign assembly residing in a juridical state of nature is by definition ill-equipped to generate legitimacy and stability, both of which Arendt treats under the rubric of "authority."[39] In her view, the constitutional history of France—"where even during the revolution constitution followed upon constitution while those in power were unable to enforce any of the revolutionary laws and decrees"—could be read as "one monotonous record" attesting to the fact that the authority of a new constitution cannot be based on and certainly not secured by sovereign decisions or hegemonic fiat.[40]

On this score, there was indeed a sharp contrast between the American and French Revolutions, and the practices of constitution-making they fostered. In a passage worth quoting at length, Arendt notes:

> The great and fateful misfortune of the French Revolution was that none of the constituent assemblies could command enough authority to lay down the law of the land; the reproach rightly levelled against them was always the same: they lacked the power to constitute by definition; they themselves were unconstitutional. . . . Conversely, the great good fortune of the American Revolution was that the people of the colonies, prior to their conflict with England, were organized in self-governing bodies, that the revolution—to speak the language of the eighteenth century—did not throw them into a state of nature, that there never was any serious questioning of the *pouvoir constituant* of those who framed the state constitutions and, eventually, the Constitution of the United States.[41]

To be sure, the last remark is hardly accurate. The framing of a new constitution in the Philadelphia Convention was fiercely questioned and contested by the anti-Federalists, and the legality of the act was (and still is) a matter of controversy. On the whole, however, Arendt has a point, and in fact an important one. In the American case, even if the exercise of constituent power was not strictly legal, it was not legally unbounded either; and certainly it was not positioned in a juridical state of nature but anchored in the "self-governing bodies" of the people themselves. Therefore, it was capable of laying claim to authority in ways the French National Assembly was not.

As Arendt's choice of words such as "fortune" and "misfortune" already indicates, however, the difference between the American and French trajectories of constitution-making (at least in this respect) was due more than anything else to the contingent historical circumstances under which revolution took place in the two countries. In France, unlike the "new world," the revolution exploded the ancien régime, and created an absolute break with its institutional edifice. The French National Assembly of 1789 was not in a position to draw on already existing institutions, and to derive its constituent power from a number of subordinate self-organizations of the people. Thus, as Andrew Arato observes, it is possible to criticize Arendt for "making a virtue of the fortunate—but entirely contingent—state of affairs that the American Constitution could legitimately become more the product of already constituted governments as against the French Constitution of 1791."[42]

In one sense, it is not difficult to reply to such criticism. The fortune and misfortune of the historical cases in focus do not compromise the theoretical validity of Arendt's main point: once the constituent power is located in a juridical void and concentrated in the hands of a single organ—whether it be construed along the lines of "extraordinary representation" (in the manner of Sieyès) or "sovereign dictatorship" (in the manner of Schmitt)—it inevitably leads to a legitimacy crisis. The bottom line of the argument is that a *potestas legibus soluta* cannot claim genuine authority and hence generate the right kind of stability. A reply of this sort, however, leaves Arendt with a more compelling question. How is it possible for a revolutionary act of constitution-making to avoid the juridical state of nature, and "not to be trapped in the vicious circle of *pouvoir constituant* and *pouvoir constitué*?"[43] How can a revolution, a new beginning carried out by spontaneous popular action, save itself from degenerating into a normative vacuum? Does Arendt have a *theoretical* answer that does not heavily draw on the historically contingent and arguably "exceptional" features of the American case?

The Problem of Authority and the Search for an Absolute

Actually, Arendt does not think that the American Revolution, despite all its "good fortune," was spared what she calls the "most troublesome of all problems in revolutionary government,"[44] namely, the problem of how to ensure the status of the constitution as the "higher law." In her view, given the foregoing critique of constituent power, the appeal to "the people" as a counterfactual macro-subject would hardly offer a stable solution. And once we turn from "the people" to the "people themselves," we are inevitably confronted with a fundamental question of modern constitutionalism. To paraphrase Jeremy Waldron: in what sense (if any) are future generations bound to take *this* event (the founding) and *this* body of law (the constitution) as the starting point and the point of reference for their own politics?[45] Or as Arendt herself puts it:

> For the men of the Revolution, who prided themselves on founding republics, that is, governments "of law and not of men," the problem of authority arose in the guise of the so-called "higher law," which would give sanction to positive, posited laws. No doubt, the laws owed their factual existence to the power of the people and their representatives in the legislatures; but these men could not at the same time represent the higher source from which these laws had to be derived in order to be authoritative and valid for all, the majorities and the minorities, the present and the future generations. Hence the very task of laying down a new law of the land, which was to incorporate for future generations the "higher law" that bestows validity on all man-made laws, brought to the fore, in America no less than in France, the need for an absolute.[46]

This is not to say that the power of the people does not contain any normative value for Arendt. On the contrary, as we have already seen, her conception of power highlights its intersubjective texture, its relation to collective action and shared opinion. However, it is precisely because power is anchored in "opinion" that it cannot secure the normative validity of the higher law. After all, what makes the constitution binding for those who are not of the same opinion? What makes it "higher" than the majority decision? What makes it the law of the land for future generations? Hence Arendt's remark about "the need for an absolute," of which some further clarification is now in order.

Arendt finds it highly intriguing that both the American and the French revolutionaries sought a transcendent (and more specifically, divine) source of authority. This quest revealed itself in a variety of ways. Robespierre introduced the cult of the "supreme being," Adams appealed to "the great legislator of the universe," and Jefferson, in his draft of the Declaration of Independence, referred not only to the "laws of nature" and "self-evident truths," but also to "nature's God."[47] One is almost tempted, as it were, to conclude with Rousseau that "it would require gods to give men laws."[48] This is all the more striking, Arendt further observes, given the fact that both American and French revolutionaries deliberately set out to constitute the secular realm of politics in the first place.

Of course, this appeal to divinity can be explained by the deistic mindset of the educated eighteenth-century thinkers. Alternatively, one can read off here the age-old prudence of the statesman who wants to mobilize religious sentiment for patriotic purposes (of which Rousseau is again illuminative). Still, whatever the truth of such explanations might be, Arendt's hunch is that the search for an absolute is symptomatic of something deeper and deeply intriguing. On the one hand, what makes revolutions possible in the modern world is the gradual dissolution of all absolute grounds of authority under the pressure of secularization. In Marx's terms, revolution becomes possible only when "all that is solid melts into air, all that is holy is profaned."[49] On the other hand, this process brings to the foreground the taxing problem of how to establish a new authority. That is, the very condition that makes revolution possible in the first place seems to undermine at the same time the revolutionary agenda to lay down new and lasting foundations. According to Arendt, this situation paradoxically "drove the very 'enlightened' men of the eighteenth century to plead for some religious sanction at the very moment when they were about to emancipate the secular realm."[50]

In the case of the American Revolution, she observes, the quest for an absolute, which was to serve as the fountain of authority, found its ultimate expression in the Declaration of Independence. Appealing to the "laws of nature and of nature's God," to "unalienable rights" and "self-evident truths," the Declaration indeed points toward a solution to the problem of authority. According to this solution, in Arendt's view, while the consent of the people is the source of the power embodied in political institutions, the authoritative source of the law resides in the higher order of transcendental moral truths.[51] Arendt celebrates the distinction between "authority" and "power." By placing the authority of the constitution next to the power of the people, she claims, Americans avoided the perilous recourse to a lawless constituent power, which resides in a normative vacuum and turns the higher law into the expression of a performative fiat.

Yet, this is only half the story since Arendt also (and emphatically) takes issue with the Declaration's appeal to natural law. She picks up on the intriguing statement of the Declaration, "we hold these truths self-evident," with a view to unpacking its inherent tension between the opinion-centric discourse of deliberation ("we hold") and the truth-centric discourse of natural law ("self-evident truths"). "Jefferson's famous words," she argues, "combine in a historically unique manner the basis of agreement between those who have embarked upon revolution, an agreement necessarily relative because related to those who enter it, with an absolute, namely with a truth that needs no agreement since, because of its self-evidence, it compels without argumentative demonstration or political persuasion."[52] The appeal to self-evident truths, she further argues, goes against the grain of the public realm and its inherent plurality because it refers to norms which are "beyond disclosure and argument," which "inform reason but are not its product" and which, therefore, "stand in no need of agreement."[53]

Notice that this critique of the appeal to natural law leaves Arendt between a rock and a hard place. On the one hand, she denounces the classical doctrine of constituent power and along with it the attempt to derive the authority of the constitution from the allegedly united will of "the people." On the other hand, she rejects the recourse to natural law for its moral foundationalism and for imposing on the political realm a transcendental source of authority, which is detached from the actual agreement of the many. The outstanding question, the inevitable question, is of course how to make sense of constitutional authority if it is neither anchored in transcendental moral truths nor reducible to the sovereign will of "the people." What is it that ensures the authority of the constitution and gives it the status of the higher law? To reiterate a question that we have already asked: does Arendt have a theoretical answer?

Actually, she does have an answer—but it is yet to be seen whether it is a tenable one. Of all the claims put forward in *On Revolution*, her most ambitious and perhaps theoretically most suggestive claim is that the act of constitution-making itself can serve as an *immanent* source of authority. And it is to this claim that we must turn now.

A Beginning That Contains Its Own Principle

At the outset of the present chapter, I already mentioned what seems to me Arendt's guiding insight on this score. Let us recall: "What saves the act of beginning from its own arbitrariness is that it carries its own principle within itself, or, to be more precise, that beginning and principle, *principium* and principle, are not only related to each other, but are coeval. The absolute from which the beginning is to derive its own validity and which must save it, as it were, from its inherent arbitrariness is the principle which, together with it, makes its appearance in the world."[54] The passage invites a number of questions. What does Arendt mean by "principle"? What is the sense in which the inherently arbitrary or contingent act of beginning, the groundless act of foundation, has nonetheless a principle residing in itself? How does this principle "save" the beginning, and ensure the validity or legitimacy of the founding act? How does it turn itself into a source of authority, one that is neither transcendentally anchored nor identified with the sovereign will of "the people"? All in all, what exactly does Arendt mean here?

Perhaps the first thing to be noted is that Arendt uses the term "principle" in an obviously non-Kantian manner. For her, as Margaret Canovan rightly observes, a principle is not a "stateable theoretical maxim," constructed by practical reason, such as "promises ought to be kept."[55] Rather, she takes her point of departure from Montesquieu's distinction between the "forms" and "principles" of government. According to this distinction, roughly speaking, while the form of government is a static quality concerning the structure of the regime and the arrangement of its basic institutions, the principle of government is a dynamic quality concerning the human passions the regime sets in motion. Principles in this sense do not tell us what we "ought" to do. Yet they orient action in a different way, by "inspiring" certain kinds of conduct and certain patterns of interaction among citizens (hence their relation to the "spirit" of the laws). To recall Montesquieu's classification of regimes in accordance with their principles: republics are animated by virtue and love of equality, monarchies turn on honor and distinction, and tyrannies radiate fear and mistrust.[56]

In "What Is Freedom?" Arendt situates this notion within her theory of action. She contrasts the inspiring principle of an action to its motive, on the one hand, and to its intended purpose, on the other.[57] Unlike the motives or incentives of action, which are rooted in the will, principles do not belong to or operate from within the self (they "inspire, as it were, from without"). And unlike the intended purpose or goal of an action, which is set by practical reason, principles are not achieved but exemplified ("the inspiring principle becomes fully manifest only in the performing act itself"). In other words, Arendt holds that principles such as "honor or glory, love of equality, . . . fear or distrust or hatred" appear to us only in and through actions that exemplify them. We may perhaps draw an analogy here (one that is close to the nerve of Arendt's thought) between the principle of an action and the "meaning" of a story. Just as a well-narrated story brings within the reach of human understanding a meaning that cannot be readily grasped by concepts and arguments, the performance of an action exemplifies and manifests its inspiring principle in a manner unattainable by prescriptive maxims. Hence, genuine action is always an exemplar, "a particular that in its very particularity reveals the generality that otherwise could not be defined."[58]

Suggestive as they are, Arendt's remarks on action-inspiring principles hardly add up to a full-fledged account, remaining somewhat vague in the end.[59] Getting back to *On Revolution*, then, how would this notion help Arendt (and her readers) address the problem of authority? How are we supposed to understand her claim that the principle inherent in the act of beginning can "save" it from its own arbitrariness? As I see it, the short answer is something like this: the authority of a new constitution is neither derived from a transcendental "absolute" nor simply rooted in "the people" but related to the *act* itself, to the *manner* or *spirit* in which the constitution is made and enacted.[60] In Arendt's view, the American Revolution was exemplary in that it was not accomplished in the manner of "dictating violence, necessary for all foundations and hence supposedly unavoidable in all revolutions."[61] On the contrary, she claims, "the principle which came to light during those fateful years when the foundations were laid—not by the strength of one architect but by the combined power of the many—was the interconnected principle of mutual promise and common deliberation."[62] In other words, the way in which the republic was founded *performatively embodied* the political ideals to which it was committed. According to Arendt, it was this performative embodiment that turned out to be crucial in establishing the authority of the new constitution in America, and therefore in reconciling novelty and permanence, the freedom of revolutionary "action" and the stability of the "world" that it helped bring about.

Two comments are in order. First, on Arendt's account of the American Revolution, authority is primarily a matter of "how," concerning the modus operandi of the constitution-making process.[63] This emphasis on "how" would be best understood if we juxtapose it to the "who" and the "what" of a new constitution. Arendt maintains that authority cannot be exclusively a matter of "who," regarding the constitutional subject. This is why the appeal to "the people" as the locus of constituent power does not suffice in and of itself to ensure the legitimacy of a new beginning. Nor is it exclusively a matter of "what," regarding the content of the constitution. And therefore, the appeal to natural law, to right reason, to self-evident first principles, and so on does not suffice either. To avoid misunderstanding, I do not mean to suggest that the dimensions of "who" and "what" do not matter, or that they are irrelevant to the question of authority. Arendt's point is rather that they would not ensure legitimacy on their own, once they are isolated from the dimension of "how," that is, from the way in which the process of constitution-making unfolds.

Second, despite the *normative* nature of the question under consideration, Arendt does little to justify her proposed solution in corresponding terms. The important insight that acts of beginning bring with them their own principles is in the final analysis a phenomenologically descriptive claim. While it may offer a lens through which we can focus on the *performative meaning* of the act, it can hardly explain what gives a certain kind of performance its *normative validity* and turns it into a separate source of authority.[64] In Arendt's story of the American Revolution, the justificatory work seems to be done by the "interconnected principle of mutual promise and common deliberation." Yet it is not quite clear what Arendt has to say, or even perhaps what she wants to say, about its normative significance, and more specifically about its relation to the process of political legitimation. Hence the question remains: why *this* principle? What is it that makes a "promissory" and/or "deliberative" founding normatively superior both to the classical doctrine of constituent power and to the kind of moral foundationalism inherited from the natural law tradition? On this score, like much of her political thought in general, Arendt's reflections contain a disturbing "normative lacuna."[65]

The Question of Legitimacy Reconsidered

Without a theoretical justification of sorts Arendt's insistence on the modality of the founding act is bound to remain somewhat inconclusive. The appeal to the "interconnected principle of mutual promise and common deliberation" as a source of immanent authority, a source of legitimacy and stability, has to be supported by reasons. One hopes to find something to this effect in her views on promising. In *The Human Condition*, for instance, Arendt presents the human faculty to make and keep promises as a "control mechanism" that arises from "the will to live together with others in the mode of acting and speaking," and that can contain or limit the "enormous risks of action"—its boundlessness and unpredictability—without compromising the autonomy of the political realm.[66]

In an important passage of *On Revolution*, worth quoting at length, Arendt brings this insight to bear on the problem of founding:

> Hence, binding and promising, combining and covenanting are the means by which power is kept in existence; where and when men succeed in keeping intact the power which sprang up between them during the course of any particular act or deed, they are already in the process of foundation, of constituting a stable worldly structure to house, as it were, their combined power of action. There is an element of the world-building capacity of man in the human faculty of making and keeping promises. Just as promises and agreements deal with the future and provide stability in the ocean of future uncertainty where the unpredictable may break in from all sides, so the constituting, founding and world-building capacities of man concern always not so much ourselves and our own time on earth as our "successors," and "posterities."[67]

This conception of "promissory founding"[68] combines the basic normative insights of the social contract tradition with Arendt's distinctive understanding of "action qua beginning" and her phenomenological notion of the "world." Every promise is an act of freedom based on the assumption that the promiser is a *causa libera*, who is capable of making a new beginning and binding herself for the future. As such, those who participate in a mutual pledge place themselves and one another at the beginning of a shared projection. Equally important here is the fact that an intersubjective praxis of this sort brings about a matrix of mutual expectations among those who perform it, thereby creating a sphere of relative predictability vis-à-vis future uncertainties. Promises are "world-building" in this specific sense. They establish new relations (here we must also keep in mind Montesquieu's definition of the law as a "rapport" rather than a command), help coordinate mutual expectations, and provide some measure of stability, all of which find their tangible counterparts in the building of new institutions.

This appeal to the stabilizing power of promises is subjected to a withering criticism by Bonnie Honig.[69] She maintains that the foregoing argument is bound up with the tension it claims to resolve since the act of promising is likely to be absorbed into the very gap—into the "abyss of freedom," to use a catch-phrase of Arendt's—which it is meant to bridge in the first place. In other words, instead of creating "little islands of stability" in the ocean of future uncertainty, promises are prone to sink into that ocean because they are themselves purely performative speech acts. According to Honig, thus, the profound problem is that if action is as "contingent and unpredictable" as Arendt claims it to be, then a performative speech act such as promising would hardly serve as a "source of reassurance and stability." Even more importantly, Honig further observes, this also means that the sought-for stability probably comes from elsewhere—something other than mutual pledges expressive of the will to live together. In her view, it is precisely an insight of this sort that guides Derrida's deconstructive reading of the Declaration of Independence.

For Derrida, as we have already seen at some length in Chapter 2, the Declaration involves an "undecidability" about whether independence is thereby "stated" or "produced," whether the speech act in question is a "constative" or a "performative" one. "This obscurity, this undecidability," says Derrida, "is *required* in order to produce the sought-after effect."[70] A performative cannot secure its own validity, and therefore it stands in need of a heteronomic support to establish itself. Of course, Arendt did not ignore the quest for a heteronomic support in both the American and the French Revolutions—suffice it to recall her remarks on the "search for an absolute," and her critical take on the Declaration's appeal to "self-evident truths." However, she thought that this search was futile, the performative "we hold" must stand on its own, and the act of foundation could secure its own authority. Drawing on Derrida, Honig now challenges this assumption. She argues contra Arendt "that no signature, promise, or performative—no act of foundation—possesses resources adequate to guarantee itself, that each and every one necessarily needs some external, systematically illegitimate guarantee to work."[71] In this view, thus, Arendt's reading of the American Revolution has a notably "fabulist" character. "It claims to be a dereification, a recovery of origins; but it erases the violence and the ambiguity that marked the original act of founding. And the effect of Arendt's fable is the same as that of all legitimating fables: to prohibit further inquiry into the origins of the system and protect its center of illegitimacy from the scrutiny of prying eyes."[72]

In response to this compelling criticism, David Ingram offers a quite different—one would even say, diametrically opposite—interpretation of Arendt. An act of foundation based on "mutual promises and common deliberation" is capable of generating authority without external or heteronomic supports, according to Ingram, because the fundamental norms of constitutional democracy are explicit formulations of those implicit presuppositions—or, if you like, "principles"—by which participants in the process of constitution-making are already bound to abide performatively. To spell out what this means, he writes:

> In other words, acts of promising and deliberating both enact—bring to finality—and constate (present) their a priori conditions of possibility. They constitute substantive rights in a manner that accords with, interprets, and realizes the universal idea of right—the very procedure that constitutes the constituting (the democratic act of promising and deliberating). In acts of promising and dialogic deliberation, revolutionary lawmakers *factually* assume the equality, autonomy, mutual openness and responsibility of their fellow interlocutors *and* they *normatively* enjoin and *constitute* it.[73]

As it stands, this formulation is more indebted to Habermas than to Arendt. The extent to which it is persuasive as a defense of the latter is therefore open to question. For Habermas, as we shall see in greater detail in the next chapter, the implicit presuppositions of deliberative constitutional authorship are based on the universal pragmatics of communication, and they turn on the cognitive value of validity claims. For Arendt, by contrast, the "principles" inherent in action lack any such universal cognitive ground. They are contingent modalities of public experience, and bound up with the performance in and through which they happen to become manifest.[74]

This being said, there is merit to Ingram's reading. He rightly emphasizes, contra Derrida and Honig, the central significance Arendt attributes to "common deliberation" in the process of constitution-making. Indeed, Arendt does not simply rely on the stabilizing power of promises, or the performative felicity of the Declaration's "we hold," as Honig seems to assume. Speaking of the American Revolution, for instance, she writes: "while power, rooted in a people that had bound itself by mutual promises and lived in bodies constituted by compact, was enough 'to go through a revolution' (without unleashing the boundless violence of the multitudes), it was by no means enough to establish a 'perpetual union,' that is, to found a new authority."[75] More important than "mutual promises" is the *political process* in which they are made, and the practice of "common deliberation" by virtue of which the constitution comes to take shape. Yet, pace Ingram, Arendt does not see this deliberative process from the standpoint of a theory of rational discourse, or in light of the "universal idea of right." Nor does she project onto it a proceduralist story of normative validity, for that matter. Rather, her appeal to "common deliberation" has primarily to do with the experience of public freedom. We have already seen the crucial role of public freedom in Arendt's critique of constituent power and the monological theory of popular sovereignty. It is equally crucial, I want to suggest now, to her understanding of constitutional authority.

Founding Moments and the Ethos of Public Freedom

Arendt's conception of public freedom has a twofold structure, involving both a performative and a communicative dimension.[76] Here I use the term "performative" in the sense that freedom is not something we *possess*, like a status, but something we *experience*; and we experience it, according to Arendt, in and through action.[77] Particularly important in this regard is the inherent tendency of action "to force open all limitations and cut across all boundaries,"[78] its power to bring about new realities and initiate something new that may as well have not existed. A defining feature of public freedom is therefore political agency and efficacy not in the manner of sovereign self-determination but in the manner of taking initiative and making a new beginning. However, just as action is intrinsically bound up with speech on Arendt's account, so the experience of public freedom has an equally intrinsic "communicative" side. It is essentially a matter of participation in discourse, in processes of opinion exchange and dialogue, debate and deliberation, contestation and persuasion, all of which are indispensable to the handling of public affairs.

A central thesis of *On Revolution* is that public freedom in this twofold sense enjoyed the pride of place in the drama of modern revolutions. Revolutionary politics reclaimed it in a hitherto unprecedented way and scale— ordinary people taking initiative, creating new public spaces, and interrupting the course of history through collective action. Furthermore, the original task of revolution in both America and France was the *constitutio libertatis*, namely, "the foundation of a body politic which guarantees the space where freedom can appear."[79] My contention is that Arendt's insistence on the modality of the founding act must be seen in light of this (perhaps quasi-normative) priority accorded to public freedom in the argument of *On Revolution*. If it is to become the fountain of authority in the new republic, the process of constitution-making must remain anchored in a talkative public space, accommodate the communicative practices by virtue of which freedom is experienced, and hence *performatively manifest* what it aspires to institute. This is the sense in which, I think, Arendt traces authority back to the act of foundation, to its modus operandi, and more specifically to the "interconnected principle of mutual promise and common deliberation." Only a founding act that makes good on these "principles," she seems to suggest, would be able to mediate between revolution and constitution, between "event" and "form," thereby growing into an immanent source of authority without either drawing on a transcendental absolute or degenerating into dictatorship.

The lingering question is whether Arendt provides us with yet another "fable." Or to put it slightly differently: does she replace the political mythology of "the people" with that of a democratic founding accomplished in common deliberation? In defending a view of this sort, as we have seen, Bonnie Honig claims that Arendt ignores the "undecidability" inherent in the act of foundation and erases its violence because she seeks in the American founding a "moment of perfect legitimacy."[80] To be sure, a crucial incentive of Arendt's storytelling is to move our imagination with a view to reenchanting our political life, expanding its horizons and disclosing new possibilities. This applies to *On Revolution* as well, and there is indeed an element of "fabulism" in her story of the American founding.[81] Yet, does she seek a "moment of perfect legitimacy"? My view is that the theoretical backbone of Arendt's story defies this claim, and for reasons that will prove important for our current discussion.

Despite her insistence on the modality of the founding act, Arendt does not see authority simply as a sort of fait accompli. The point here is not only that authority is not bestowed upon the constitution from without but generated in and through the process of constitution-making. The point is also that it is not generated at once and completely. To borrow Josiah Ober's fine phrase, the constitution is an "artifact of revolution" for Arendt.[82] Yet the endurance of this artifact is crucially a matter of its being invented anew. Arendt thus writes: "Political institutions, no matter how well or how badly designed, depend for continued existence upon acting men; their conservation is achieved by the same means that brought them into being. Independent existence marks the work of art as a product of making; utter dependence upon further acts to keep it in existence marks the state as a product of action."[83] Viewed from the vantage point of this "dependence upon further acts"—or better yet, this orientation toward the *future*—authority is crucially incomplete and stands in need of "augmentation," that is, future practices of citizenship and new experiences of public freedom. Albrecht Wellmer puts the point aptly: "Institutions of freedom must be *invented*—and their preservation in some sense amounts to their continuous re-invention. The establishment of such institutions can more or less succeed or fail, and their invention, where successful, will bring about a new grammar of political discourse, new experiences and attitudes, while, conversely, they remain dependent upon such experiences and attitudes, on judgment and political virtue."[84]

The phenomenological insight that "the beginning contains its own principle" takes on a further meaning here. It is not only about how the act of foundation could stabilize revolutionary politics and create stable, worldly institutions, thereby avoiding the twin dangers of permanent revolution and restoration, but also and as much about what sort of *political culture* stems from the act of foundation. To be sure, there is no such thing as crafting or creating an ethos of public freedom from scratch. But we should also embrace the possibility that certain "events" have a role in the transformations of political culture. It is the hallmark of revolutionary episodes to challenge the given perceptions of social and political reality, and to effect a shift from one way of doing things to another. After all, this is why, to again cite Josiah Ober, "revolution matters."[85] Such episodes inscribe themselves not only in the institutional structure of the new polity but also in the soft flesh of habits, emotions, and mentalities, leaving their "imprint" on political imagination and memory. These are the stuff that political culture is made of. Getting back to Honig's claim, then, it seems to me that Arendt insists on the importance of "how" the political community begins not so much because she seeks a "moment of perfect legitimacy," but because she sees an elective affinity between the act of foundation and the kind of politics that it "inspires." It is in this sense, I think, that she writes: "origin can never become entirely a thing of the past."[86]

* * *

This chapter has examined two aspects of Arendt's argument in *On Revolution*: first, her critique of the classical doctrine of constituent power; and second, the central significance that she attributed to the modality of the founding act. These two points are no doubt interrelated. The notion of "the people" understood as a counterfactual macro-subject, residing in a juridical state of nature and holding a *potestas legibus soluta*, Arendt claims, is a dangerous fiction. It stands in contradiction to the essential traits of a talkative public space, that is, to the plurality of acting and speaking agents, the diversity of their opinions and perspectives, and the practices of deliberation, contestation, and persuasion, all of which are indispensable to the experience of public freedom in her account. The classical doctrine of constituent power, she therefore claims, is ill-equipped to cope with the problem of authority—of legitimacy and stability—which pertains to the politics of founding by definition. Against the backdrop of this criticism and in search of an alternative way of thinking about authority, Arendt turns to the modality of the founding act and argues for a deliberative process of constitution-making.

In the view that I defend here, this move is important, for one, because it resists a crucial dilemma that stems from the paradox of democratic founding. If the people themselves are never "the people" in whose name democratic constitutions claim to speak, then, are we not supposed to conclude that there is an unavoidable moment of "performative force," a moment of "original violence," which impugns every act of foundation with a democratic claim? While rejecting the political mythology of a unified constituent power, Arendt also takes a critical distance to the assumption of an unavoidable founding violence. Instead, she seeks to steer through the horns of the dilemma by shifting the burden of legitimacy from the allegedly united will of "the people" to the process in which this people, in their "manyness," strive to establish for themselves a space of public freedom. This shift from the "subject" to the "act" points toward what Andrew Arato aptly calls the "post-sovereign paradigm" of democratic founding.[87] In the next chapter, following Arendt's lead, I focus on this paradigm more closely as it unfolds in contemporary theories of deliberative democracy.

Chapter 6

Law and Democracy in Founding Moments

Deliberative Constitution-Making

Hannah Arendt's insistence on the modality of the founding act as an immanent source of authority—more specifically, her argument for a process of constitution-making carried out in "mutual promise" and "common deliberation"—appears to suggest an elective affinity with deliberative democratic theory. In one sense, there is nothing wrong with this appearance. From the standpoint of deliberative democratic theory, the process of constitution-making is as important as its outcome, or "how" the constitution is framed matters as much as "what" it prescribes. Yet, there are also crucial differences. And they, too, are worth emphasizing. As we have already seen in the previous chapter, Arendt does not see the importance of constitutional pedigree through the lens of a proceduralist conception of normative validity. And she certainly does not thematize the value of deliberation in terms of a theory of rational discourse. Her interest in deliberative constitution-making has rather to do with the experience of public freedom. As such, it is grounded in a phenomenological rather than a normative mode of theorizing. By contrast, deliberative democratic theory has first and foremost a normative agenda in which questions of rights and justice, legitimacy and justification, are of central significance. The present chapter aims to explore what follows from this agenda with regard to the problem of democratic founding.

The basic issue we shall focus on is the relationship between law and democracy in the context of foundation. In the previous chapter, we have already seen with Arendt why the notion of constituent power, located in a juridical state of nature as a *potestas legibus soluta*, is deeply problematic. But what happens when the appeal to legal resources turns out to be circular, as it typically does, at moments of constitutional founding? Its merits notwithstanding, Arendt's argument for an act of foundation carried out in "common deliberation" does not squarely face up to the question of legal rupture. In her story of the American Revolution, she could avoid this question only by virtue of the historically contingent aspects of the American case. Can we find a better answer in deliberative democratic theory now?

After all, a central tenet of deliberative democratic theory is that law and democracy belong together, or that they presuppose one another at a fundamental level. In *Between Facts and Norms*, Jürgen Habermas has developed this point into a full-fledged theory of legitimacy structured around the thesis of "co-originality."[1] Simone Chambers sums it up aptly: "There is no People's will to speak of without rights and there are no rights without some theory of popular sovereignty to create an original justification. The relationship between constitutional rights and popular sovereignty mirrors the relationship between law and democracy. The rule of law is inherent in democracy and democracy cannot function without the rule of law. We are legal persons protected by rights only to the extent that we are authors of those laws. We are authors only to the extent that we are persons under the law."[2] But then, is it possible to retain the interdependence of law and democracy at moments of foundation? Or to put it differently: how to exercise popular sovereignty in such a way as to create a new constitution while at the same time remaining "under the law"? This is the central question that will guide our discussion in the present chapter. Since the discussion will unfold in the form of a critical dialogue with Habermas, let me begin with a sketch of some key points in his "discourse theory of law and democracy."

In Search of the Founding Act of Positive Law

One of the main tasks Habermas undertakes in *Between Facts and Norms* is to offer a "postmetaphysical"[3] account of the normative content of modern positive law as a "system of rights." This indicates a twofold challenge that is appropriately mirrored in the title of the book. On the one hand, to be postmetaphysical, such an account must abandon all appeals to a transcendental source of normativity such as the constructions of the natural law tradition; on the other hand, it must also avoid falling into the trap of legal positivism if it is to redeem the normative content of law after all. With this agenda of steering "between facts and norms," Habermas develops a reconstructive approach to law. Instead of appealing to foundationalist arguments, this approach takes its cue from the "self-understanding" of actually existing legal orders. "No one can credit herself with access to a system of rights in the singular, independent of the interpretations she already has historically available. 'The' system of rights does not exist in transcendental purity. But two hundred years of European constitutional law have provided us with a sufficient number of models. These can instruct a generalizing reconstruction of the intuitions that guide the intersubjective practice of self-legislation in the medium of positive law."[4] An approach of this sort, thus, proceeds from the assumption that there exists some crucial points of convergence between particular legal orders despite their specific historical and cultural backgrounds.

Habermas's inquiry into these points of convergence underscores three main features of positive law. First, a duality between "facticity and validity" resides at the heart of modern legal orders. Laws are enforced by coercive measures, while at the same time laying claim to legitimacy. As such, the addressees of the law can comply with it either for prudential reasons generated by the facticity of penal sanctions or for moral reasons based on an affirmation of the normative validity of the law. Second, these fundamental dimensions of facticity and validity are not isolated from each other but instead tied together by virtue of rights. The force of law is justified to the extent that it protects the equal freedom of all, while each person is thereby offered a good reason to comply with the law not only in instrumental but also in moral terms. Understood as a "system of rights," thus, law can be said to mediate between coercion and freedom. Finally, modern legal orders regulate rights around the basic categories of private and public autonomy, which are embodied in the catalogs of human rights and the rights of citizens respectively. While the protection of human rights ensures the private autonomy of individuals, the public autonomy of citizens is based on the exercise of popular sovereignty enabled by the rights of political participation. A significant insight follows from this reconstructive reading: human rights and popular sovereignty are *the* fundamental norms that modern legal orders claim to embody in their own specific ways. Or, to put it differently, they are the principal sources of legitimation from which positive law derives its normative authority.

According to the thesis of "co-originality," at its most basic, public and private autonomy, or popular sovereignty and human rights, mutually presuppose each other.[5] We could see this claim from two different though complementary perspectives. In one sense, it brings to our attention the *functional* interdependence of democracy and the rule of law. Democratic processes of collective decision-making require the background assurance of legally regulated rights, while the latter can be politically protected insofar as the exercise of power is channeled by participatory decision-making processes. This makes perfect sense, but it is not the sole point Habermas wants to make. Equally important is that neither principle has priority over the other, that they are not only functionally interdependent but also *normatively* co-original in the order of justification. What is of particular significance for our discussion is the way in which Habermas defends this point. In order to show that law and democracy presuppose each other at a fundamental conceptual level, he moves from the "system of rights" to its *constitutional genesis*, and undertakes a reconstructive analysis of constitution-making as a deliberative practice. "I try to develop the system of rights from the historical model of constitution-making through an analysis of the constitutive features of such a practice."[6]

We will see in a moment how this justificatory strategy works. Before that, however, a clarification is in order. Habermas's reconstructive account of constitution-making bears a family resemblance to the design of social contract theories in that it begins with the counterfactual motif of an indefinite number of individuals entering into the practice of instituting a political community. Yet, this resemblance can also be deceptive. Habermas does not design a hypothetical thought experiment such as Rawls's "original position," and he certainly does not speculate about what rational individuals *would* agree to if they were to deliberate impartially. But he takes it for granted that they would engage in *deliberation*, namely that they would have a commitment to resolve their issues by talking with one another in the manner of reasoned argument. The task of the reconstructive theorist is to analyze what they *do* when they deliberate, thereby unpacking the *performative meaning* of constitution-making as a deliberative practice.

Also notice that the participants who engage in such a practice must be *already* willing to coordinate their living together through a mutually granted system of rights: "they are united by a common resolution to legitimately regulate their future life together by means of positive law."[7] This common resolution stipulates what we might call a "pre-constitutional commitment." Insofar as the commitment to positive law is not the product but the prior condition of the constitution-making practice, it raises the question why the participants have come to take positive law as *the* means of regulating their common life. In response, Habermas does not claim to offer a normative justification for law as such: "We are not under an *obligation* to regulate our living together by means of positive law."[8] Rather, he gives a functionalist explanation, according to which there is no viable functional equivalent to the medium of positive law in modern societies.[9]

A claim of this sort, in its turn, can be defended only at the level of social theory because it requires an account of the increasingly abstract processes of social integration that modern societies have gone through. From this sociologically and historically informed perspective, the pre-constitutional commitment to positive law is not an arbitrary starting point. Rather, it is imposed on the participants themselves by the *facticity* of modern societies where the traditional sources of authority have largely dried up, while law has become the sole viable medium of social integration and solidarity among strangers. Hence, the participants of Habermas's counterfactual constitution-making practice draw on a historical learning process, one that emerges from the "crumbling edifice of substantial ethical life"[10] and provides them with an intuitive understanding of why they should regulate their common life by means of positive law.

The Performative Meaning of Constitution-Making

In the "Postscript" to *Between Facts and Norms*, Habermas explains why the theme of constitutional founding comes to the foreground in his attempt to give a theoretical justification for the co-originality thesis:

> what rights must citizens mutually grant one another if they decide to constitute themselves as a voluntary association of legal consociates and legitimately to regulate their living together by means of positive law? The performative *meaning* of this constitution-making practice already contains *in nuce* the entire content of constitutional democracy. The system of rights and the principles of the constitutional state can be developed from what it means to carry out the practice that one has gotten into with the first act in the self-constitution of such a legal community.[11]

Of course, the passage stands in need of some unpacking. What does Habermas mean by the "performative meaning" of the constitution-making practice? More specifically, what exactly does it mean that this practice "already contains *in nuce*" the normative content of constitutional democracy? Or to put it differently, how are the normative principles of human rights and popular sovereignty, the rule of law and democracy, co-originally inscribed in the act of constitution-making itself?

To answer such questions, we need to recall that Habermas conceives the act of constitution-making as a deliberative practice in which participants try to achieve an agreement. That is, they talk about constitutional essentials in order to come up with a text that will appeal to all participants and command their allegiance. As a matter of fact, this deliberative process turns on a variety of substantive topics about which participants are very likely to hold different views. Despite their disagreements on what ought to become the specific and concrete content of the constitution, however, they have something important in common. In committing themselves to a deliberative enterprise, they adopt a certain kind of performative attitude toward one another—an attitude without which they could not have initiated and carried forward the process of framing the constitution in the manner of reasoned speech.

Once the performative attitude of participants comes into focus this way, our attention turns from the content of constitutional debate to its modus operandi. The question of what topics the participants talk about is now replaced by the question of what they *do* in talking about them. In the course of their constitutional debate, regardless of the content of their respective positions, the participants argue about the essentials of the future constitution, offer what they take to be good reasons in favor of their own proposals, and critically challenge the proposals made by others. In doing so, they first and foremost exercise what Habermas calls "communicative freedom,"[12] the freedom to take part in a discourse by making arguments (or, in Habermas's parlance, by raising "criticizable validity claims") and taking affirmative or negative ("yes/no") positions in response to the arguments of others.

In the course of exercising their communicative freedom collectively, the participants are at the same time practically bound to abide by several implicit commitments. For instance, they must recognize the like freedom of one another to propose topics and to take positions, without which deliberation cannot progress. Moreover, they must accept the obligation to give reasons with a view to justifying their claims if and when they are challenged by others because a refusal to do so disrupts the deliberative process and abandons the possibility of reaching agreement. Thus, if they are willing to carry the process forward, they must be ready to try to convince one another through a constant exchange of reasons. Finally, the participants also commit themselves to the further obligation of regulating the subsequent course of their actions in accordance with the propositional content of an accepted validity claim when they actually happen to reach agreement. Without a commitment of this sort, deliberation would remain ineffective and pointless since participants would not take the deliberative process seriously if they did not expect their future agreement to be binding for everyone. For Habermas, commitments of this sort, when they are taken together, add up to the "communicative structures of reciprocity."[13]

It is crucial to keep in mind that these structures are not given to the participants prior to deliberation as explicitly thematized guidelines to be followed. Rather, they are "pragmatic presuppositions" that need to be fulfilled if a meaningful deliberation is to take place at all. Therefore, they reveal themselves first and foremost in the performative attitude of the participants. The deliberative practice of constitution-making can begin, proceed, and bring about an agreement only if participants actually abide by these presuppositions throughout the process. What follows from this analysis is that communicative freedom and communicative reciprocity belong together. The participants in the process can exercise their communicative freedom only insofar as they abide by the requirements of communicative reciprocity, while the latter, in turn, reveals itself only in and through the exercise of the former.[14]

As I see it, this insight is *the* conceptual kernel of Habermas's reconstruction of the constitution-making practice, and it is meant to offer a solution to the problem of "reconciling private and public autonomy at a fundamental conceptual level."[15] According to this solution, the co-originality of rights and popular sovereignty mirrors the performative unity of communicative freedom and reciprocity—hence the sense in which the performative meaning of constitution-making "contains *in nuce*" the normative content of constitutional democracy. More specifically, a system of rights that ensures the private and public autonomy of citizens can be understood as an explicit expression or rearticulation of the implicit presuppositions that enable the deliberative practice of constitution-making in the first place.

On this account, the fundamental norms of constitutional democracy, conceived in terms of human rights and popular sovereignty, are not transcendental principles guiding the act of foundation from without, as if those who frame the constitution implement a suprasensible code.[16] Instead, these principles originate from the performative attitude that the participants in the constitution-making process are bound to take if they want to achieve a shared understanding of how to coordinate their common life through a system of positive law. Thus, when the participants in the constitution-making process eventually come to an agreement to enact a system of rights structured around the categories of private and public autonomy, they essentially give a normative and legally binding formulation to the performative meaning of their own practice. On the view defended by Habermas, as Andreas Kalyvas aptly recapitulates, "the act of constituent higher lawmaking enacts those principles that are also the very conditions of its possibility."[17]

Thus far, then, we have outlined a highly abstract and counterfactual model of deliberative constitution-making. Throughout the complicated argument of *Between Facts and Norms*, however, Habermas does not address himself to the question of how this model relates to historical moments of foundation. In a way, of course, this is not unexpected. Although the model has a toehold in actual practices of constitution-making, whose performative meaning it claims to reconstruct and explicate, Habermas does not intend it for purposes of "application," but rather for purposes of "justification." In other words, the foregoing argument is meant to theoretically demonstrate the co-originality of self-determination and rights, thereby offering a postmetaphysical account of legitimation. In order to see how the democratic practice of self-determination and a legally structured system of rights mediate one another in actual political processes, Habermas writes, we need to "move from the horizontal association of consociates who reciprocally accord rights to one another to the vertical organization of citizens within the state."[18] With this move from the counterfactual model of deliberative constitution-making to the institutional functioning of an *already* established constitutional democracy, however, a number of questions remain intact.

Supposing that Habermas's model does the theoretical and justificatory work it is intended to do, how does it actually relate to the *politics* of constitution-making? In other words, what does deliberative democratic theory have to tell us about the *making* of the democratic constitution? How are we supposed to design the constitution-making process, if we are to meet the standards of deliberative legitimacy? Is it possible, for instance, to retain the interdependence of law and democracy at moments of foundation? Or, to put it slightly differently, is it possible to fulfill the demands of proceduralism in the very process of establishing the procedures of legislation? If the "democratic procedure for the production of law evidently forms the only postmetaphysical source of legitimacy,"[19] as Habermas emphatically holds, then what sort of constitutional process does it take to establish the legitimacy of a new constitution? All in all, how can citizens themselves get to underwrite their constitution—and make it *their own* constitution—in a deliberative manner?

To elaborate on these questions, it would be helpful to bring the paradox of founding to bear on Habermas's model of deliberative constitution-making. This is not to disregard the fact that the model is designed for justificatory purposes in the first place. Rather, it is to ask whether or to what extent the deliberative model, once it is *restored* to the gray area in which the enterprise of democratic founding takes place, would encounter the paradox under consideration. In Chapter 2, we saw that the paradox of democratic founding can be stated in two main ways: *substantively* (as a matter of democratic ethos) and *procedurally* (as a matter of legal form). In the next two sections, I discuss how each of these versions may apply to deliberative democracy, and what deliberative democratic theory has to say in response.

Deliberative Democracy and Rousseau's Paradox of Founding

A broader discussion between Habermas and his critics, which turns on the role of "democratic ethos" in deliberative politics, can offer us some initial guidance. Even some of Habermas's most sympathetic readers raise objections against the rigid distinction he draws between the pragmatic presuppositions of communication and the substantial content of a concrete form of life committed to democratic values, insisting that these two are indistinguishable in practice. Richard Bernstein puts the point clearly: "there is no adequate discourse theory of democratic procedure that avoids presupposing a democratic ethos—an ethos that conditions and affects *how* discussion, debate, and argumentation are *practiced*."[20]

In his earlier work, Habermas indeed downplays the role of democratic ethos in favor of the universal pragmatics of communication.[21] In *Between Facts and Norms*, however, his position is more nuanced. He concedes that deliberative politics depends on "a liberal political culture and an enlightened political socialization," on "a rationalized lifeworld that meets it halfway."[22] In response to Bernstein, more specifically, he argues that his theory makes room for "democratic ethos," should this be understood not in the strong sense of an overtaxing civic virtue but in the weaker sense of a "postconventional *Sittlichkeit*," or the dispositions of a "population accustomed to freedom."[23]

Now, taking our cue from this exchange and narrowing down the scope of Bernstein's criticism to the deliberative model of constitution-making in particular, we can attempt to restate Rousseau's paradox of founding. If the practice of deliberation draws upon liberal patterns of political culture and socialization, as Habermas maintains, then, does not his notion of deliberative constitutional founding entail, in somewhat the same circular manner perceptively described by Rousseau, the prior existence of those politico-cultural resources which can nevertheless be at the disposal of only a mature and functioning democratic society? Isn't it the case that, to put it in Rousseau's words, "the effect would have to become the cause, the social spirit [or, in this case, the political culture of deliberation] which is to be the work of the institution would have to preside over the institution itself"?

The answer depends on where one looks. Recall that Habermas presents the deliberative model of constitution-making against the broad historical background of a *modern* society. A starting point of this sort already involves an implicit response to Rousseau's paradox. For Habermas, the formation of the politico-cultural resources that can enable a democratic constitutional founding is ultimately a matter of historical development. In this respect, Habermas's theory is through and through Hegelian. It is the gradual rationalization of what he calls the "lifeworld structures," of the ways we make sense of our world and ourselves, that brings about the practical dispositions and moral intuitions conducive to the establishment of a constitutional democracy based on the twin principles of private and public autonomy. To be sure, the participants in the founding process cannot have at their disposal the kind of concrete, specific, and explicit public culture that we would today associate with a functioning democratic society. But this does not mean they have nothing at their disposal. The elements of a "postconventional *Sittlichkeit*," or the stuff that the political culture of a mature democracy is to be made of, are already built into the lifeworld of modern individuals in implicit, amorphous, and incomplete ways.

Furthermore, Habermas does not claim that normative political theory can account for the historical development of these lifeworld structures. Obviously it cannot. At the level of normative analysis, the outcome of this process needs to be taken for granted. Any claim regarding the rationalization of the lifeworld, in turn, must be justified at the level of social theory, by explaining the evolution and increasing differentiation of reasons and symbolic forms of interaction human beings employ in making sense of their world.[24] Even though we cannot here explore this social-theoretical register of the argument, it has an interesting implication for our discussion. Viewed from the standpoint of Habermas's social theory, Rousseau seems to have encountered the paradox of founding due to his own social-theoretical premises, according to which human sociality is perverted in self-destructive directions through the very process of historical development. In other words, Rousseau invokes a "great lawgiver" because his pessimistic outlook on history leaves no room for understanding the formation of a democratic ethos as an outcome of long-range trends over which no one has strict control. For Habermas, by contrast, what would save us from getting entrapped in Rousseau's paradox of founding is not so much the educative authority of a "great lawgiver" but the long process of rationalization and moral learning.

Despite its merits, this is a "grand theory" kind of answer. While it would help us take a critical stance vis-à-vis some of the background assumptions that shape and inform Rousseau's paradox, it says little about the self-evident *political* problem Rousseau points out. It suffices to recall the sometimes desperately painful transitions to democracy or the failure thereof, like the one we have been observing in Egypt today. Regardless of his background assumptions, the kind of circularity Rousseau so acutely diagnosed in *The Social Contract* is hard to miss in such transitional cases where mutual trust, civic habits, and a deliberative public cannot be taken for granted, but need to be promoted, as much as possible, in and through the politics of founding. How would a deliberative process of constitution-making get off the ground under such circumstances?

This was precisely the challenge that confronted the constitutional assembly of South Africa in 1994. Established by the national parliament after the first nonracial elections, the assembly was commissioned with the task of drafting the new constitution. Although the importance of widespread public deliberation and citizen consultation was acknowledged, it was by no means clear how this could be done.

> The assembly's main challenge was to find ways to enter into effective dialogue and consultation with a population of more than forty million people. South Africa had a large rural population, most of which was illiterate and without access to print or electronic media. Moreover, South Africa had never had a culture of constitutionalism or human rights, which made it difficult to consult with people who did not recognize the importance of a constitution. Meeting this

challenge, thus, had to include raising awareness to empower people to be able to participate meaningfully in the process.[25]

In this graphic description of a largely illiterate rural population "who did not recognize the importance of a constitution," one cannot help but hear the echoes of Rousseau's pressing question: "How will a blind multitude," he (in)famously asked, "carry out an undertaking as great, as difficult as a system of legislation?"[26]

The challenge in South Africa was no doubt daunting, but the response turned out to be equally astounding. To solicit public input from every possible corner of the country, the assembly initiated a massive participation program on a hitherto unprecedented scale. Hundreds of educational workshops and public consultation meetings were held. Many of them took place especially in the rural areas. Citizens were both informed and consulted in face-to-face settings; members of the assembly met with associations of all sorts; and a "hearing system," composed of a phone line and website, was put to work in order to facilitate constitutional submissions. The assembly also sponsored a biweekly newspaper devoted to "constitutional talk," bearing the same title, as well as numerous radio broadcasts. Radio was especially effective in reaching out to villages since it was the primary and in many cases the only means of media access. By the end of the program, the constitutional assembly received more than two million submissions from the public, suggesting a broad and active citizen interest in the constitution-making process.

From a skeptical point of view, of course, all this might seem a little too good to be true, or perhaps too similar to what we would like to believe rather than what actually happened. As Christina Murray reports, some observers of the constitutional process in South Africa saw it as an elaborate public relations campaign. The final document, they claimed, did not so much reflect the submissions as the negotiation among the elites:

> In support of this argument, people pointed to the huge volume of submissions and asked if any politicians could be expected to review them all. Moreover, these critics might have added, if the politicians had reviewed the submissions, they would have found vague wish lists, more often concerned with poverty and the standard of living than with matters appropriately dealt with in a constitution.... Even those who read through the submissions found repetition rather than inspiration, and in many painful requests based on deep

poverty, they found the legacy of apartheid rather than a design for the future.[27]

While this criticism was not entirely unwarranted, according to Murray, it sidesteps the fact that the process had "broader and less instrumental goals," which had to do with generating a sense of ownership in the constitution and facilitating its taking root in the political culture of an emerging civic nation. On this approach, the process had a twofold character, serving both as a school of democratic citizenship and a time-extended forum where major issues are collectively thematized in public. Moreover, the expected deliberative effect was not that the ideas of the participants would directly make their way into the constitution. As another commentator puts it aptly, public deliberation was rather meant to be a "process of integration through which the imagination of all parties steadily evolved toward the embrace of potentially sustainable alternatives."[28]

Getting back to Rousseau's paradox of founding in light of these considerations, I think that it is possible to see the South African experience in deliberative constitution-making as a fairly successful attempt in coping with it. In Chapter 2, I already suggested that we would be well-advised not to hypostatize the paradox under consideration but to take it as a *heuristic problem*. Viewed as such, Rousseau's version of the paradox brings home to us the intricate question of how to envision a democratic founding if its politico-cultural conditions—or if you like, the kind of "democratic ethos" required to enable it—cannot be taken for granted, but need to be promoted, as much as possible, in and through the politics of founding itself. The case of South Africa offers a real world illustration of how this could be done in practice. Although no single case can serve as a "model," particularly when the question in focus is that of "democratic ethos," we can nonetheless underline some key points which were crucial to the success of deliberative constitution-making in South Africa.

The first one is about numbers. From the outset, the sponsors of the "constitutional talk" wanted to bring as many people as possible into the process. They believed, in my view rightly, that only broad participation could turn the process into a shared experience of democratic citizenship for a population with no tradition of constitutional democracy to draw on. Although the kind of ethos required to sustain democratic institutions cannot be generated at will, or at any specific point in time, a participatory process of constitution-making can nonetheless help foster its formation by restoring the dignity of politics as a public activity and serving as a school of civic capacity. After all, to put it with Aristotle, "we learn by doing," we become flute players by playing the flute, and we become citizens by taking part in political decision-making.[29]

The second point has to do with the principles that actually guided the course of public deliberation. "The citizen participation program brought people together in a process that itself was governed by the very principles that South Africans were attempting to enshrine: the process treated citizens (many of them for the first time) as equal, free, and deserving of respect. It did this by adhering to high standards of publicity, accountability, and dialogue."[30] In other words, the basic normative content of the democratic constitution was already performatively manifest in the process of public deliberation aiming to frame it. This makes it easier to understand how the constitutional process could progressively negotiate Rousseau's paradox of founding. It is simultaneously both a process of education *and* one of agency. That is to say, it introduces the basic principles of constitutional democracy to citizens, while at the same time involving them in the shaping of the constitution that is to give a concrete formulation to the very same principles.

Finally, the observers of the process also draw attention to the kind of public rhetoric practiced, most notably, by Nelson Mandela. Acting as a "deliberative orator," Simone Chambers notes, Mandela facilitated the process of nation-wide discussion, influenced the broad public sphere, and eventually managed to prevent it from being dominated by the plebiscitary rhetoric that is typical of mass politics.[31] This point implies that Rousseau's own solution to the paradox of founding, the appeal to the lawgiver, may not be irrelevant to a democratic theory of deliberative constitution-making, but rather would have to be incorporated into it. In Chapter 3, I already suggested that we could see Rousseau's lawgiver as an "interpreter" interacting with the people rather than an "architect" creating a new ethos from scratch. The point can be restated from the standpoint of deliberative democratic theory now. Especially in cases of extraordinary politics, as episodes of constitution-making typically are, the attitude of the political elite is a crucial variable in setting the tone of public debate. After all, it would be implausible to expect meaningful deliberation to take place under the pressure of plebiscitary appeals to "the people." And it is precisely in this respect that the presence of a "deliberative orator" matters a great deal.

The Problem of Infinite Regress: Habermas Versus Michelman

I have been arguing that deliberative democratic theory can effectively respond to Rousseau's paradox of founding. Whether it can also cope with the other version of the paradox—such as the procedural version which troubled Sieyès and Madison—is, however, yet to be examined. As we have already seen in Chapter 2, Frank Michelman picks up on this version of the paradox and brings it to bear on the deliberative model of constitution-making propounded by Habermas. To recall briefly, Michelman does not object that law and democracy stand in a circular relationship: "A truly democratic process is itself inescapably a legally conditioned and constituted process."[32] His point is rather that, when pressed doggedly, the interdependence of law and democracy dissolves into an infinite regress: "If it takes a legally constituted democratic procedure to bring forth valid fundamental laws, then the (valid) laws that frame *this* lawmaking event must themselves be the product of a conceptually prior procedural event that was itself framed by (valid) laws that must, as such, have issued in their turn from a still prior (properly) legally constituted event. And so on, it would appear, without end."[33] But what exactly, one might want to ask at this point, is the problem with infinite regress?

The problem is that it seems to leave us with a most unwelcome dilemma. Either the buck does not stop at all or it stops somewhere but only arbitrarily. In the former case, the democratic process cannot even begin. "Where in history," Michelman asks, "can this 'originary' constitutive moment ever be fixed or anchored?"[34] If the procedural presuppositions of deliberative legitimacy lead to an infinite regress, then, the founding act could never be "anchored" in history and thus could never make the kind of beginning it claims to make. In the latter case, the constitution gets enacted but in a procedurally arbitrary way which cannot vouch for its own democratic credentials. Hence, there is no guarantee that the higher law enables a "truly democratic" process and delivers the kind of procedural legitimacy that it is supposed to confer on subsequent legislation. In this respect, Michelman's point is quite similar to Derrida's: the act of foundation, understood as a new beginning, cannot guarantee its own legitimacy.

In response to Michelman, Habermas writes: "I prefer not to meet this objection by recourse to the transparent objectivity of ultimate moral insights that are supposed to bring the regress to a halt. Rather than appeal to a moral realism that would be hard to defend, I propose that we understand the regress itself as the understandable expression of the future-oriented character, or openness, of the democratic constitution."[35] Apparently, what Habermas proposes here is to recast the problematic groundlessness of the founding act in terms of the promising openness of the democratic constitution. Is this a question-begging move?

As I see it, the answer is both yes and no. No insofar as, by appealing to the "future-oriented character" of the democratic constitution, Habermas takes up the challenge on its own terms of temporality. As Ciaran Cronin observes: "Habermas's response amounts to the claim that the riddle of the 'polity's groundless discursive self-constitution' (Michelman) cannot be solved as long as the founding is viewed as an isolated event which must vouch for its own democratic credentials."[36] But the answer is also yes, provided Habermas does not say anything about how to negotiate the problem of infinite regress—that is, the problem of democratic legitimacy in view of its relation to law—at moments of foundation. As we will see shortly, this aspect of the challenge cannot be set aside without a certain cost, which eventually compromises the cogency of Habermas's response to Michelman.

To get a grasp of why this is the case, let us take a closer look at Habermas's response. On the one hand, he seems to admit—even if implicitly—that for the constitution-making practice to set out, its originary procedures have to be laid down by a "decision" that cannot have been achieved through a legally regulated democratic deliberation. Michelman is right on this point. He convincingly picks up on what we might call the "facticity" of founding. After all, this is why political foundings are always susceptible to a legitimation deficit. On the other hand, however, acknowledging the unavoidable facticity of founding, Habermas also turns the tables on Michelman. If we are to understand the founding act in the temporal sense of a "new beginning," as Michelman rightly wants us to do, then we cannot treat it as an isolated event anymore. A beginning has to be the beginning of something. A constitutional founding initiates a process, an open-ended normative debate in and through which the principles of the democratic constitution are constantly applied, challenged, revised, and reapplied. Thus, we find ourselves, once again, "between facts and norms." The facticity of the founding act links up with the normative process that it sets in motion.

For Habermas, unlike Michelman (and, by implication, unlike Derrida), there is no devastating or insurmountable aporia here. Rather, the groundlessness of the founding compels us to admit its "fallibility." If the originary procedures are not fully inclusive, for instance, the enacted constitution may fall short of its own democratic promise in significant ways. But notice that the proviso of fallibility already applies to all deliberative politics in one way or another. In fact, it is *the* reason why deliberation is inherently open-ended. It is open-ended because perfect legitimacy cannot be ensured at any given moment, and the founding moment of a polity is no exception in this regard. In other words, Habermas grants that there is no perfectly legitimate founding, but he also adds that there does not have to be one. Constitutional democracy is not realized at once. It is a work in progress, "a tradition-building project with a clearly marked beginning in time."[37] Introducing a constitutional order, a system of rights, the act of foundation initiates this project. But it is only the later generations who can unfold its latent normative content and retroactively redeem its democratic promise by "tapping" the system of rights on an ongoing basis.

Nevertheless, this is not yet a full response. On the ground of what has been said so far, it is by no means clear whether we can tell that the later generations are actually bootstrapping and not simply caught up in a vicious circle that constantly reproduces itself in ever new forms over time. After all, this is part of the question posed by Michelman. If the founding of our polity is problematic in some fundamental way, if it is implicated in a deficit of legitimacy, then how do we know that we are doing better today? The question can be understood in two ways, which have different implications. First, what are the grounds on which we can claim to *know* that we are doing better? And second, what are the grounds on which we can claim that we are *doing better* today? Habermas is aware of the problem. "To be sure," he writes, "this fallible continuation of the founding event can break out of the circle of a polity's groundless discursive self-constitution only if this process—which is not immune to contingent interruptions and historical regressions—can be understood in the long run as a self-correcting learning process."[38] Hence the crux of Habermas's response: the deficit of legitimacy, which apparently attends to every act of foundation, gets to be dissolved over time in and through the progressively evolving "learning processes" that the political community undergoes.

This claim is based upon two premises. The first one concerns the reflexive nature of a constitutional beginning with a democratic intent. "On this premise," Habermas writes, "each founding act also creates the possibility of self-correcting attempts to tap the system of rights ever more fully."[39] The "possibility" of self-correction is built into the democratic logic of political rights by virtue of which citizens can interpret and revise their legal and political system. Second, Habermas adds, if citizens are to effectively make use of this possibility, they must take the founding event and its normative commitments as the point of reference for their own politics. As he puts it quite emphatically (but also, as we will see, problematically):

> Of course, the interpretation of constitutional history as a learning process is predicated on the nontrivial assumption that later generations will start with the same standards as did the founders. . . . The descendants can learn from past mistakes only if they are "in the same boat" as their forebears. They must impute to all the previous generations the same intention of creating and expanding the bases for a voluntary association of citizens who make their own laws. All participants must be able to recognize the project as *the same* throughout history and to judge it from *the same* perspective.[40]

In this view, then, the founding act opens up a horizon within which its own deficiencies and shortcomings, whatever they turn out to be, can be thematized, addressed, and gradually overcome, should the later generations commit themselves to the same normative project of creating and sustaining a self-legislating political community, and hence carry the project progressively forward. The problem of infinite regress is thereby replaced, or so Habermas claims, by an open-ended process of learning, self-correction, and constant bootstrapping.

Habermas's notion of constitutional history as a progressive learning process has been the subject of various criticisms. One common concern is that it is not clear what he means by "the same boat." Habermas seems to have in mind the generic project of constitutional democracy as such. Yet, this is just too general a point of reference. If citizens are to be in the same boat with *their* founders, they must be able to attach themselves not only to the generic project of constitutional democracy but also to the concrete shape it has taken in a specific constitutional history. Otherwise, it should have been possible for, say, Canadian citizens to regard themselves in the same boat as American framers—which, of course, is not the case.[41] Once the project is embedded, however, another question arises. In an evolving learning process, later generations cannot by definition share "the same perspective" with the preceding ones. "If, as Habermas's model requires, the project constitutes a learning process, then later generations must surely adopt *different*, continually evolving perspectives on the constitution as they reinterpret and revise it."[42] Or as another commentator puts it pointedly: "as a U.S. citizen, I might plausibly *deny* that I share the same project with a founding generation that constitutively excluded so many from political citizenship."[43] Finally, a perhaps more pressing criticism has to do with whether the appeal to "learning processes" can actually escape the challenge of interpretive pluralism, that is, whether we can come to an agreement on what we are supposed to have learnt through the political and interpretive battles of the past.[44]

From the standpoint of our investigation, however, the problem with Habermas's argument is neither about the meaning of constitutional learning nor about its possibility as such. The problem is rather that, in his response to Michelman, Habermas does not address the challenge of infinite regress *on its own terms*. That is, he does not even attempt to make a case about how a deliberative practice of constitution-making can engage with the problem of infinite regress, or how the interdependence of law and democracy can be retained and realized at moments of foundation. At times, in fact, Habermas's argument sounds as if it does not matter how the project of constitutional democracy gets off the ground insofar as the possibility of "self-correction" is already built into it. But then can we hope to initiate a self-correcting constitutional process from any starting point whatsoever?

Actually, Habermas himself argued otherwise in his practically oriented interventions in the German unification debate.[45] In opposition to an executive-driven unification process in the wake of 1989, he defended a process of democratic constitution-making in which East and West German citizens would take part on equal terms and publicly reflect on the principles of their political association. According to him, only a deliberative act of constitution-making, which would have to culminate in a popular referendum, could grant democratic legitimacy to the constitutional system in a unified Germany, while at the same time serving as a founding moment "around which the republican self-understanding of future generations can crystallize."[46]

Although we cannot here get into the specifics of the German unification debate, it is worth noting that in this context Habermas pressed for a democratic founding instead of appealing to the future possibility of self-correction. And he insisted on the mode of the unification process not only for normative considerations but also for reasons regarding its long-term effects. This view is quite different from—though, not necessarily contradictory to—the position he adopted in his critical exchange with Michelman. In the context of the

German unification debate, Habermas puts the emphasis not so much on how the future generations would retrospectively redeem the promise of a democratic constitution as on how the present generation shapes its own politics and what sort of legacy it leaves to the future. The gist of his argument is that the future is not independent of what we do here at the moment.[47]

In Chapter 3, juxtaposing Rousseau and Kant on the importance of founding moments, we already faced a different version of this issue. Founding is everything (or almost everything) for Rousseau precisely because he does not put his trust in progress, in gradual reform, and in political development. By contrast, Kant is decidedly indifferent to the way in which the political community happens to be established because, in his view, once a "rightful condition" effectively replaces the juridical state of nature, it sets in motion a process of rationalization toward the republican constitution. If we take Rousseau and Kant as representing two opposite poles—the former emphasizing the singular significance of founding and its impact on the future prospects of the republic, the latter emphasizing continuous reform and gradual development—we can ask the following question: where does Habermas stand on the spectrum?

While he leans toward the Kantian pole in his critical encounter with Michelman, I would suggest that one finds a more Rousseauean bent in Habermas's interventions in the German unification debate.[48] Indeed, a theory of democratic founding would do well to seek a middle ground. On the one hand, contra Rousseau, it is important to insist (as Habermas himself does) on the open-ended and future-oriented character of the democratic constitution, and consequently on the possibility of constitutional learning and self-correction. On the other hand, Kant's indifference toward the politics of founding would only make sense in a world where the prospect of progressive reform is firmly anchored in the reassuring "facts of reason." Once this backdrop is gone, along with the metaphysics of practical reason (namely, in a world devoid of transcendental guarantees), the making of the democratic constitution and the prospect of constitutional development can hardly be detached from one another. This means that the processes of constitutional learning cannot be clearly severed from the way in which they are set in motion. Under postmetaphysical circumstances, in other words, we must also take into consideration the Rousseauean end of the spectrum, that is, the role of founding moments in opening up or precluding different future prospects, and in setting the paths of constitutional development.[49] This is the kind of insight, I think, that underpinned Habermas's more Rousseauean interventions in the German unification debate. Viewed in light of this insight, it is not sufficient to point toward the future possibility of self-correction vis-à-vis the challenge of infinite regress. If how we begin is a matter of concern, then the challenge must be taken up on its own terms.

Law and Democracy in Founding Moments

The question is still on the table then: how to remain under the law, paradoxical as it may seem, while making the higher law? The anomalous status of amendment can provide us with some initial guidance here. Stephen Holmes and Cass Sunstein draw attention to the difficulties confronted by French constitutional theorists who painfully tried to classify the "amending power":

> Following usage established by Abbé Sieyès in the late eighteenth century, French constitutionalists distinguish between the framing power—*le pouvoir constituant*—and the three established branches of government—*les pouvoirs constitués*. The amending power does not fit comfortably into either category. It inhabits a twilight zone between authorizing and authorized powers. To classify it, therefore, French constitutionalists resort to farfetched terms, such as *le pouvoir constituant institué* and *le pouvoir constituant derivé*. They might as well have confessed their embarrassment and called it *le pouvoir constituant constitué*. Strangely enough, there is something to this oxymoron. The amending power is simultaneously framing and framed, licensing and licensed, original and derived, superior and inferior to the constitution. This acrobatic both/and pattern alerts us to the undertheorized dilemma posed by the constitutionally regulated power to revise constitutional regulations of power.[50]

Actually, this "acrobatic both/and pattern" not only alerts us to the dilemmas of amendment but also points toward something arguably more important. It brings home to us a situation in which the distinction between constituent and constituted powers is blurred, and their standing to one another is relativized. Something *like* this, I want to argue, is essential to an understanding of how to retain the interdependence of law and democracy at moments of foundation.

The question of how to remain under the law while making the higher law came to the foreground in many cases of "transition" from dictatorship to democracy in the wake of 1989. First in Central and Eastern Europe, then in South Africa, constitutional framers deliberately avoided models of constitution-making based on the classical doctrine of constituent power.[51] That is, instead of locating the constituent power in a juridical state of nature as a *potestas legibus soluta*, "power absolved from the law" and unbound by any legal proviso, they attempted to ensure some form of legal continuity in the context of large-scale political transformation. A common pattern was that the constitutional politics of founding the new regime tapped into the legal and institutional provisions provided by or left over from the old one. For instance, framers used the amendment rule of the old regime as a leverage to make the new constitution, thereby ensuring at least some degree of formal legal continuity. Thus, the observers of the process rightly maintained that while we in fact witnessed "constitutional revolutions," they were nonetheless "cloaked as constitutional revisions."[52]

What was innovative in those episodes, however, was not simply the employment of amendment rules for the sake of formal (and in a sense necessarily liquidated) legal continuity. Rather, as Andrew Arato puts it aptly, "the underlying idea, unfortunately all too poorly understood, is to apply constitutionalism not only to result but also to the democratic process of constitution-making."[53] According to Arato, this reflexive application of constitutionalism to the politics of founding itself suggests a new model or a "post-sovereign paradigm" of democratic constitution-making, one which rivals the classical doctrine of constituent power.[54]

At its most basic, the central element of this new model is a multi-stage process. It involves the making of an interim constitution, a provisional higher law typically negotiated by a "round table" (or a functional equivalent), followed by free elections and the formation of a democratic assembly, which is then to draft the final constitution. The final work is done by the democratically elected assembly and in consultation with the broader public, but also in compliance with the rules and principles foreseen in the interim constitution. In this way, the distinction between constituent and constituted powers is progressively relativized. The model opens the floor for multiple constitutional actors instead of investing the plenitude of constituent power in a sovereign "organ." This is the basic sense in which the model is "post-sovereign." All actors and participants are brought under legal rules throughout the process, and no single instance or institution is authorized to embody "the people" as such. As illustrated by the successful case of South Africa, this multi-stage model even makes room for the institution of judicial review in the course of constitutional founding. The provisional supreme court, set up by the interim constitution, is entitled to review whether the final document complies with the principles of the interim constitution.

Can this new paradigm of constitution-making save us from the vexing problem of infinite regress? Again, the answer is both yes and no. Obviously, it is possible to keep pushing the question. One would argue (à la Michelman) that the reflexive use of constitutionalism in the process of constitution-making does not make a *logical* difference, if for no other reason than that the regress problem now applies to the interim constitution. Either the interim constitution itself has to be framed in accordance with legally valid procedures (in which case we inevitably fall back on infinite regress) or we must admit that there is a foundational moment of facticity, a moment of "decision" that escapes the demand for procedural validity. I would certainly agree: the problem is logically insurmountable at a formal level of analysis.

And yet, I would also argue that the reflexive use of constitutionalism in the process of constitutional founding is capable of making a *political* difference. This claim is premised on the assumption that it is *normatively* significant whether the buck stops anywhere arbitrarily (including the likelihood that the constitution is to be made by a sovereign assembly, speaking in the name of "the people" en masse, but dominated by those who hold the power to impose their terms, as most recently happened in Egypt) or whether a multi-track space opens for bargaining, negotiation, and deliberation on the essentials of the final constitution, allowing different groups and actors to participate, make their cases, and try to effect the outcome. After all, even if the problem is logically irresolvable, there are normatively better and worse ways of arresting infinite regress in practice, and the difference between them is far from insignificant.

Notice that the problem of infinite regress can also help us understand what is truly innovative in this new model of multi-stage constitution-making. The process does *not* begin with the assumption of either full legality or democratic legitimacy. On the contrary, in all relevant cases, the interim constitutions have been the product of negotiations among major political forces around the "round table." Thus, the provisional higher law, which is to regulate the making of the final constitution, clearly lacks the kind of democratic legitimacy that only free elections, fair representation, and widespread public deliberation could provide. As for the initial legality of the interim constitution, it is often only formal since it relies on the amendment rule of the old regime, and sometimes even formal legal continuity is hard to establish.

"Indeed," argues Arato, "the legality that is being preserved in many of the cases is fictional or is rather created for the occasion, since the old regimes were dictatorships with paper constitutions that may have routinely disregarded and not only violated their own ritualized legality."[55] Hence, the kind of legitimation deficit (in terms of both legal and democratic legitimacy) that the problem of infinite regress brings to our attention is obviously there at the initial stage. To its merit, however, the new model of constitution-making is precisely premised on the recognition of this legitimation deficit, and offers a bootstrapping process in which it is to be worked through. The key point in this process is the reciprocal establishment of legal authority and democratic legitimacy, step by step, in a series of back and forth movements—so that the interdependence of law and democracy are performatively retained and realized in the course of building a constitutional democratic regime.

* * *

In his 1991 essay, "Democracy and Territoriality," having elaborated on Rousseau's paradox of founding, William Connolly extends the hermeneutics of suspicion to his own argument and raises the following question:

> But how does one prove that the "paradox of sovereignty" is not itself the result of a contestable interpretation of politics? Is it necessarily true that Rousseau is right in identifying it, but wrong in concealing it (if he does, indeed, attempt the latter)? . . . Is it not possible, for instance, to read historical experiences of discordance in the structure of politics through the optics of a teleological ontology that promises the possibility of closing this gap in the future (or the memory of being closed in the past)? These questions are never likely to become settled by a definitive answer. One does not *prove* the truth of the interpretation offered here, and the teleological option does remain open for pursuit. These two conditions/limitations, indeed, should affect the way any and every interpretation is advanced on this terrain.[56]

For some, Habermas's argument about learning processes falls into this category of "teleological option."[57] My reading of Habermas, however, points toward a different assessment. Take for instance the following statement: "the allegedly paradoxical relation between democracy and the rule of law resolves itself in the dimension of historical time, provided one conceives the constitution as a project that makes the founding act into an ongoing process of constitution-making that continues across generations."[58] What I primarily see here is not so much a reluctant teleology as a mode of theorizing schooled in the tradition of Hegelian *contextualism*: we are always already embedded in history, and the "historical experiences of discordance in the structure of politics," as Connolly calls them, are experiences in bootstrapping.

The argument of the present chapter can be said to yield a twofold conclusion. First, without rejecting the contours of Habermas's conception of constitutional history as a bootstrapping process, I have sought to show that how the project of constitutional democracy gets off the ground should be a matter of concern for deliberative democratic theory. More specifically, vis-à-vis contemporary restatements of the paradox of democratic founding, it is not sufficient to establish the future possibility of self-correction, especially if the future is not independent of what we do here at the moment. The way the constitutional process gets off the ground would jeopardize or constrain the prospects for learning in myriad ways. I have been therefore arguing that deliberative democratic theory must address the paradox of founding on its own terms.

The second conclusion is that this is possible, and with regard to both versions of the paradox under consideration. In other words, deliberative democratic theory is able to creatively negotiate both the problem of how to engage in widespread public deliberation if the kind of democratic ethos required to sustain it cannot be taken for granted, *and* the problem of how to retain the interdependence of law and democracy in the context of constitutional foundation. This is not to say that the paradox of founding is thereby *solved* for good. The point of the matter is rather that should we approach the paradox as a heuristic problem, as I have been proposing throughout this study, we can better make sense of the idea of democratic foundation in spite of its paradoxical structure. Deliberative democratic theory offers the most developed paradigm to pursue this possibility.

Conclusion

"The Act by Which a People Is a People"

The Epigraph in Retrospect

Our inquiry opened with an epigraph from Rousseau: "it would be well to examine the act by which a people is a people."[1] Thus far, I have not commented on this phrase directly, if for no other reason than that its relevance to the present study seems only (and even pedantically) self-evident. After all, "to examine the act by which a people is a people" is precisely what I have set out to do in this book. Yet, there is a further and deeper sense in which the epigraph links up with the nerve of our inquiry. Rousseau's phrase implies that action is prior to and constitutive of peoplehood. The people is not given as a self-contained subject which precedes action, but rather we *become* (and keep becoming) who "we" are as a people in and through acting. Hence the reason why, I want to emphasize now, "it would be well to examine *the act*."

This study proceeds from a sense of dissatisfaction about the ways in which such examination is carried out—namely, the ways the problem of democratic founding is thematized and analyzed—in contemporary political theory. More specifically, the overarching argument that I tried to develop in the previous chapters takes a critical stance vis-à-vis two approaches. One of them is the *process-based* conception of constitutional democracy. On this view, what primarily matters is not so much how the project of constitutional democracy gets off the ground at a purported founding moment but rather how it moves on, that is, whether it keeps going in such a way as to progressively realize its own guiding aspirations. We came across different versions of this approach in discussing the contours of dynamic constitutionalism (Chapter 1), Kant's argument for progressive reform (Chapter 3), and Habermas's interpretation of constitutional history as a learning process (Chapter 6).

The other approach I have taken issue with is *paradox-centric*. It focuses on the inevitably circular relationship between the people and the constitution, suggesting that this circularity is symptomatic of an elementary violence, a moment of performative force, and an instance of speaking in the name of a people which does not yet exist as such. The heteronomous intervention that marks the act of foundation, so the argument goes, not only indicates a foundational deficit of legitimacy, but also impugns all subsequent democratic practice and tangles it up in irresolvable paradoxes. I presented an exposition of contemporary perspectives on the paradox of founding in Chapter 2, and critically revisited them in the rest of the study.

In a sense, the way I engage with both approaches takes its point of departure from the Rousseau epigraph, though not in the same way. In partial contrast to the process-based conception of constitutional democracy, I argue for the significance of founding *moments*. In the view pressed here, the act that marks a founding moment—"the act by which a people is a people"—is important for both the original legitimation *and* the future prospects of a new constitution. This being said, it should also be noted that my argument is not meant to challenge dynamic constitutionalism in and of itself—hence the reason why the contrast is only "partial." In other words, without rejecting the importance of learning and self-correction, bootstrapping and incremental reform, I nonetheless insist that how the project of constitutional democracy is launched matters, and it matters precisely because we cannot hope to initiate a democratic process from any starting point.

My disagreement with the paradox-centric approach cuts deeper. While taking the paradox of democratic founding seriously, I criticize its contemporary restatements for hypostatizing that paradox and hence turning a primarily political problem into a logical puzzle. In contrast to this interpretive strategy, I proposed to take the paradox of democratic founding as a heuristic problem to begin with. My guiding aspiration has been to show that even though the paradox remains logically irresolvable, it can be politically negotiated. The phrase "to examine the act by which a people is a people" acquires a further meaning here, one which has to do with navigating the gray area where the people is neither an "amorphous multitude" nor a constitutionally organized "corporate body" but a community of action in the making. Accordingly, to counter the tendencies of hypostatization, this study inquired into the formation of democratic peoplehood in and through collective action.

Taken together, then, these two strands of argument—one engaging with the underestimation of founding moments in dynamic constitutionalism, the other with the hypostatization of the paradox of founding in contemporary political theory—converge around the motif of democratic founding. By way of conclusion, I want to highlight now some key points as to why this motif is still important in the current state of democratic theory, while at the same addressing some possible criticisms and lingering questions. These concluding reflections are presented in three steps: the first has to do with "event" and "form" in democratic politics; the second turns on the issue of "original legitimation" in the context of foundation; and finally, the third reconsiders the temporal dimension of constitutional democracy, elaborating on the relationship between "moment" and "process."

"Form" and "Event" in Democratic Politics

For a wide variety of theorists working in different traditions, democracy is first and foremost a political "form," that is, one type of regime among others. It is embodied in a certain kind of constitution, which serves as an instrument or better yet a medium of self-government.[2] On this view, to recall an important distinction that we have already seen, a democratic constitution functions not only or not even primarily like "regulative rules" which govern practices that exist regardless of the rule (e.g., parking is prohibited during work hours), but like "constitutive rules" which make a certain kind of practice possible in the first place (e.g., the queen can move in all directions on the chess board).[3] The basic idea is easy to grasp: instead of simply limiting power, a democratic constitution is meant to enable the exercise of power in a certain way. It establishes the basic institutions and procedural forms in and through which citizens can get to make binding decisions and collectively govern themselves.

In contrast to this widely held view, others emphasize the importance of unruliness for a vibrant democratic politics, and turn it into *the* definitional moment of democracy.[4] To get a better grasp of this standpoint, recall the oldest charge set against democracy in the history of political thought (most notably by Plato and to a lesser degree by Aristotle): it is not only a corrupt regime but also and perhaps more important a "quasi-regime" due to its intrinsic propensity towards instability and unruliness. Some contemporary theorists of democracy pick up on this charge and make a virtue out of it. They argue that democracy is not essentially a settled form or regime, but rather an unsettling practice whose spirit becomes manifest in the "event."

In this context, the term "event" designates something that happens in such a way as to interrupt the conventional or established order. Every regime has its own presuppositions; it takes certain things for granted and defines the boundaries of political experience accordingly. These are the boundaries that determine what is sayable and doable, who is entitled to speak and when, what counts as a valid reason, and so on. We can thus make a distinction between what comes to pass within these boundaries and what interrupts them (and by extension between the two kinds of politics, say, ordinary and extraordinary, that correspond to each state). The "event" refers us to the latter.

For a certain kind of democratic theory, "event" in this specific sense is paradigmatic for both the historical beginnings and the enduring political promise of democracy. "Democracy was born in transgressive acts," Sheldon Wolin maintains, "for the *demos* could not participate in power without shattering the class, status, and value systems by which it was excluded."[5] Or as Jacques Rancière puts it, democratic politics is "an intervention in the visible and the sayable," and this is why "the people (*demos*) exists only as a rupture."[6] According to this kinetic conception, democracy does not stand for one kind of regime or political form among others. Rather, its spirit reveals itself in transgressive acts that challenge established political forms and the given boundaries of political experience. As such, its hallmark is to make visible what has been hitherto repressed, excluded, and rendered invisible.

The category of event has been an important background theme in our discussion as it helps us move beyond the rigid dichotomy between two images of the people, which structure the paradox of democratic founding: people as an "amorphous multitude" incapable of any positive action, on one hand, and as a constitutionally organized "corporate body" capable of acting only in and through the state, on the other. A different mode of peoplehood becomes manifest in the event, even if only episodically or "fugitively," when scattered experiences of injustice are fused into a popular practice of transgression and claim-making. In such episodes, the people disclose themselves as neither a multitude nor a corporate body but a community of action reclaiming the public stage, sometimes by setting up that stage in the first place.

An exclusive emphasis on the event has nonetheless its own shortcomings. Those who take it as the epicenter of democratic politics often draw a too neat distinction between form and event, and associate the act of foundation with the closure of that extraordinary moment. Consider, for example, Sheldon Wolin's rhetorical question: "When a democratic revolution leads to a constitution, does that mark the fulfillment of democracy, or the beginning of its attenuation?"[7] Wolin argues that the latter is the case, condemning the idea of constitutional founding in the name of the spirit that animates the democratic event. Thus, from the standpoint of democracy-as-event, constitutions are not the enabling medium of democratic politics. On the contrary, they lead to its pacification, absorb the *élan vital* of unruly action, and chasten the spirit of insurgency.[8] In my view, the problem with this claim is not only its reductionist approach to constitutionalism. It also impoverishes our understanding of the event itself by neglecting the ways democratic events can foster new organizational forms and new laws and institutions, or radically transform the existing ones.

In thinking through the possibility of democratic founding, this book has sought to interrupt the rigid dichotomy between form and event. Taking my cue from Hannah Arendt's insights about the "lost treasure" of modern revolutions, I view the overstatement of such a dichotomy as a "loss" for democratic theory.[9] As Patchen Markell observes, it is a dichotomy that leaves us with a torn political imagination, "caught between the ideal of popular sovereignty, in which the people jointly exercise control over their collective destiny, and the ideal of popular insurgency, in which the people spontaneously shatter the bonds of established political forms."[10] I did not seek for—nor do I claim to have found—a felicitous middle ground reconciling these two aspirations. What I tried to do instead was to relativize the terms of the dichotomy in such a way as to recover the "jurisgenerative" potential of the event.[11]

In the foregoing, I pursued this possibility along two lines. First, the episodic appearance of the-people-in-action is not only the hallmark of the democratic event, but it also paves the way for constitutional (re)founding. In Chapter 3, through a close reading of some key passages in Rousseau's work, we came to see that the emergence of a new constitutional form is not simply the work of a great lawgiver but anchored in the agency of a people insofar as their collective efforts, no matter how inchoate and episodic those efforts might be, generate the suitable conditions for legislation. On this alternative scenario, it is the people who call forth the lawgiver and not the other way around. Second, by engaging with Arendt's *On Revolution* in Chapter 5, we explored how the action-orienting principles that animate the revolutionary event can make their way into the constitutional form by means of which they are to be preserved. What is of utmost significance in this respect is the *modus operandi* of constitution-making praxis. If the gap between event and form is to be bridged, if the revolution is to culminate in the *constitutio libertatis* and to establish an organized space "housing" the public freedom of citizens along with their shared capacity to act, as we have seen with Arendt, then, the exercise of constituent power must remain faithful to the intersubjective experience of collective action which brings about such power in the first place. On the view defended here, this amounts to a deliberative praxis of constitution-making.

Deliberation, Constitutional Negotiation, and Democratic Legitimacy

The argument for deliberative constitution-making, expounded in Chapter 6, stems from *the* central thesis of this book, namely, from the claim that *how* a constitution is made is as important as *what* it prescribes. From a normative point of view, this claim hinges on a specific conception of popular sovereignty, according to which the legitimacy of a new constitution cannot be severed from what citizens themselves actually have to say in their own voices on the form and principles of their own political organization. Or to put it differently, popular sovereignty is not modelled "hypothetically" (based on arguments about what everyone *would* agree to if they were rational) but related to the actual deliberation of citizens themselves.

A claim of this sort is of course subject to some critical questions and by extension to some possible objections. For instance, a skeptical interlocutor might suggest that an exclusive focus on public deliberation is prone to highlight "legitimacy" at the expense of "justification." What exactly is the difference? To put it in terms of a distinction familiar from the liberal tradition, while legitimacy is about consent, justification is about the *reasons* for consent.[12] It is important to emphasize this difference since consent as such is subject to deep contingency and exposed to all sorts of distortions such as misinformation and manipulation, all of which compromise its credibility as a normative criterion. Insofar as actual deliberation is exposed to similar risks, our skeptical interlocutor might go on, we would be well-advised to take the idea of justification more seriously and to focus on the *content* of the constitution rather than its pedigree. What primarily matters in this view is whether the normative content of the constitution is justified to citizens on the basis of good reasons, and not necessarily whether they have participated in the process of making the constitution.

In response to such criticism, I want to stress that my argument does not intend to downplay the importance of constitutional content as such. After all, a democratic constitution must enable the practice of self-government;

and to do so, its content must cover the norms and normative institutional arrangements required to regulate such practice. What I have been arguing is rather that democratic constitution-making is not *only* about getting the content right but it is also about getting it right *in the right way*. This point brings home to us the generic difference between normative theories centered on "public reason" and those centered on "public deliberation." At its most basic, while the former is primarily concerned with the content of reasons given in a justification process, the latter is primarily concerned with the process of reason-giving itself, that is, the procedural constraints and intersubjective dynamics it involves, such as reciprocity, publicity, inclusiveness, and so on.[13] But then, of course, the real question is about why we should focus on the process of reason-giving rather than on the reasons themselves. On this register, there are at least two different types of answers: while one of them highlights the *epistemic* value of deliberation, the other one takes its point of departure from the *moral* notions of autonomy and respect.

The central claim of the epistemic account is that you need a deliberative process to achieve an outcome based on good reasons—that is, a process in which claims are made, arguments are aired and all are critically tested before the public. Here, the process of reason-giving is instrumental to the formation of public reason. Although my argument about the significance of constitutional pedigree does not rest on an epistemic account of deliberation, I do think that there is merit to a "weak" version of it. Proper public deliberation— understood as a process of assessing arguments, exercising enlarged mentality, and forming judgments about the common good—is likely to increase the intersubjective validity of the outcome (hence its epistemic value). Yet I find it difficult to think of this epistemic value in terms of approximating "truth" (and hence the reason why it is "weak"). Seyla Benhabib, it seems to me, makes a similar point when she says: "A deliberative model of democracy suggests a necessary but not sufficient condition of practical rationality, because . . . procedures can neither dictate outcomes, nor can they define the quality of the reasons advanced in argumentation."[14]

The other type of answer, which is central to my argument, is moral rather than epistemic. It proceeds from the notions of autonomy and respect. Here, the basic claim is that all interested parties must be able to participate in the deliberative process, not only because what they have to say would expand the range of reasons relevant to the debate and might eventually increase the epistemic quality of the outcome, but also because it is *intrinsically* important to allow someone to speak in her own voice. Or conversely, not to allow someone to speak in her own voice is a fundamental failure in respecting her autonomy. On this view, not to be asked is an instance of injustice in and of itself even though, had I been consulted, I would indeed agree with the content of the specific proposal and the reasons given in support of it. As such, this is not an argument from the epistemic idea of good reasons but, to put it somewhat pointedly, an argument from the "moral causality" of the will. A deliberative process structured around principles such as equality, reciprocity, and inclusiveness is worth defending even when it does not explicitly enhance the rationality of the outcome.

To be sure, these two accounts of deliberation are in no way mutually exclusive, and a good many deliberative theorists endorse some version of both. Nonetheless, when these two conceptions are brought to bear on the politics of constitution-making, they open up to us quite different problem areas along with quite different prospects. From the standpoint of an epistemic account, constitutional deliberation is primarily outcome-oriented. The ultimate question is what kind of deliberative process would help foster the force of the better argument. Yet, this is an especially difficult question to answer in the case of constitution-making because different types of deliberation have their respective merits and pitfalls.

What I have specifically in mind here is the split between "open" and "closed" deliberation. Open deliberation in public is likely to have certain salutary effects concerning the epistemic value of the outcome: it enables the circulation of different views and relevant information, increases awareness of the central issues in debate, and indirectly compels the participants to frame their arguments in terms of common good—in ways that would appeal to public rather than private reasons. This being said, widespread public deliberation has also its own drawbacks. As Jon Elster convincingly argues, publicity is prone to decrease the quality of deliberation in certain ways because when speakers discuss before the broad public, they are less likely to change their minds in response to reasoned objections. This, in turn, jeopardizes the prospect of agreement. Besides, in public deliberation, "large audiences serve as a resonance box for rhetoric."[15] In my view, the problem here is not rhetoric as such but the plebiscitary direction that it would easily take, especially when constitutional issues are at stake.

It is possible to avoid (or at least more easily manage) such risks in a closed setting. Shielded from the public eye and the pressure that comes with it, framers can engage in serious discussion, share viewpoints, revise their positions, and seek resolutions acceptable to all without worrying about how they would appear on the public stage. However, like publicity, secrecy has drawbacks as well. Apart from the obvious and serious problem of democratic deficit, closed deliberation opens the floor for partisan interests and private reasons, which are less likely to be expressed before the public. Here, the risk awaiting meaningful deliberation is that of horse trading. Elster illustrates the point by contrasting the Constitutional Convention in Philadelphia (1787) with the National Assembly in Paris (1789). In the records of the Philadelphia Convention, which was held in secrecy, "we come across some exceptionally fine instances of rational discussion" but also "some exceptionally hard bargains"—by contrast, "in the records of the French Assembly," whose deliberations were held in public, under the pressure of the hissing and applauding galleries, "we find neither."[16]

With regard to the epistemic value of deliberation, then, both publicity and secrecy have their own respective merits and pitfalls. The problem is how to achieve an optimally rational outcome under such circumstances. It may be true that there was too little publicity in the Philadelphia Convention of 1787, and too much in the National Assembly of 1789.[17] It may also be true that both types of deliberation must have their place in the constitution-making process.[18] But where does the mean lie? Or is it a matter of steering a middle ground in the first place? Perhaps a better way of framing the question is how to counterbalance the pathologies of constitutional negotiation in each setting, i.e., how to protect the deliberative process from the domination of plebiscitary rhetoric in public, and from the domination of private reasons in closed sessions.[19] These issues are not directly addressed in the foregoing chapters, but they point towards a research field into which the central thesis of this study can be expanded.

My defense of deliberative constitution-making in this book takes its cue, primarily, from the moral account of deliberation (in the sense mentioned above) rather than an epistemic one. More specifically, I have sought to answer the following question: if the classical doctrine of constituent power (and hence the counterfactual picture of "the people" as a macro-subject) is no longer tenable, then how are we supposed to understand constitutional claims of popular sovereignty? As we have already seen, one kind of answer is that such claims are inherently paradoxical. Dissatisfied with this line of argument, however, I maintain that a deliberative praxis of constitution-making would help us make sense of the original exercise of popular sovereignty. Such a praxis gives voice to the "people themselves" without stipulating "the people" in advance as a unified macro-subject.

On this view, what matters is the *process* of deliberation, and the emphasis on process has a twofold signification here. First, it suggests a critical distance towards models of popular sovereignty structured around the act of ratification, say, through a national referendum. One finds such a model in Carl Schmitt, for instance: "The people's constitution-making will always expresses itself only in a fundamental yes or no and thereby reaches the political decision that constitutes the content of the constitution."[20] By contrast, in a deliberative model, citizen consultation and participation during the drafting of the new constitution come to the foreground. As we have seen in the case of South Africa (in Chapter 6), this entails large-scale public deliberation, and the exercise of popular sovereignty is not tied to a single act such as the ratification vote, but to the deliberative process itself. This being said, I see no principled reason why ratification through referendum should not be incorporated into the deliberative model of constitution-making, provided that the burden of legitimacy is placed on the process.[21]

Second, we must also pay attention to the distinction between process and its outcome. No matter how the process unfolds, the constitution as outcome would hardly reflect a full and actual agreement among all citizens under contemporary conditions of diversity and plurality. The outcome cannot stand for "the people" as an object of all-embracing consensus. Nonetheless, it may convincingly lay claim to popular sovereignty depending on how the process of constitution-making is *experienced* by citizens themselves. The constitutional process would make room for civic agency in ways much richer than an episodic referendum. Citizens can relate to it in their own voices, get on and off along the way so to speak, and eventually develop a sense of joint ownership in the constitution, despite their ongoing disagreements. As such, the deliberative process of constitution-making offers a model of exercising popular sovereignty without stipulating in advance an already unified "we the people" or claiming to achieve universal consensus. On this model, citizens can exercise popular sovereignty by taking part in the process, which in turn allows them to consider themselves (and one another) as participants in the collective enterprise of shaping their destiny.

Constitutional Democracy in Time: Founding Moments and Learning Processes

Throughout this study, I have insisted on the importance of founding moments not only for normative reasons related to popular sovereignty and the original legitimation of a new constitution, but also for reasons regarding the future prospects of the political community. Along this line, the key idea is that how we begin makes a difference in our future prospects, in the paths of constitutional development, in the patterns of political culture and socialization, and eventually in the kind of "we" that we want to be. Or to put it differently, the effects of founding as a crucial historical experience are woven—for better and for worse—into the very fabric of the political community, lingering in its institutions, practices, and identity.

In one sense, of course, this is a descriptive claim, and the extent to which it can be verified in any specific way depends on empirical evidence. Admittedly, in the foregoing chapters, I did not seek to provide "hard evidence" through comparative case studies, but confined myself to the more general task of establishing the intuitive plausibility of the main idea. Several suggestions were made to this effect, exploring the politics of founding in view of its relation to the transformations of political culture (Chapter 3), to the formation of collective identity (Chapter 4) and to the experiential sources of democratic peoplehood (Chapters 5 and 6). To conclude this line of inquiry now, I want to elaborate on how it relates to the conception of constitutional democracy as an open-ended learning process.

Habermas offers a vivid statement of such conception. We have already seen its outline in Chapter 6. But to recall the main idea, it would be helpful to consider the following passage from his seminal essay, "Constitutional Democracy":

> in my view, a constitution that is democratic—not just in its content but also according to its source of legitimation—is a tradition-building project with a clearly marked beginning in time. All the later generations have the task of actualizing the still-untapped normative substance of the system of rights laid down in the original document of the constitution. According to this dynamic understanding of the constitution, ongoing legislation carries on the system of rights by interpreting and adapting rights for current

circumstances.... To be sure, this fallible continuation of the founding event can break out of the circle of a polity's groundless discursive self-constitution only if this process—which is not immune to contingent interruptions and historical regressions—can be understood in the long run as a self-correcting learning process.[22]

On the one hand, I don't see any outright tension between my argument for the importance of founding moments and the sort of dynamic constitutionalism outlined here. Quite to the contrary, one would easily argue that how constitutional democracy begins should be a matter of concern precisely because under consideration is a tradition-building project.

On the other hand, however, there is something in the idea of constitutional history as a "learning process" that seems to urge us not to overestimate the importance of "founding moments." Without denying that how we begin must be a matter of some concern, one would suggest that it is not "that important" after all because we can also fix things as we go on. In fact, one would further insist, we must already keep rebuilding the ship at sea anyway since constitutional democracy is an open-ended project. The point is clear enough: how we begin may not be irrelevant or inconsequential, but insofar as every act of foundation with a democratic intent is by definition future-oriented (and hence should be accompanied by learning, openness to change, and self-correction), what eventually matters is how we keep moving on.

This is an important point, and it has an intuitive appeal. In the end, nothing is carved in stone. Just as a good beginning is not and cannot be a guarantee for the future, a bad one is not necessarily a recipe for disaster. Nonetheless, I doubt whether we can theoretically sort out the respective significance of "founding" and "bootstrapping," "moment" and "process," at a fundamental conceptual level, and hence conclusively show that one is "more important" than the other.

Take for example two quite different cases that we previously mentioned: the Canadian Constitution Act of 1982 and the Egyptian Revolution of 2011. In the former case, the patriation of the constitution despite Québec's disagreement had a largely negative impact on Canadian politics in the years that followed. Two serious attempts were made to "fix" the problem and to bring Québec back into the reach of constitutional agreement: the Meech Lake process in 1987 and the Charlottetown Accord in 1992.[23] Both of them officially failed, and their failure exacerbated the situation in the short run. Nonetheless, after three decades, it seems less of a wound today. Why? Not because it is water under the bridge but because Québec's concerns were explicitly discussed, negotiated, and made their way into the ongoing constitutional conversation. The process had begun in a wrong way, but Canadians managed to keep the dialogue open. Observing such a case, thus, one would conclude that the "heart of constitutional politics does not reside in a privileged contractual or founding moment but in sustaining a conversation over time."[24]

What has recently happened in Egypt, however, might suggest a quite different lesson. Although the 2011 revolution was a promising "event," things went wrong in the process of constitution-making, and partisan imposition prevailed over collective deliberation.[25] The result was a military coup, and a politics of restoration has been under way now. Things could have been drastically different if the constitution-making process unfolded in the right way. But it did not, and Egypt had a very bad start (compared to Tunisia, for instance, where the constitutional negotiation did not break down). Does this mean that the prospect of democratization is now over for Egypt? Perhaps not permanently—but how long? No one quite knows what it will take to set the country back on the track of democratization. For the moment, a historical opportunity appears to have been missed, and it has been missed badly. Now what is the lesson to be drawn from such a case? My short answer would be that we cannot hope to initiate a "tradition-building project" or a "self-correcting learning process" from any starting point whatsoever. From the perspective of the present study, this is one crucial reason why founding moments matter.

To be sure, a skeptical interlocutor would point out that the Egyptian case is too recent or too fresh to serve as a counter example vis-à-vis the Canadian case. Egypt might have had a bad start but democratization takes time anyway. It involves endless and sometimes very incremental bootstrapping. And therefore, our interlocutor might go on, we should think of the significance of founding moments in reverse relation to time passing. Indeed, it sounds plausible that the more a political community accumulates democratic experience over time (which would of course include failures, dead ends, and so on as well as learning and improvement), the less decisive becomes the impact of founding moments. The "tainted origins" or the birth defects of the polity, in other words, would turn out to be less of an issue in the long run, provided that the polity keeps striving to realize the normative substance of constitutional democracy.[26]

My ultimate answer would be a cautious one: it depends. Tocqueville once commented that it is a privilege "to have the chance to make mistakes that can be retrieved."[27] While some mistakes are repairable, others are less so. What makes the difference? When does a mistake turn out to be harder or perhaps impossible to correct? Sometimes, it has to do with the nature of the mistake. What is done is done, and we cannot undo it. But sometimes, it is *our relation* to the mistake that makes it harder to recover. For instance, a mistake which cuts deep into our way of doing things is likely to have a strong tendency to reproduce itself over time; or one which cuts deep into our self-understanding would not appear to us as a "mistake" in the first place. In such cases, self-correction is considerably more difficult.

The idea of "path dependency" offers one way to bring this insight to bear on constitutional politics. In a path-dependent process, generally speaking, the sequence of events is of crucial importance since what happens at an earlier stage is able to shape the conditions of possibility for later ones, making certain things more likely and others less likely to occur in the future. As Paul Pierson puts it aptly, the key mechanism at work is self-reinforcement: "Initial steps in a particular direction may encourage further movement along the same path. Over time, 'roads not chosen' may become increasingly distant, increasingly unreachable alternatives. Relatively modest perturbations at early stages may have a large influence on these processes. In many cases, the significance of early events or processes in the sequence may be amplified, while that of later events or processes is dampened. Thus, *when* a particular event or process occurs in a sequence will make a big difference."[28]

Constitutional development is an especially suitable candidate to be analyzed through the lens of path dependency because, as Kevin Olson rightly observes, constitutions are by definition meant to "establish political ground rules, institutional mechanisms, and terms of discourse for what comes after, increasing the likelihood of some later events and decreasing the likelihood of others."[29] Viewed in this light, interestingly enough, the impact of founding (both for better and for worse) does not seem to stand in reverse relation to time passing, but rather the other way around. Some of the choices and decisions made at the beginning may tend to grow more and more influential— may tend to cut deeper and deeper both into our way of doing things and our self-understanding as a political community—as we move along a certain path. Or, in Tocqueville's words, some "mistakes" would become increasingly harder to "retrieve" as time goes by.[30]

Let me emphasize that these remarks are not intended to undermine the conception of constitutional history as a learning process. I find it absolutely important that such a conception highlights the fallibilistic and always provisional nature of constitutional settlement in a democratic polity, keeps us alert about the dangers of closure, and accommodates the possibility of learning, self-correction, and innovation without which the project of collective self-determination cannot reproduce itself on an ongoing basis. At the same time, however, I have been also arguing that, in any specific context, the relationship between founding and bootstrapping, moment and process, is more complicated than it might seem at first sight. The learning processes, which are supposed to redeem the normative promise of the constitution, take place against the background and within the context of social meanings and institutional arrangements which are generated, at least in part, by acts of foundation in the first place. What this means is that the founding of the polity does not reveal itself to later generations merely as a *generic* constitutional beginning with a universal normative content, but it is always also a *specific* event which makes a particular claim on us, and in a sense which claims to have made *us*. In various ways, it shapes the very people who are supposed to do the learning and tapping, fixing and correcting. In the view defended here, therefore, this is one of the main reasons as to why founding moments matter—and to return to our epigraph, as to why "it would be well to examine the act by which a people is a people."

Notes

INTRODUCTION

Epigraph: Jean-Jacques Rousseau, *The Social Contract*, in *The Social Contract and Other Later Political Writings*, ed. and trans. Victor Gourevitch (Cambridge: Cambridge University Press, 1997), 49.

1. Hannah Arendt, *On Revolution*, rev. ed. (New York: Viking, 1965), 141.
2. It is needless to say that such a thesis, at this level of abstraction, is by no means original. Especially after the revolutions of 1989, many find it less and less plausible for a democratic constitution to be justified exclusively in terms of its substantive content. Also important, we are told, is the pedigree of the constitution, that is, the way it is drafted and enacted. Accordingly, citizen consultation and participation in the process of constitution-making (of which making the post-apartheid constitution in South Africa is still exemplary) have become crucial markers of democratic legitimacy in the contemporary world. For similar statements that inspired my project in the first place, see Andrew Arato, "Forms of Constitution Making and Theories of Democracy," *Cardozo Law Review* 17 (1995): 191–231; Simone Chambers, "Democracy, Popular Sovereignty, and Constitutional Legitimacy," *Constellations* 11, 2 (2004): 153–73.
3. See, for example, Iris M. Young, *Justice and the Politics of Difference* (Princeton, N.J.: Princeton University Press, 1990); James Tully, *Strange Multiplicity: Constitutionalism in an Age of Diversity* (Cambridge: Cambridge University Press, 1995); William Connolly, *The Ethos of Pluralization* (Minneapolis: University of Minnesota Press, 1995).
4. The claim that the "how" of constitution-making is as important as the "what" of the constitution is subject to an important objection inspired by the case of more or less successful constitutional democracies, such as Germany and Japan, which clearly have undemocratic origins. I address this objection in Chapter 1 below.
5. The literature on deliberative democracy is vast. For some representative statements of the basic tenets of deliberative democratic theory, see Joshua Cohen, "Deliberation and Democratic Legitimacy," in *The Good Polity*, ed. Alan P. Hamlin and Philip Pettit (Oxford: Blackwell, 1989), 17–34; Seyla Benhabib, "Deliberative Rationality and Models of

Democratic Legitimacy," *Constellations* 1, 1 (1994): 26–52; Jürgen Habermas, "Three Normative Models of Democracy," in *The Inclusion of the Other*, ed. Ciaran Cronin and Pablo De Greiff (Cambridge, Mass.: MIT Press, 1998), 239–52. On the relevance of deliberative democracy to the politics of constitution-making, see Jon Elster, "Deliberation and Constitution Making," in *Deliberative Democracy*, ed. Jon Elster (Cambridge: Cambridge University Press, 1998), 97–122; Jürgen Habermas, "Constitutional Democracy: A Paradoxical Union of Contradictory Principles?" *Political Theory* 29, 6 (2001): 766–81; Simone Chambers, "Open Versus Closed Constitutional Negotiation," in *Deliberative Democracy in Practice*, ed. David Kahane et al. (Vancouver: UBC Press, 2010), 77–91.

6. Jürgen Habermas, *Between Facts and Norms*, trans. William Rehg (Cambridge, Mass.: MIT Press, 1996), 301; also see "Popular Sovereignty as Procedure," Appendix I to *Between Facts and Norms*, 463–90. As I try to show in Chapter 6, however, Habermas's political theory, especially when it is read in relation to his contributions to the German unification debate, would make room for a deliberative politics of constitution-making more friendly to concrete forms of agency.

7. While its role in political discourse can hardly be denied and its significance for democratic theory can hardly be overestimated, the notion of "the people" is to a large extent vague, ambiguous, and controversial. The vast and sophisticated literature in democratic theory has often taken "the people" for granted rather than approaching it as a proper object of theoretical inquiry, at least until quite recently. For a good starting point, see Margaret Canovan, *The People* (Cambridge: Polity, 2005); and its synopsis "The People," in *The Oxford Handbook of Political Theory*, ed. John Dryzek, Bonnie Honig, and Anne Phillips (Oxford: Oxford University Press, 2006), 349–62. Some of the other important contributions to the analysis of "the people" in contemporary democratic theory are cited below.

8. Robert A. Dahl, *Democracy and Its Critics* (New Haven, Conn.: Yale University Press, 1989), 193. This problem has been noted under different names such as the "boundary problem," the "unit problem," or the "domain problem," though terminology is of little importance here. See Frederick Whelan, "Democratic Theory and the Boundary Problem," *Nomos* 25 (1983): 13–47; Sofia Näsström, "The Legitimacy of the People," *Political Theory* 35, 5 (2007): 624–58; David Miller, "Democracy's Domain Problem," *Philosophy and Public Affairs* 37, 3 (2009): 201–28; Paulina Ochoa Espejo, "People, Territory, and Legitimacy in Democratic States," *American Journal of Political Science* 58, 2 (2014): 466–78.

9. Bernard Yack, "Popular Sovereignty and Nationalism," *Political Theory* 29, 4 (2001): 529.

10. On this point, especially see Habermas, *The Inclusion of the Other*, 114–17, 140–42.

11. This issue has far-reaching implications in contemporary political theory, particularly with regard to the debates on immigration and citizenship. See Michael Walzer, *Spheres of Justice* (New York: Basic Books, 1983), 31–63; Joseph Carens, "Aliens and Citizens: The Case for Open Borders," *Review of Politics* 49, 2 (1987): 251–73; Seyla Benhabib, *The Rights of Others* (Cambridge: Cambridge University Press, 2004); Arash Abizadeh, "Democratic Theory and Border Coercion," *Political Theory* 36, 1 (2008): 37–65.

12. G. W. F. Hegel, *Elements of the Philosophy of Right*, ed. Allen Wood, trans. H. B. Nisbet (Cambridge: Cambridge University Press, 1991), §279.

13. Canovan, *The People*, 6.

14. Bruce Ackerman, *We the People: Transformations* (Cambridge, Mass.: Harvard University Press, 1998), 187. For the essentials of Ackerman's account of how the interaction between political elites and ordinary citizens comes to acquire the voice of "the people" at certain historical junctures, see *We the People: Foundations* (Cambridge, Mass.: Harvard University Press, 1991).

15. Jason Frank, *Constituent Moments: Enacting the People in Postrevolutionary America* (Durham, N.C.: Duke University Press, 2010), 3.

16. Paulina Ochoa Espejo, *The Time of Popular Sovereignty: Process and the Democratic State* (University Park: Pennsylvania State University Press, 2011), 6, 13.

17. In *Sharing Democracy* (Oxford: Oxford University Press, 2012), Michaele L. Ferguson holds a similar view, while at the same time distinguishing between the monological model of "sovereign agency" and the dialogical model of what she calls "democratic interagency." The former is typically located in state institutions and takes the people as a single macro-subject whereas the latter emerges between a plurality of acting and speaking persons who engage in the experience of collectively shaping their shared world. To a certain extent, my own argument about the dynamics of peoplehood converges with Ferguson's "democratic interagency" and its Arendtian background. Unlike Ferguson's project, however, this book is ultimately about the politics of democratic constitution-making.

18. For an extensive discussion on the category of "extraordinary" as it applies to founding moments, see Andreas Kalyvas, *Democracy and the Politics of the Extraordinary* (Cambridge: Cambridge University Press, 2008).

19. Claude Lefort's much celebrated thesis, stated in *Democracy and Political Theory*, trans. David Macey (Cambridge: Polity, 1988), 39, is relevant here: the site of "the people" is an "empty space," Lefort argues, and *must* remain empty for the sake of democratic openness because democracy is a "regime founded upon the legitimacy of a debate as to what is legitimate and what is illegitimate—a debate which is necessarily without any guarantor and without any end."

20. See Rogers M. Smith, *Stories of Peoplehood: The Politics and Morals of Political Membership* (Cambridge: Cambridge University Press, 2003).

21. Margaret Kohn and Keally McBride, *Political Theories of Decolonization: Postcolonialism and the Problem of Foundations* (Oxford: Oxford University Press, 2011), 153.

22. Plato, *Republic*, trans. G. M. A. Grube (Indianapolis: Hackett, 1992), 414b–15d. For a detailed analysis, see Malcolm Schofield, *Plato* (Oxford: Oxford University Press, 2006), 284–309.

23. Rousseau, *The Social Contract*, 71.

24. In Chapter 6, I will revisit the case of South Africa in order to analyze how the constitutional framers (in my view successfully) coped with Rousseau's paradox of founding.

25. For some representative statements, see Jacques Derrida, "Declarations of

Independence," *New Political Science* 15 (1986): 7–15; William Connolly, *The Ethos of Pluralization* (Minneapolis: University of Minnesota Press, 1995), 135–61; Frank I. Michelman, "Constitutional Authorship," in *Constitutionalism: Philosophical Foundations*, ed. Larry Alexander (Cambridge: Cambridge University Press, 1998), 64–98; Bonnie Honig, "Between Decision and Deliberation: Political Paradox in Democratic Theory," *American Political Science Review* 101, 1 (2007): 1–17.

26. There is a sense in which this interpretive strategy implicitly builds on Machiavelli's well-known account of the violent origins of the political community. Especially see Niccolò Machiavelli, *The Prince*, ed. Quentin Skinner and Russell Price (Cambridge: Cambridge University Press, 1988), ch. 6; *Discourses on Livy*, trans. Julia C. Bondanella and Peter Bondanella (Oxford: Oxford University Press, 1997), Book I, ch. 9. Machiavelli's relevance to contemporary restatements of the paradox of founding is well captured in Paul Ricoeur, "The Political Paradox," in *History and Truth*, trans. Charles A. Kelbley (Evanston, Ill.: Northwestern University Press, 1965), 258.

27. Edmund Burke, "Speech on Opening of Impeachment," in *Empire and Community: Edmund Burke's Writings and Speeches on International Relations*, ed. David P. Fidler and Jennifer M. Welsh (Boulder, Colo.: Westview, 1999), 217.

28. To be sure, the criticism posed here is not meant to apply to all agonistic interpretations of the paradox of founding as such. Remaining committed to such an interpretation, Jason Frank's *Constituent Moments*, for example, deliberately avoids the trap of hypostatization: "the affirmation of political paradox that characterizes so much contemporary democratic theory, especially in its radically democratic guise, is at once historically insightful, and yet perhaps also too formal in its central preoccupations" (33).

29. Of course, there are different strategies of navigation as well. According to Bonnie Honig, for instance, the primary value of navigating this gray area has to do with "the fecundity of undecidability, a trait that suggests that our cherished ideals—law, the people, general will, deliberation—are implicated in that to which deliberative democratic theory opposes them: violence, multitude, the will of all, decision" ("Between Decision and Deliberation," 8). In this book, I argue for a different strategy of navigation, one that is attentive to the practices of democratic bootstrapping that politically respond to such "undecidability."

CHAPTER 1. ORIGINS AND FOUNDATIONS: TWO FEATURES OF
THE MODERN CONSTITUTION

1. The phrase "reflection and choice" refers, of course, to Alexander Hamilton's opening statement in the first issue of *The Federalist*, ed. J. R. Pole (Indianapolis: Hackett, 2005).

2. See Charles H. McIlwain's classic discussion in *Constitutionalism: Ancient and Modern* (Ithaca, N.Y.: Cornell University Press, 1947), 1–23.

3. As a number of theorists rightly emphasize, constitutions are always enacted within

some pre-constituted context, drawing on existing laws, institutions, and practices in myriad ways. See, for example, Alessandro Ferrara, *Justice and Judgment* (London: Sage, 1999), 133–49; Andrew Arato, *Civil Society, Constitution, and Legitimacy* (Lanham, Md.: Rowman and Littlefield, 2000), 167–97; Jacob Levy, "Not So *Novus* an *Ordo*: Constitutions Without Social Contracts," *Political Theory* 37, 2 (2009): 191–217. In full agreement, I hold that a theory of democratic founding should reject the myth of ex nihilo creation or the model of an absolute new beginning, especially as it has been stated in the classical doctrine of "constituent power." The reader will find a more extensive discussion on this issue in Chapter 5.

4. János Kis, *Constitutional Democracy*, trans. Zoltán Miklósi (Budapest: Central European University Press, 2003), 140.

5. Robert Filmer, "Observations upon Aristotles Politiques," in *The Patriarcha and Other Writings*, ed. J. P. Sommerville (Cambridge: Cambridge University Press, 1991), 277.

6. For the details of this argumentative battle, see Edmund S. Morgan, *Inventing the People* (New York: Norton, 1988), 17–93.

7. Filmer, "Observations upon Aristotles Politiques," 277.

8. Filmer, "Observations upon Aristotles Politiques," 277.

9. For some commentators, it is precisely the abstract character of "the people" that distinguishes the modern doctrine of popular sovereignty from the traditional accounts of democratic rule. See, for example, Istvan Hont, "The Permanent Crisis of a Divided Mankind: 'Contemporary Crisis of the Nation State' in Historical Perspective," *Political Studies* 42 (1994): 166–231; Bernard Yack, "Popular Sovereignty and Nationalism," *Political Theory* 29, 4 (2001): 517–36.

10. David Hume, "Of the Original Contract," in *Political Essays*, ed. Knud Haakonssen (Cambridge: Cambridge University Press, 1994), 192.

11. Hume, "Of the Original Contract," 189–90.

12. Hume, "Of the Original Contract," 192.

13. David Hume, *A Treatise of Human Nature*, ed. David F. Norton and Mary J. Norton (Oxford: Oxford University Press, 2000), 362.

14. Hume, *A Treatise of Human Nature*, 362.

15. Jacques Derrida, "Force of Law: 'The Mystical Foundation of Authority,'" in *Deconstruction and the Possibility of Justice*, ed. Drucilla Cornell, Michel Rosenfeld, and David Gray (New York: Routledge, 1992), 35.

16. In "Democracy, Popular Sovereignty, and Constitutional Legitimacy," *Constellations* 11, 2 (2004): 155, Simone Chambers labels this kind of argument "hypothetical popular sovereignty" insofar as "it does not directly call on real people but rather deduces from general principles what the 'people' would want and by extension would agree to." In what follows, I basically draw on this definition in speaking of hypothetical conceptions of popular sovereignty.

17. Immanuel Kant, "Theory and Practice," in *Practical Philosophy*, ed. and trans. M. J. Gregor (Cambridge: Cambridge University Press, 1996), 296.

18. Immanuel Kant, *The Metaphysics of Morals*, in *Practical Philosophy*, ed. and trans. M. J. Gregor (Cambridge: Cambridge University Press, 1996), 459.

19. Kant, "Theory and Practice," 296–97.

20. Thomas Hobbes, *Leviathan*, ed. Edwin Curley (Indianapolis: Hackett, 1994), 492, 127.

21. Hobbes, *Leviathan*, 128.

22. Kant, *The Metaphysics of Morals*, 462.

23. Hobbes, *Leviathan*, 106.

24. For a detailed and careful exposition, see Arthur Ripstein, *Force and Freedom: Kant's Legal and Political Philosophy* (Cambridge, Mass.: Harvard University Press, 2009), 182–231.

25. See Patrick Riley, *Will and Political Legitimacy* (Cambridge, Mass.: Harvard University Press, 1982), 125–27.

26. Immanuel Kant, "The Contest of Faculties," in *Political Writings*, ed. H. S. Reiss, trans. H. B. Nisbet (Cambridge: Cambridge University Press, 1991), 187.

27. Kant, "Theory and Practice," 297.

28. John Rawls, *Political Liberalism* (New York: Columbia University Press, 1993), 304–10. Of course, the "original position" is not meant to make an argument about popular sovereignty in the narrow sense. It is nonetheless pertinent to our discussion as it involves an influential model of hypothetical agreement.

29. Jürgen Habermas, "Reconciliation Through the Public Use of Reason," in *The Inclusion of the Other*, ed. Ciaran Cronin and Pablo De Greiff (Cambridge, Mass.: MIT Press, 1998), 69–70.

30. Habermas, "Reconciliation Through the Public Use of Reason," 71.

31. Habermas, "Reconciliation Through the Public Use of Reason," 69.

32. Chambers, "Democracy, Popular Sovereignty, and Constitutional Legitimacy," 156.

33. As Frank Michelman notes in "Constitutional Authorship," in *Constitutionalism: Philosophical Foundations*, ed. Larry Alexander (Cambridge: Cambridge University Press, 1998), 67: "The connection we draw between normative authority and perceived historical facts of authorship ('we ought to because they said so') . . . is a sitting duck for critique." This is true as long as the problem is stated from the retrospective standpoint of later generations. Unlike Michelman, however, I argue that such connection between authority and authorship is essential to the democratic legitimacy of a *new* constitution. Here the exemplary statement is not "we ought to because *they said* so" but rather "we ought to because *we say* so."

34. In a sense, this is the crux of Paulina Ochoa Espejo's recent *The Time of Popular Sovereignty: Process and the Democratic State* (University Park: Pennsylvania State University Press, 2011). Taking her point of departure from an observation quite similar to Filmer's ("they which are the people this minute, are not the people the next minute"), Espejo argues that we need to think of the people as a "process" instead of seeking to locate popular sovereignty at some privileged "moment." While there is much I agree with in Espejo's book, I think that the fundamental problem with traditional notions of popular sovereignty (the problem that she calls "the indeterminacy of popular unification") has to do

with the requisite of substantive agreement rather than the positioning of such agreement at a single point in time. Once that requisite is abandoned, it becomes possible to emphasize the importance of founding moments as experiments in democratic peoplehood, while at the same time endorsing a dynamic, open-ended and processual conception of constitutional democracy.

35. Christopher F. Zurn, "The Logic of Legitimacy: Bootstrapping Paradoxes of Constitutional Democracy," *Legal Theory* 16 (2010): 216.

36. Zurn, "The Logic of Legitimacy," 225.

37. Zurn, "The Logic of Legitimacy," 225.

38. Zurn, "The Logic of Legitimacy," 226.

39. Zurn, "The Logic of Legitimacy," 197.

40. Donald P. Kommers, *The Constitutional Jurisprudence of the Federal Republic of Germany*, 2nd ed. (Durham, N.C.: Duke University Press, 1997), 30.

41. Chambers, "Democracy, Popular Sovereignty, and Constitutional Legitimacy," 165.

42. Kommers, *The Constitutional Jurisprudence of the Federal Republic of Germany*, 30.

43. To be sure, a heated debate took place about whether a unified Germany would have to adopt a new constitution, one which was to be based on a "free decision by the German people," as Article 146 clearly asked for. For some, the existing Basic Law had already proven itself over four decades. Accordingly, so the argument goes, to open the floor for a full-scale constitutional debate would only lead to destabilization. For others, however, even if the content of the Basic Law did not require major re-engineering, the unification of Germany would have to be crowned by a democratic act of constitution-making. This was required, they argued (in my view rightly), not only in order to address the deficit of democratic legitimacy left over from 1949, but also (and more important) in order to facilitate the integration of Western and Eastern Germans into a shared understanding of democratic peoplehood. For an excellent defense of this view, see Ulrich Preuss, "Political Institutions and German Unfication," in *German Unification: Expectations and Outcomes*, ed. Peter C. Caldwell and Robert L. Shandley (New York: Palgrave Macmillan, 2011), 137–51. We will revisit the German unification debate in more detail in Chapter 6.

44. For an overview of the major changes, see Peter H. Russell, *Constitutional Odyssey*, 3rd ed. (Toronto: University of Toronto Press, 2004), 124–25.

45. James Tully, *Strange Multiplicity: Constitutionalism in an Age of Diversity* (Cambridge: Cambridge University Press, 1995), 11–12.

46. For the major points of disagreement, see Charles Taylor, "Shared and Divergent Values," in *Reconciling the Solitudes* (Montreal: McGill-Queen's University Press, 1993), 155–86.

47. Simone Chambers, "Contract or Conversation? Theoretical Lessons from the Canadian Constitutional Crisis," *Politics and Society* 26, 1 (1998): 147–48.

CHAPTER 2. THE PARADOX OF DEMOCRATIC FOUNDING:
CANONICAL STATEMENTS AND CONTEMPORARY PERSPECTIVES

1. Jean-Jacques Rousseau, *The Social Contract*, in *The Social Contract and Other Later Political Writings*, ed. and trans. Victor Gourevitch (Cambridge: Cambridge University Press, 1997), 71 (emphasis mine).

2. Rousseau, *The Social Contract*, 68.

3. The most systematic discussion of the lawgiver is still to be found in Roger D. Masters, *The Political Philosophy of Rousseau* (Princeton, N.J.: Princeton University Press, 1968), 354–417. For an extensive bibliography on the lawgiver, see note 2 in Chapter 3.

4. Sheldon Wolin, "Transgression, Equality, and Voice," in *Dēmokratia: A Conversation on Democracies, Ancient and Modern*, ed. Josiah Ober and Charles W. Hedrick (Princeton, N.J.: Princeton University Press, 1996), 73. See also Arthur Melzer, *The Natural Goodness of Man* (Chicago: University of Chicago Press, 1990), 233–36; Seyla Benhabib, "Deliberative Rationality and Models of Democratic Legitimacy," *Constellations* 1, 1 (1994): 28–30.

5. See, for instance, William Connolly, *The Ethos of Pluralization* (Minneapolis: University of Minnesota Press, 1995), 135–61; Steven Johnston, *Encountering Tragedy: Rousseau and the Project of Democratic Order* (Ithaca, N.Y.: Cornell University Press, 1999), 45–74; Alan Keenan, *Democracy in Question* (Stanford, Calif.: Stanford University Press, 2003), 41–53; Bonnie Honig, "Between Decision and Deliberation: Political Paradox in Democratic Theory," *American Political Science Review* 101, 1 (2007): 1–17.

6. Emmanuel Joseph Sieyès, "What Is the Third Estate?" in *Political Writings*, ed. and trans. Michael Sonenscher (Indianapolis: Hackett, 2003), 135.

7. Sieyès, "What Is the Third Estate?" 135.

8. John Searle, *Speech Acts* (Cambridge: Cambridge University Press, 1969), 33. In fact, Sieyès himself seems to point toward a similar distinction when he argues that the constitution must "subject a government to fixed forms, both internal and external" ("What Is the Third Estate?" 136).

9. I take it for granted that in the context of Sieyès's writings the term "nation" is interchangeable with that of the "people," and does not bear the connotations of "nationalism" as it applies to considerations of identity, ethnicity, and culture.

10. Sieyès, "What Is the Third Estate?" 136.

11. Sieyès, "What Is the Third Estate?" 136.

12. Sieyès, "What Is the Third Estate?" 138.

13. Sieyès, "What Is the Third Estate?" 139.

14. For a detailed discussion of how this problem unfolded in historical context, see Keith Michael Baker, *Inventing the French Revolution* (Cambridge: Cambridge University Press, 1990), 224–51.

15. Alexander Hamilton, James Madison, and John Jay, *The Federalist*, ed. J. R. Pole (Indianapolis: Hackett, 2005), No. 40.

16. For an insightful discussion on how Rousseau and Madison try to navigate the

paradox of founding by tapping into informal registers of normativity, see Jason Frank, "'Unauthorized Propositions': *The Federalist Papers* and Constituent Power," *Diacritics* 37, 2–3 (2007): 103–20.

17. G. W. F. Hegel, *Elements of the Philosophy of Right*, ed. Allen W. Wood, trans. H. B. Nisbet (Cambridge: Cambridge University Press, 1991), §279.

18. Recall, for instance, Tocqueville's conviction (expressed in less than a decade following Hegel's death) that "the democratic revolution occurring before our eyes is an irresistible fact." Alexis de Tocqueville, *Democracy in America*, trans. George Lawrence (New York: Anchor, 1969), 417–18.

19. See Shlomo Avineri, *Hegel's Theory of the Modern State* (Cambridge: Cambridge University Press, 1972), 176–93; Paul Franco, *Hegel's Philosophy of Freedom* (New Haven, Conn.: Yale University Press, 1999), 154–87, 306–30.

20. According to Hegel, there is no action without determination; to act means to be determined. In this respect, the abstract notion of "the people" is not only "garbled" but also extremely precarious for him. Abstracted from the institutional edifice of the state and its system of determinations, "the people" can reveal itself in the realm of action only in a destructive way. This issue looms large in Hegel's analysis of the French Revolution in general and his well-known critique of the Terror in particular. See G. W. F. Hegel, *Phenomenology of Spirit*, trans. A. V. Miller (Oxford: Oxford University Press, 1977), §§582–95; *Philosophy of Right*, §258.

21. János Kis, *Constitutional Democracy*, trans. Zoltán Miklósi (Budapest: Central European University Press, 2003), 140.

22. Stephen Holmes, "Precommitment and the Paradox of Democracy," in *Constitutionalism and Democracy*, ed. Jon Elster and Rune Slagstad (Cambridge: Cambridge University Press, 1988), 230.

23. Ulrich K. Preuss, *Constitutional Revolution: The Link Between Constitutionalism and Progress*, trans. D. L. Schneider (Atlantic Highlands, N.J.: Humanities Press, 1995), 18–19. Also see Ulrich Preuss, "Constitutional Powermaking for the New Polity: Some Deliberations on the Relations Between Constituent Power and the Constitution," *Cardozo Law Review* 14 (1992): 639–60. For an earlier statement of this view from within the paradigm of legal positivism, see Hans Kelsen, *General Theory of State and Law*, trans. A. Wedberg (Cambridge, Mass.: Harvard University Press, 1949), 261: "the people—from whom the constitution claims its origin—comes to legal existence first through the constitution."

24. Hegel, *Philosophy of Right*, §273.

25. Nevertheless, it is possible to read certain sections of the *Phenomenology of Spirit* as a rich reflection on "founding moments" in the sense that what comes to pass in those moments destroys an existing form of life, while at the same time initiating a new one and paving the way for the recognition of new values. For an excellent discussion of Hegel's interpretation of *Antigone* (in *Phenomenology*, §§446–76) along these lines, see Ido Geiger, *The Founding Act of Modern Ethical Life* (Stanford, Calif.: Stanford University Press, 2007), 50–70.

26. J. L. Austin, *How to Do Things with Words* (Oxford: Oxford University Press, 1962), 1–11.

27. Jacques Derrida, "Declarations of Independence," *New Political Science* 15 (1986): 9.

28. Derrida, "Declarations of Independence," 10.

29. For a criticism to this effect, see Seyla Benhabib, "Democracy and Difference: Reflections on the Metapolitics of Lyotard and Derrida," *Journal of Political Philosophy* 2, 1 (1994): 15.

30. Austin, *How to Do Things with Words*, 14.

31. Jacques Derrida, "Living On," in Jacques Derrida et al., *Deconstruction and Criticism* (London: Continuum, 1979), 81. For the full exposition of Derrida's critique of Austin, see "Signature Event Context," in *Margins of Philosophy*, trans. Alan Bass (Chicago: University of Chicago Press, 1982), 307–30. For insightful commentaries, see Jonathan Culler, *On Deconstruction* (Ithaca, N.Y.: Cornell University Press, 1982), 110–25; Ian Maclean, "Un dialogue de sourds? Some Implications of the Austin-Searle-Derrida Debate," *Paragraph* 5 (1985): 1–26; Stanley Fish, "With the Compliments of the Author: Reflections on Austin and Derrida," in *Doing What Comes Naturally* (Durham, N.C.: Duke University Press, 1989), 37–67; Sandy Petrey, *Speech Acts and Literary Theory* (New York: Routledge, 1990), 3–21; Stanley Cavell, "What Did Derrida Want of Austin?" in *Philosophical Passages: Wittgenstein, Emerson, Austin, Derrida* (Cambridge, Mass.: Blackwell, 1995), 42–65.

32. Austin, *How to Do Things with Words*, 118.

33. For a brilliant analysis exploring this reversal in the context of revolutionary France, see Sandy Petrey, *Realism and Revolution* (Ithaca, N.Y.: Cornell University Press, 1988), 17–51.

34. Jacques Derrida, "Force of Law: 'The Mystical Foundation of Authority,'" in *Deconstruction and the Possibility of Justice*, ed. Drucilla Cornell, Michel Rosenfeld, and David Gray (New York: Routledge, 1992), 13–14.

35. See Geoffrey Bennington, *Interrupting Derrida* (London: Routledge, 2000), 18–33; Margaret Davies, "Derrida and Law: Legitimate Fictions," in *Jacques Derrida and the Humanities*, ed. Tom Cohen (Cambridge: Cambridge University Press, 2001), 213–37.

36. Edmund Burke, "Speech on Opening of Impeachment," in *Empire and Community: Edmund Burke's Writings and Speeches on International Relations*, ed. David P. Fidler and Jennifer M. Welsh (Boulder, Colo.: Westview, 1999), 217.

37. For further discussion, see Bonnie Honig, "Declarations of Independence: Arendt and Derrida on the Problem of Founding a Republic," *American Political Science Review* 85, 1 (1991): 97–113.

38. Most notably in *The Ethos of Pluralization*, 135–61; but also see William Connolly, *Political Theory and Modernity* (Oxford: Blackwell, 1988), 53–57; *Pluralism* (Durham, N.C.: Duke University Press, 2005), 134–36.

39. Connolly, *Ethos of Pluralization*, 138.

40. Connolly, *Ethos of Pluralization*, 139. Paul Ricoeur, on whom Connolly also draws, makes a similar point with regards to Machiavelli in "The Political Paradox," in

History and Truth, trans. Charles A. Kelbley (Evanston, Ill.: Northwestern University Press, 1965), 258: "Machiavelli raised the true problem of political violence, not that of ineffectual violence, of arbitrary or frenetic violence, but that of calculated and limited violence designed to establish a stable state. Of course, one can say that by means of this calculation, inceptive violence places itself under the judgment of established legality; but this established legality, this 'republic' is marked from its inception by violence, which was successful. All nations, all powers, and all regimes are born in this way. Their violent birth then becomes resorbed in the new legitimacy which they foster and consolidate. But this new legitimacy always retains a note of contingency, something strictly historical which its violent birth never ceases to confer upon it."

41. Connolly, *Ethos of Pluralization*, 139.

42. For a rich discussion on the theme of the foreign founder in Rousseau, see Bonnie Honig, *Democracy and the Foreigner* (Princeton, N.J.: Princeton University Press, 2001), 15–40.

43. Connolly, *Ethos of Pluralization*, 138.

44. As Ernest Renan was among the first to notice, forgetting is at the heart of national self-understanding: we become who we are by forgetting the crimes that forged the foundations of our political community. See Ernest Renan, "What Is a Nation?" in *Nation and Narration*, ed. Homi K. Bhabha (London: Routledge, 1990), 11. On the relationship between "founding" and "forgetting," also see Jacques Derrida, *On Cosmopolitanism and Forgiveness*, trans. Mark Dooley and Michael Hughes (London: Routledge, 2001), 57: "all states . . . have their origin in an aggression of the *colonial* type. This foundational violence is not only forgotten. The foundation is made *in order to* hide it; by its essence it tends to organise amnesia, sometimes under the celebration and sublimation of the grand beginnings."

45. Honig, "Between Decision and Deliberation," 3.

46. Honig, "Between Decision and Deliberation," 6.

47. Rousseau entertains the possibility that the alleged lawgiver might turn out to be a charlatan. *The Social Contract*, 71: "Any man can carve tablets of stone, bribe an oracle, feign secret dealings with some divinity, train a bird to speak in his ear, or find other crude ways to impress the people." For more discussion on this point and its implications, see Geoffrey Bennington, *Legislations* (London: Verso, 1994), 218–22; Ronald Beiner, *Civil Religion* (Cambridge: Cambridge University Press, 2011), 356–57.

48. Honig, "Between Decision and Deliberation," 6–7.

49. Keenan, *Democracy in Question*, 50.

50. Keenan, *Democracy in Question*, 52.

51. Keenan, *Democracy in Question*, 53.

52. To be sure, depending on one's conception of "constitutionalism," its relation to democracy can be problematized in different ways. On a "rights foundationalist" conception of constitutionalism, according to which certain basic rights must be constitutionally entrenched and insulated from popular mandate, the tension is between the rights of the individual and the will of the majority. In the context of Michelman's discussion, however,

constitutionalism primarily refers to the distinction between ordinary law-making and the "higher law" that frames it. See Frank Michelman, *Brennan and Democracy* (Princeton, N.J.: Princeton University Press, 1999), 6.

53. Frank Michelman, "Law's Republic," *Yale Law Journal* 97, 8 (1988): 1500–1501.

54. Frank Michelman, "How Can the People Ever Make the Laws?" in *Deliberative Democracy: Essays on Reason and Politics*, ed. James Bohman and William Rehg (Cambridge, Mass.: MIT Press, 1997), 147. The phrase "in some nonfictively attributable sense" suggests a critical take on "hypothetical" conceptions of popular sovereignty we explored in Chapter 1.

55. Frank Michelman, "Review of Jürgen Habermas, *Between Facts and Norms*," *Journal of Philosophy* 93 (1996): 310.

56. Jürgen Habermas, "Reconciliation through the Public Use of Reason," in *The Inclusion of the Other*, ed. Ciaran Cronin and Pablo De Greiff (Cambridge, Mass.: MIT Press, 1998), 69.

57. Jürgen Habermas, *Between Facts and Norms*, trans. William Rehg (Cambridge, Mass.: MIT Press, 1996), 447–48.

58. Frank Michelman, "Constitutional Authorship," in *Constitutionalism: Philosophical Foundations*, ed. Larry Alexander (Cambridge: Cambridge University Press, 1998), 91.

59. Michelman, "Constitutional Authorship," 91.

60. Michelman, "How Can the People Ever Make the Laws?" 164.

61. I borrow this way of juxtaposing "circularity" and "infinite regress" from David Ingram, *Law* (London: Continuum, 2006), 75. Ingram argues that while the former frames a question of "legitimacy," the latter frames a question of "legality." Although he has a point, the distinction does not easily fit Michelman's argument, according to which legality is an essential component of legitimacy.

62. Michelman, "Review of Jürgen Habermas, *Between Facts and Norms*," 308.

63. Michelman, "Constitutional Authorship," 86.

64. Michelman, "How Can the People Ever Make the Laws?" 165.

65. Michelman, "Constitutional Authorship," 91–92.

66. This is not to say that contemporary treatments of the paradox of founding do nothing but hypostatize the problem. Rather, I draw attention to "tendencies" of hypostatization within a broad scope of arguments that prove to be fruitful in a variety of other ways. Nor do I argue that the charge of hypostatization applies to all treatments of the paradox of founding in contemporary political theory. For a recent study committed to the persistence of the paradox, while at the same time avoiding hypostatization, see Jason Frank, *Constituent Moments: Enacting the People in Postrevolutionary America* (Durham, N.C.: Duke University Press, 2010).

67. Michelman, "How Can the People Ever Make the Laws?" 151.

68. Hannah Arendt, "Lying in Politics," in *Crises of the Republic* (New York: Harcourt Brace, 1972), 5. For a similar point, also see Sigmund Freud, *Moses and Monotheism*, trans. Katherine Jones (New York: Vintage, 1939), 22.

69. In making the distinction between "absolute" and "relative" new beginnings, I

follow Andreas Kalyvas's interpretation of Arendt in *Democracy and the Politics of the Extraordinary* (Cambridge: Cambridge University Press, 2008), 223–31.

70. Bonnie Honig, "The Time of Rights: Emergent Thoughts in an Emergency Setting," in *The New Pluralism: William Connolly and the Contemporary Global Condition*, ed. David Campbell and Morton Schoolman (Durham, N.C.: Duke University Press, 2008), 88.

71. Honig, "Between Decision and Deliberation," 1.

72. But then Honig names these moments of responding as "re-foundings" ("Between Decision and Deliberation," 8). If the paradox is not one of founding, as she claims, it is hard to see why the response would be a re-founding.

73. Honig, "Between Decision and Deliberation," 8.

74. For the philosophical exposition of hermeneutic experience and its circular structure, see Hans-Georg Gadamer, *Truth and Method*, rev. ed., trans. Joel Weinsheimer and Donald G. Marshall (New York: Continuum, 2003), 265–379.

CHAPTER 3. THE PEOPLE AND THE LAWGIVER: ROUSSEAU ON
THE POSSIBILITY OF DEMOCRATIC FOUNDING

1. Jean-Jacques Rousseau, *The Social Contract*, in *The Social Contract and Other Later Political Writings*, ed. and trans. Victor Gourevitch (Cambridge: Cambridge University Press, 1997), 69. In what follows, I refer to the same volume for *Considerations on the Government of Poland* and *The Discourse on Political Economy*.

2. The literature on Rousseau's lawgiver is vast. I find the following helpful: Roger D. Masters, *The Political Philosophy of Rousseau* (Princeton, N.J.: Princeton University Press, 1968), 354–417; Judith Shklar, *Men and Citizens* (Cambridge: Cambridge University Press, 1969), 127–64; Andrew Levine, *The Politics of Autonomy* (Amherst: University of Massachusetts Press, 1976), 159–85; Hilail Gildin, *Rousseau's Social Contract* (Chicago: University of Chicago Press, 1983), 67–91; Arthur Melzer, *The Natural Goodness of Man* (Chicago: University of Chicago Press, 1990), 232–52; Patrick Riley, "Rousseau's General Will," in *The Cambridge Companion to Rousseau*, ed. Patrick Riley (Cambridge: Cambridge University Press, 2001), 124–53. What is nonetheless missing in these monographic studies of Rousseau's political thought is a discussion of the ways the eighteenth-century French political and intellectual context informed his views on the lawgiver. David A. Wisner's *The Cult of the Legislator in France 1750–1830* (Oxford: Voltaire Foundation, 1997) fills this gap elegantly, by exploring how almost all major figures of the French Enlightenment—including Rousseau, Voltaire, Diderot, Helvétius, and d'Alembert—had a notion of *legislateur* and how their reflections on the topic were tied to the decisive events in French politics.

3. Although I do not raise this question in terms of the history of political thought, it is important to note here Rousseau's debt to Machiavelli in particular. See Niccolò Machiavelli, *Discourses on Livy*, trans. Julia C. Bondanella and Peter Bondanella (Oxford: Oxford University Press, 1997), Book I, chs. 1, 9–13; Book III, ch. 1; *The Prince*, ed. Quentin

Skinner and Russell Price (Cambridge: Cambridge University Press, 1988), ch. 6. For an extensive discussion of the theme of (re)founding in Machiavelli, see Hanna F. Pitkin, *Fortune Is a Woman* (Chicago: University of Chicago Press, 1984), 230–82. For an overview of Rousseau's modification of the Machiavellian conception of founding, see Masters, *The Political Philosophy of Rousseau*, 364–68. A penetrating assessment of Machiavelli's influence on *The Social Contract* in general and Rousseau's notion of the lawgiver in particular can be found in Lionel A. McKenzie, "Rousseau's Debate with Machiavelli in the *Social Contract*," *Journal of the History of Ideas* 43, 2 (1982): 209–28. Particularly important for both Machiavelli and Rousseau is the political use of religion in the context of foundation; for a vivid and insightful discussion, see Ronald Beiner, *Civil Religion* (Cambridge: Cambridge University Press, 2011), 29–36, 79–80.

4. William Connolly, *The Ethos of Pluralization* (Minneapolis: University of Minnesota Press, 1995), 137.

5. Bonnie Honig, "Between Decision and Deliberation: Political Paradox in Democratic Theory," *American Political Science Review* 101, 1 (2007): 3.

6. For analytical difficulties of defining political culture, see Patrick Chabal and Jean-Pascal Daloz, *Culture Troubles: Politics and the Interpretation of Meaning* (London: Hurst, 2006), 5–34.

7. Rousseau, *The Social Contract*, 81.

8. Immanuel Kant, "Toward Perpetual Peace," in *Practical Philosophy*, ed. and trans. M. J. Gregor (Cambridge: Cambridge University Press, 1996), 335.

9. Especially see Rousseau, *Considerations on the Government of Poland*, 189–93; *Discourse on Political Economy*, 13–23; *Letter to M. d'Alembert*, trans. Allan Bloom (Ithaca, N.Y.: Cornell University Press, 1968), 67–75.

10. Rousseau, *Letter to M. d'Alembert*, 74.

11. Rousseau, *The Social Contract*, 72.

12. Rousseau, *The Social Contract*, 77.

13. Jean-Jacques Rousseau, *Discourse on the Origin and the Foundations of Inequality Among Men*, in *The Discourses and Other Early Political Writings*, ed. and trans. Victor Gourevitch (Cambridge: Cambridge University Press, 1997), especially see 164–70.

14. Rousseau, *The Social Contract*, 72.

15. Rousseau, *Considerations on the Government of Poland*, 180–82.

16. For an especially forceful statement of this standard view, see Melzer, *The Natural Goodness of Man*, 232–36.

17. As Judith Shklar perceptively notes in *Men and Citizens*, 129: "He wanted to believe in his Plutarchian heroes, and such figures as the Legislator, Emile's tutor and M. de Wolmar show how well he could imagine men capable of reordering the lives of others."

18. The analogy of "architect" comes from *The Social Contract*, 72. I borrow the analogy of "interpreter" from Josiah Ober's studies on the Cleisthenic revolution in Athens. See especially Josiah Ober, *The Athenian Revolution* (Princeton, N.J.: Princeton University Press, 1996), 32–52.

19. Rousseau, *Considerations on the Government of Poland*, 184.

20. Sheldon Wolin, "Transgression, Equality, and Voice," in *Dēmokratia: A Conversation on Democracies, Ancient and Modern*, ed. Josiah Ober and Charles W. Hedrick (Princeton, N.J.: Princeton University Press, 1996), 73.

21. Rousseau, *The Social Contract*, 73.

22. Rousseau, *Considerations on the Government of Poland*, 180.

23. Alan Keenan, *Democracy in Question* (Stanford, Calif.: Stanford University Press, 2003), 52.

24. Rousseau, *Letter to M. d'Alembert*, 66 (emphasis mine).

25. This point is nicely emphasized in Honig, "Between Decision and Deliberation," 6.

26. Jean-Jacques Rousseau, *Plan for a Constitution for Corsica*, in *The Collected Writings of Rousseau*, vol. 11, ed. Christopher Kelly, trans. Christopher Kelly and Judith Bush (Hanover, N.H.: University Press of New England, 2005), 123–65.

27. Rousseau, *The Social Contract*, 78.

28. See Rousseau, *Plan for a Constitution for Corsica*, 124–25; *The Social Contract*, 78.

29. For a discussion of background theoretical and methodological issues as to reading meaningful action as a text, see Paul Ricoeur, "The Model of the Text: Meaningful Action Considered as a Text," in *Hermeneutics and the Human Sciences*, ed. and trans. John B. Thompson (Cambridge: Cambridge University Press, 1981), 197–221.

30. Rousseau, *The Social Contract*, 71.

31. Ober, *The Athenian Revolution*, 35.

32. Rousseau, *The Social Contract*, 109.

33. William Connolly, *Pluralism* (Durham, N.C.: Duke University Press, 2005), 135.

34. Rousseau, *The Social Contract*, 69; Kant, "Toward Perpetual Peace," 335.

35. See Immanuel Kant, *Metaphysics of Morals*, in *Practical Philosophy*, ed. and trans. M. J. Gregor (Cambridge: Cambridge University Press, 1996), 455–56.

36. Kant, *Metaphysics of Morals*, 456.

37. Kant, "Toward Perpetual Peace," 339. Also see the "Appendix" to *Metaphysics of Morals*, 506.

38. Kant, "Toward Perpetual Peace," 339.

39. Rousseau, *The Social Contract*, 71.

40. Kant, *Metaphysics of Morals*, 480.

41. Immanuel Kant, "Theory and Practice," in *Practical Philosophy*, ed. and trans. M. J. Gregor (Cambridge: Cambridge University Press, 1996), 296.

42. Margaret Canovan, *The People* (Cambridge: Polity, 2005), 100.

CHAPTER 4. BUILDING A HOMELAND: FOUNDING AND IDENTITY IN HANNAH ARENDT'S JEWISH WRITINGS

1. Reported by Elisabeth Young-Bruehl, *Hannah Arendt: For Love of the World* (New Haven, Conn.: Yale University Press, 1982), 405. Arendt's self-description was careful

enough to imply that phenomenology was not for her a philosophical program to be developed in and of itself but a way of philosophizing that she adopted in a flexible manner in her own political inquiries. Hence the accuracy of her self-description as a "*sort of* phenomenologist."

2. Hannah Arendt, *The Jewish Writings*, ed. Jerome Kohn and Ron. H. Feldman (New York: Schocken, 2007). Hereafter *JW*.

3. Hannah Arendt, *The Origins of Totalitarianism*, 3rd ed. (New York: Harcourt, 1968), 155.

4. Arendt, *The Origins of Totalitarianism*, 8.

5. Hannah Arendt, "On Humanity in Dark Times: Thoughts About Lessing," in *Men in Dark Times* (New York: Harcourt Brace, 1968), 17–18. Also see Arendt, "The Enlightenment and the Jewish Question," *JW*, 3–18.

6. Arendt, "On Humanity in Dark Times," 18.

7. Arendt, "Stefan Zweig: Jews in the World of Yesterday," *JW*, 328.

8. Arendt, "The Jewish Army—The Beginning of a Jewish Politics?" *JW*, 137.

9. Arendt, "Ceterum Censeo," *JW*, 142.

10. For explicit statements of her disappointment, see particularly "The 'So-called Jewish Army,'" *JW*, 157–60, and "If You Don't Resist the Lesser Evil," *JW*, 165–67.

11. Arendt, "Ceterum Censeo," *JW*, 143.

12. For the complexities of Arendt's take on Zionism, see Ron Feldman, "The Jew as Pariah: The Case of Hannah Arendt," in *The Jew as Pariah: Jewish Identity and Politics in the Modern Age*, ed. Ron Feldman (New York: Grove, 1978), 15–52; Dagmar Barnouw, *Visible Spaces: Hannah Arendt and the German Jewish Experience* (Baltimore: Johns Hopkins University Press, 1990), 72–134; Seyla Benhabib, *The Reluctant Modernism of Hannah Arendt* (Thousand Oaks, Calif.: Sage, 1996), 35–46; Richard Bernstein, *Hannah Arendt and the Jewish Question* (Cambridge: Polity Press, 1996), 101–22; Ronald Beiner, "Arendt and Nationalism," in *The Cambridge Companion to Hannah Arendt*, ed. Dana Villa (Cambridge: Cambridge University Press, 2000), 44–62.

13. Arendt, "The Jewish State," *JW*, 377.

14. See her discussion in "Zionism Reconsidered," *JW*, 357, 362.

15. Arendt, "Herzl and Lazare," *JW*, 338–42.

16. See her discussions in "Zionism Reconsidered," *JW*, 353, 358–60; "The Jewish State," *JW*, 381–82; and *The Origins of Totalitarianism*, 7–10.

17. Arendt, "The Jewish State," *JW*, 382. Arendt does not fail to note the Eurocentric arrogance of imagining Palestine as a "country without a people." See her remarks in "Peace or Armistice in the Near East," *JW*, 432.

18. Arendt, "The Jewish State," *JW*, 382.

19. Arendt, "Zionism Reconsidered," *JW*, 367.

20. Arendt, "The Jew as Pariah," *JW*, 275.

21. Beiner, "Arendt and Nationalism," 49.

22. Arendt, *The Origins of Totalitarianism*, ix.

23. Arendt, "The Jew as Pariah," *JW*, 297.

24. Arendt, "To Save the Jewish Homeland," *JW*, 394–95.
25. Arendt, "To Save the Jewish Homeland," *JW*, 396.
26. Arendt, "To Save the Jewish Homeland," *JW*, 396.
27. Arendt, "Peace or Armistice in the Near East?" *JW*, 435.
28. Hannah Arendt, "What is Existenz Philosophy?" *Partisan Review* 13, 1 (1946): 55.

29. See in particular Arendt's discussion of the activity of "work" as distinguished from "labor" and "action" in *The Human Condition* (Chicago: University of Chicago Press, 1958), 136–74. For an insightful treatment of the political implications of "artificiality" in Arendt's political thought, see Margaret Canovan, *Hannah Arendt: A Reinterpretation of Her Political Thought* (Cambridge: Cambridge University Press, 1992), 105–10.

30. See Arendt, *The Origins of Totalitarianism*, 296–302.
31. Arendt, "Peace or Armistice in the Near East?" *JW*, 435.
32. Bernard Yack, "The Myth of the Civic Nation," in *Theorizing Nationalism*, ed. Ronald Beiner (New York: SUNY Press), 105.
33. Yack, "The Myth of the Civic Nation," 106.
34. Yack, "The Myth of the Civic Nation," 106.
35. Arendt, "Peace or Armistice in the Near East?" *JW*, 438. For a good discussion of Arendt's relation to this tradition, see Amnon Raz-Krakotzkin, "Binationalism and Jewish Identity: Hannah Arendt and the Question of Palestine," in *Hannah Arendt in Jerusalem*, ed. Steven E. Ascheim (Berkeley: University of California Press, 2001), 165–80.
36. Arendt, "Zionism Reconsidered," *JW*, 352.
37. See in particular the discussion in "The Crisis of Zionism," *JW*, 329–37, where she also advocated with perspicacity the prospect of a federal Europe.
38. Arendt, "To Save the Jewish Homeland," *JW*, 400.
39. Arendt, "To Save the Jewish Homeland," *JW*, 396.
40. Arendt, "To Save the Jewish Homeland," *JW*, 400.
41. Arendt, "Peace or Armistice in the Near East?" *JW*, 446.
42. See, for example, Benhabib, *The Reluctant Modernism of Hannah Arendt*, 42.
43. Arendt, "Peace or Armistice in the Near East?" *JW*, 428.
44. Arendt, "Peace or Armistice in the Near East?" *JW*, 429.
45. Arendt, "To Save the Jewish Homeland," *JW*, 396.
46. Arendt, "Peace or Armistice in the Near East?" *JW*, 423.
47. Bernstein, *Hannah Arendt and the Jewish Question*, 27.

48. As I also briefly discussed in the Introduction, this problem has been noted under different names such as the "boundary problem," the "unit problem," or the "domain problem." For some of the important contributions to its analysis, see note 8 to the Introduction.

49. In the *Political Theories of Decolonization: Postcolonialism and the Problem of Foundations* (Oxford: Oxford University Press, 2011), Margaret Kohn and Keally McBride persuasively show how both perspectives were deployed in the context of postcolonial foundations: "The critics of colonialism discussed in this book could be divided into two groups, or perhaps more appropriately located along a continuum based on whether they

argued that the alternative values were embedded in history or created through struggle" (145).

50. Its first canonical example can be found in Plato, *Republic*, trans. G. M. A. Grube (Indianapolis: Hackett, 1992), 414b–15d. According to Rogers M. Smith, stories of this sort fall in the broad category of "ethically constitutive stories" as distinct from stories of "economic well-being" and stories of "political power"—see *Stories of Peoplehood: The Politics and Morals of Political Membership* (Cambridge: Cambridge University Press, 2003), 57–71.

51. Geoffrey Bennington, *Legislations: The Politics of Deconstruction* (London: Verso, 1994), 240.

52. The Arendtian insight that action is constitutive of identity has been the matrix of a number of brilliant studies in contemporary political theory. Especially see Patchen Markell, *Bound by Recognition* (Princeton, N.J.: Princeton University Press, 2003); Linda Zerilli, *Feminism and the Abyss of Freedom* (Chicago: University of Chicago Press, 2005); Michaele L. Ferguson, *Sharing Democracy* (Oxford: Oxford University Press, 2012).

CHAPTER 5. REVOLUTION AND CONSTITUTION:
THE LEGITIMACY OF BEGINNING IN QUESTION

1. Jacques Derrida, "Declarations of Independence," *New Political Science* 15 (1986): 10.

2. Jacques Derrida, "Force of Law: 'The Mystical Foundation of Authority,'" in *Deconstruction and the Possibility of Justice*, ed. Drucilla Cornell, Michel Rosenfeld, and David Gray (New York: Routledge, 1992), 13–14.

3. Hannah Arendt, *On Revolution*, rev. ed. (New York: Viking, 1965), 206.

4. See Bonnie Honig's important article, "Declarations of Independence: Arendt and Derrida on the Problem of Founding a Republic," *American Political Science Review* 85, 1 (1991): 97–113. Drawing on Derrida, Honig offers a sustained critique of Arendt. I will revisit her criticism below.

5. Arendt, *On Revolution*, 212.

6. Hannah Arendt, *The Origins of Totalitarianism*, 3rd ed. (New York: Harcourt, Brace, 1968), 438.

7. Hannah Arendt, "The Eggs Speak Up," in *Essays in Understanding*, ed. Jerome Kohn (New York: Schocken, 1994), 271.

8. Arendt appropriates the concept of the "world" from Heidegger, but her interpretation of it follows the lead of Jaspers and his Kantian emphasis on freedom and communication. See Seyla Benhabib, *The Reluctant Modernism of Hannah Arendt* (Thousand Oaks, Calif.: Sage, 1996), 50–56, 104–7; Dana Villa, *Arendt and Heidegger: The Fate of the Political* (Princeton, N.J.: Princeton University Press, 1996), 211–40; Jacques Taminiaux, *The Thracian Maid and the Professional Thinker: Arendt and Heidegger*, trans. Michael Gendre (Albany, N.Y.: SUNY Press, 1997), 56–88.

9. Hannah Arendt, *The Human Condition* (Chicago: University of Chicago Press, 1958), 190.

10. For more discussion on this point, see Michael Gottsegen, *The Political Thought of Hannah Arendt* (Albany, N.Y.: SUNY Press, 1993), 118–24.

11. For early examples, see Eric Hobsbawm, "Review: On Revolution. By Hannah Arendt," *History and Theory* 4, 2 (1965): 252–58; George Lichtheim, "Two Revolutions," in *The Concept of Ideology and Other Essays* (New York: Random House, 1967), 115–22.

12. See Hanna F. Pitkin, "Justice: On Relating Private and Public," *Political Theory* 9, 3 (1981): 327–52; Richard Bernstein, "Rethinking the Social and Political," in *Philosophical Profiles* (Philadelphia: University of Pennsylvania Press, 1986), 238–59; Benhabib, *The Reluctant Modernism of Hannah Arendt*, 155–66.

13. See Honig, "Declarations of Independence: Arendt and Derrida on Founding a Republic"; Alan Keenan, "Promises Promises: The Abyss of Freedom and the Loss of the Political in the Work of Hannah Arendt," *Political Theory* 22, 2 (1994): 297–322; Jason Frank, *Constituent Moments: Enacting the People in Postrevolutionary America* (Durham, N.C.: Duke University Press, 2010), 41–66; Lisa Disch, "How Could Hannah Arendt Glorify the American Revolution and Revile the French?" *European Journal of Political Theory* 10, 3 (2011): 350–71.

14. Arendt, *On Revolution*, 223.

15. For the development of the doctrine of constituent power in the context of English, American and French constitutional politics, see the following articles in *The Paradox of Constitutionalism: Constituent Power and Constitutional Form*, ed. Martin Loughlin and Neil Walker (Oxford: Oxford University Press, 2007): Martin Loughlin, "Constituent Power Subverted: From English Constitutional Argument to British Constitutional Practice," 27–48; Stephen M. Griffin, "Constituent Power and Constitutional Change in American Constitutionalism," 49–66; Lucien Jaume, "Constituent Power in France: The Revolution and Its Consequences," 67–85.

16. Thomas Paine, "Rights of Man, Part II," in *Political Writings*, ed. Bruce Kuklick (Cambridge: Cambridge University Press, 2000), 184.

17. Emmanuel Joseph Sieyès, "What Is the Third Estate?" in *Political Writings*, ed. and trans. Michael Sonenscher (Indianapolis: Hackett, 2003), 136.

18. Sieyès, "What Is the Third Estate?" 137.

19. Sieyès, "What Is the Third Estate?" 138.

20. Sieyès, "What Is the Third Estate?" 136: "Prior to the nation and above the nation there is only natural law." See also Sieyès, "Views of the Executive Means," in *Political Writings*, 13.

21. Sieyès, "What Is the Third Estate?" 139.

22. I borrow the terms "act for" and "stand for" as designating different modes of representation from Hannah F. Pitkin, *The Concept of Representation* (Berkeley: University of California Press, 1967).

23. Sieyès, "What Is the Third Estate?" 139.

24. Sieyès, "What Is the Third Estate?" 139.

25. Carl Schmitt, *Constitutional Theory*, trans. Jeffrey Seitzer (Durham, N.C.: Duke University Press, 2008), 125. Throughout the English text, the German term *verfassungsgebende Macht* is rendered as "constitution-making power" instead of the conventional "constituent power." I modify the translation in accordance with the conventional usage in the quotations that follow.

26. See, for example, Schmitt, *Constitutional Theory*, 126–30, 140–42. For a critical discussion on this aspect of Schmitt's constitutional theory, see Renato Cristi, "Schmitt on Constituent Power and the Monarchical Principle," *Constellations* 18, 3 (2011): 352–64.

27. Schmitt, *Constitutional Theory*, 109.

28. Schmitt, *Constitutional Theory*, 110.

29. Schmitt, *Constitutional Theory*, 132.

30. Nonetheless, Arendt was certainly familiar with Schmitt's *Constitutional Theory*. See Hannah Arendt, "What Is Freedom?" in *Between Past and Future* (New York: Viking, 1968), 296, n. 21.

31. Arendt, *On Revolution*, 153.

32. Andrew Arato and Jean Cohen, "Banishing the Sovereign? Internal and External Sovereignty in Arendt," *Constellations* 16, 2 (2009): 310. For a similar argument that persuasively documents the ways Arendt's critical engagement with Schmitt distorted her understanding of the French Revolution in general and her interpretation of Sieyès in particular, see William Scheuerman, "Revolutions and Constitutions: Hannah Arendt's Challenge to Carl Schmitt," *Canadian Journal of Law and Jurisprudence* 10, 1 (1997): 141–61. On Arendt's relation to Schmitt, see also Andreas Kalyvas, *Democracy and the Politics of the Extraordinary* (Cambridge: Cambridge University Press, 2008), 194–253.

33. See Arendt, "What Is Freedom?" 144–45. For further discussion, see Ronald Beiner, "Action, Natality and Citizenship: Hannah Arendt's Concept of Freedom," in *Conceptions of Liberty in Political Philosophy*, ed. Zbigniew Pelczynski and John Gray (New York: St. Martin's, 1984), 349–75.

34. For a different interpretation, see James Miller, "The Pathos of Novelty: Hannah Arendt's Image of Freedom in the Modern World," in *Hannah Arendt: The Recovery of the Public World*, ed. Melvyn A. Hill (New York: St. Martin's, 1979), 177–208. Miller sees in Arendt's own version of republicanism an intersubjective reformulation of Rousseauian ideals, and hence questions her highly critical take on Rousseau. For a criticism of Miller's argument along with a thoughtful exposition of what is at stake in Arendt's departure from will-centered models of political freedom, see Villa, *Arendt and Heidegger*, 59–77.

35. Max Weber, *The Theory of Social and Economic Organization*, trans. Talcott Parsons (New York: Free Press, 1964), 152. In her early work, however, Arendt uses the term in a primarily Weberian sense. Especially see her analysis of imperialist expansion in chapter 5 of *The Origins of Totalitarianism*, where she treats power as an instrumental capacity akin to the means of violence.

36. Hannah Arendt, *The Human Condition* (Chicago: University of Chicago Press, 1958), 200.

37. See Arato and Cohen, "Banishing the Sovereign?" 309.

38. Arendt, *On Revolution*, 156.

39. Arendt's conception of authority has a twofold structure, combining elements of both normative and phenomenological analysis. Normatively, authority involves a *legitimacy claim* which stands in opposition to force and violence. Phenomenologically, it is a *principle of permanence* rooted in the fundamental human experience of the continuity of a shared world. Notice that authority in this twofold sense is built into the very idea of founding. Insofar as every act of foundation and hence every constitution has by definition a future-oriented normative intent, it claims to be binding not only for the present generation but also for the posterity. Especially see Arendt, "What Is Authority?" in *Between Past and Future*, 91–141.

40. Arendt, *On Revolution*, 163.

41. Arendt, *On Revolution*, 165.

42. Andrew Arato, "Forms of Constitution Making and Theories of Democracy," *Cardozo Law Review* 17 (1995): 207, n. 31.

43. Arendt, *On Revolution*, 166.

44. Arendt, *On Revolution*, 158.

45. Jeremy Waldron, "Arendt's Constitutional Politics," in *The Cambridge Companion to Hannah Arendt*, ed. Dana Villa (Cambridge: Cambridge University Press, 2000), 212–13. Waldron (in my view, misleadingly) reads into Arendt the view that future generations must take the constitution as binding "not because of anything special or noticeable about this event or body of law, but simply because they acknowledge that there must *be* such a point of reference, that it is bound to be in some sense arbitrary, and that they are determined nevertheless to act from henceforth as though *this one* will do" (213). For reasons that will become clear, I disagree. In Arendt's view, as we will see, whether "this one would do" depends to a large extent on the inherent qualities of the founding act itself.

46. Arendt, *On Revolution*, 182.

47. Arendt, *On Revolution*, 184–85.

48. Jean-Jacques Rousseau, *The Social Contract*, in *The Social Contract and Other Later Political Writings*, ed. and trans. Victor Gourevitch (Cambridge: Cambridge University Press, 1997), 69. Arendt herself cites the phrase in *On Revolution*, 184.

49. Karl Marx and Friedrich Engels, *The Manifesto of the Communist Party*, in *The Marx-Engels Reader*, ed. Robert C. Tucker (New York: Norton, 1972), 476.

50. Arendt, *On Revolution*, 185–86.

51. Arendt, of course, does not fail to note that the Constitution evades the question of ultimate authority; *On Revolution*, 193–94: "If we were to understand the body politic of the American republic solely in terms of its two greatest documents, the Declaration of Independence and the Constitution of the United States, then the Preamble to the Declaration of Independence would provide the sole source of authority from which the Constitution, not as an act of constituting government but as the law of the land, derives its own legitimacy; for the Constitution itself, in its preamble as well as in its amendments which form the Bill of Rights, is singularly silent on this question of ultimate authority."

52. Arendt, *On Revolution*, 192.

53. Arendt, *On Revolution*, 192–93.

54. Arendt, *On Revolution*, 212. A few pages earlier, she articulates the same idea in a slightly different manner: "The very fact that the men of the American Revolution thought of themselves as 'founders' indicates the extent to which they must have known that it would be the act of foundation itself, rather than an Immortal Legislator or self-evident truth or any other transcendent, transmundane source, which eventually would become the fountain of authority in the new body politic. From this it follows that it is futile to search for an absolute to break the vicious circle in which all beginning is inevitably caught, because this 'absolute' lies in the very act of beginning itself" (204).

55. Margaret Canovan, *Hannah Arendt: A Reinterpretation of Her Political Thought* (Cambridge: Cambridge University Press, 1992), 173.

56. Montesquieu, *The Spirit of the Laws*, ed. and trans. Anne M. Cohler, Basia C. Miller, and Harold S. Stone (Cambridge: Cambridge University Press, 1989), 10–30.

57. Arendt, "What Is Freedom?," 152–53. In the rest of the paragraph, all phrases in quotation marks refer to these pages.

58. Hannah Arendt, *Lectures on Kant's Political Philosophy*, ed. Ronald Beiner (Chicago: University of Chicago Press, 1982), 77.

59. For a systematic reconstruction of Arendt's scattered remarks on principles of action, see Lucy Cane, "Hannah Arendt on the Principles of Political Action," *European Journal of Political Theory* 14, 1 (2015): 55–75.

60. Hence my disagreement with Waldron's claim that the constitution is held to be binding, according to Arendt, "not because of anything special or noticeable about this event or body of law." See note 45 above.

61. Arendt, *On Revolution*, 213.

62. Arendt, *On Revolution*, 214.

63. So far as I can see, only Andrew Arato has been *systematically* attentive to this dimension of Arendt's argument in *On Revolution*. Especially see his comments in the "Forms of Constitution Making and Theories of Democracy," 205–10, from which, I think, his later empirically oriented work on the models and processes of constitution-making takes its theoretical point of departure.

64. The same holds true for Arendt's reflections on the Roman origins of "authority." Based on the controversial assumption that one can recover the authentic meaning of a concept in the original experience that gave birth to it, Arendt traces the concept of authority back to its Roman roots. She thereby seeks to demonstrate that in its "authentic" form authority was not transcendentally bestowed but immanent in the act of foundation—and that this Roman model reasserted itself in the American founding (see *On Revolution*, 194–217). The problem with such speculative excursions into the deep past, or into the buried strata of allegedly "authentic" (forgotten but never completely lost) experience, is not simply that they are wrong. The problem is rather that, even if these claims were true, they would not clarify what accounts for the normative authority of the kind of action that inaugurates a new political community.

65. The phrase "normative lacuna" is from Benhabib, *The Reluctant Modernism of*

Hannah Arendt, 193. For a compelling critique of the normative deficiencies of Arendt's political thought in general, see George Kateb, *Hannah Arendt: Politics, Conscience, Evil* (Totowa, N.J.: Rowman and Allanheld, 1983). For a response defending Arendt's distance to normative political theory, see Villa, *Arendt and Heidegger*, 52–77.

66. Arendt, *The Human Condition*, 243–47. For a recent assessment on the programmatic significance of promising in Arendt's political thought, see J. M. Bernstein, "Promising and Civil Disobedience: Arendt's Political Modernism," in *Thinking in Dark Times: Hannah Arendt on Ethics and Politics*, ed. Roger Berkowitz, Jeffrey Katz, and Thomas Keenan (New York: Fordham University Press, 2010), 115–27.

67. Arendt, *On Revolution*, 175.

68. I owe the term "promissory founding" to Angélica Bernal, "Conceptions of Founding in Contemporary Political Theory," paper presented at the annual meeting of the Western Political Science Association, March 19, 2009.

69. Honig, "Declarations of Independence: Arendt and Derrida on the Problem of Founding a Republic," 101–6.

70. Derrida, "Declarations of Independence," 9.

71. Honig, "Declarations of Independence: Arendt and Derrida on Founding a Republic," 106.

72. Honig, "Declarations of Independence: Arendt and Derrida on Founding a Republic," 107.

73. David Ingram, "Novus Ordo Saeclorum: The Trial of (Post)Modernity or the Tale of Two Revolutions," in *Hannah Arendt: Twenty Years Later*, ed. Larry May and Jerome Kohn (Cambridge, Mass.: MIT Press, 1996), 236–37. Andreas Kalyvas develops a similar argument in *Democracy and the Politics of the Extraordinary*, 241–53.

74. While Ingram admits the substantial differences between Arendt and Habermas on this score (see "Novus Ordo Saeclorum," 249, n. 13), he does not take into account what follows from those differences with regard to his own reading of Arendt.

75. Arendt, *On Revolution*, 182.

76. This duality can be observed in other aspects of Arendt's work as well, and implies a tension that cuts deep into her political thought. See Peter Fuss, "Hannah Arendt's Conception of Political Community," in *Hannah Arendt: The Recovery of the Public World*, 156–76; Maurizio Passerin d'Entrèves, *The Political Philosophy of Hannah Arendt* (London: Routledge, 1994), 84–85; Benhabib, *The Reluctant Modernism of Hannah Arendt*, 123–30; Villa, *Arendt and Heidegger*, 52–59.

77. Arendt, "What Is Freedom?" 146, 151.

78. Arendt, *The Human Condition*, 190.

79. Arendt, *On Revolution*, 125.

80. Honig, "Declarations of Independence: Arendt and Derrida on Founding a Republic," 106.

81. See also Dana Villa, *Public Freedom* (Princeton, N.J.: Princeton University Press, 2008), 101–5.

82. Josiah Ober, "Revolution Matters: Democracy as Demotic Action," in *Democracy*

2500? Questions and Challenges, ed. Ian Morris, Kurt A. Raaflaub, and David Castriota (Dubuque, Iowa: Kendall Hunt, 1997), 78. Also see Arendt, *On Revolution*, 157.

83. Arendt, "What Is Freedom?" 153.

84. Albrecht Wellmer, "Hannah Arendt on Revolution," in *Hannah Arendt in Jerusalem*, ed. Steven E. Ascheim (Berkeley: University of California Press, 2001), 43. It is also possible to read in Wellmer's remark an implicit response to the charge that the "agonistic event" disappears in or written out of Arendt's account of foundation. Examples of such criticism can be found in Antonio Negri, *Insurgencies: Constituent Power and the Modern State*, trans. Maurizia Boscagli (Minneapolis: University of Minnesota Press, 1999), 15–20; Frank, *Constituent Moments*, 41–66.

85. In a series of essays, inspired in part by Arendt's work, Josiah Ober developed a cogent argument concerning the importance of the Cleisthenic revolution for the formation of democratic mentality in classical Athens. See *The Athenian Revolution: Essays on Ancient Greek Democracy and Political Theory* (Princeton, N.J.: Princeton University Press, 1996); "Revolution Matters: Democracy as Demotic Action," in *Democracy 2500?*, 67–85; " 'I Besieged That Man': Democracy's Revolutionary Start," in *Origins of Democracy in Ancient Greece*, ed. Kurt A. Raaflaub, Josiah Ober, and Robert W. Wallace (Berkeley: University of California Press, 2007), 83–104.

86. Arendt, "Understanding and Politics," *Essays in Understanding*, 321.

87. See Andrew Arato, "Redeeming the Still Redeemable: Post Sovereign Constitution Making," *International Journal of Politics, Culture, and Society* 22 (2009): 427–43; "Conventions, Constituent Assemblies, and Round Tables: Models, Principles and Elements of Democratic Constitution-Making," *Global Constitutionalism* 1, 1 (2012): 173–200.

CHAPTER 6. LAW AND DEMOCRACY IN FOUNDING MOMENTS: DELIBERATIVE CONSTITUTION-MAKING

1. Jürgen Habermas, *Between Facts and Norms*, trans. William Rehg (Cambridge, Mass.: MIT Press, 1996), 104.

2. Simone Chambers, "Deliberative Democratic Theory," *Annual Review of Political Science* 6 (2003): 310.

3. As I see it, the term "postmetaphysical" is not meant to suggest that metaphysics is now over or left behind for good. Rather, it means that any appeal to an independent/transcendental order of moral truth as a strategy of justification has become deeply controversial, and consequently that we are bound to start from "within," that is, without presumptions of a transparent reason capable of circumventing historically conditioned forms of life. For an overview, see Jürgen Habermas, *Postmetaphysical Thinking*, trans. William M. Hohengarten (Cambridge, Mass.: MIT Press, 1992), 28–53; for an exposition of the relationship between proceduralism and postmetaphysical thinking, see Simone Chambers, *Reasonable Democracy: Jürgen Habermas and the Politics of Discourse* (Ithaca, N.Y.: Cornell

University Press, 1996), 30–42; for a brief but illuminating discussion on how Habermas's "postmetaphysical reconstructivism" differs from Rawls's "nonmetaphysical constructivism," see Todd Hedrick, *Rawls and Habermas: Reason, Pluralism, and the Claims of Political Philosophy* (Stanford, Calif.: Stanford University Press, 2010), 81–85.

4. Habermas, *Between Facts and Norms*, 129.

5. Habermas, *Between Facts and Norms*, 99–104; also see Jürgen Habermas, "On the Internal Relation Between the Rule of Law and Democracy," in *The Inclusion of the Other*, ed. Ciaran Cronin and Pablo De Greiff (Cambridge, Mass.: MIT Press, 1998), 253–64.

6. Jürgen Habermas, "A Short Reply," *Ratio Juris* 12, 4 (1999): 447.

7. Jürgen Habermas, "Constitutional Democracy," *Political Theory* 29, 6 (2001): 776.

8. Jürgen Habermas, "Reply to Symposium Participants," in *Habermas on Law and Democracy*, ed. Michel Rosenfeld and Andrew Arato (Berkeley: University of California Press, 1998), 412.

9. For further discussion, see Hedrick, *Rawls and Habermas*, 133–36.

10. Habermas, *Between Facts and Norms*, 84.

11. Habermas, *Between Facts and Norms*, 453.

12. Habermas, *Between Facts and Norms*, 119.

13. Jürgen Habermas, "Remarks on Discourse Ethics," in *Justification and Application*, trans. Ciaran Cronin (Cambridge, Mass.: MIT Press, 1993), 67.

14. Note here that Habermas's argument is not meant to *describe* actual constitutional deliberation but to *reconstruct* its communicative structure so as to offer a theoretical justification for the co-originality thesis. This being said, his reconstructive approach is controversial in at least two respects. First, at this level of abstraction, we are left with a picture of transparent communication, in which manipulation, demagoguery, and so on are absent. Thus, it remains an open question how this model would be transposed to the realm of action from which it claims to take its point of departure. I take up this issue below in discussing the *politics* of deliberative constitution-making. Second, Habermas's claims about the "pragmatic presuppositions of communication" are exposed to the charge of linguistic foundationalism. Although this criticism poses a larger set of philosophical questions that it is not my purpose to explore here, let me mention that I am ambivalent on this score. On the one hand, statements such as "reaching understanding is the inherent telos of human speech" suggest that the criticism has a point; see Jürgen Habermas, *The Theory of Communicative Action*, vol. 1, trans. Thomas McCarthy (Boston: Beacon, 1984), 287. On the other hand, Habermas's evolutionary account of rationalization, outlined in Chapter 1 of *The Theory of Communicative Action*, suggests that the priority accorded to "reaching understanding" should be viewed along the model of Hegelian contextual development rather than some sort of foundationalism. For a compelling critique of Habermas's foundationalist leanings, especially as they apply to his political theory, see Margaret Kohn, "Language, Power, and Persuasion: Toward a Critique of Deliberative Democracy," *Constellations* 7, 3 (2000): 408–29.

15. Habermas, *Between Facts and Norms*, 84.

16. Habermas, *Between Facts and Norms*, 129.

17. Andreas Kalyvas, "Popular Sovereignty, Democracy, and the Constituent Power," *Constellations* 12, 5 (2005): 237.

18. Habermas, *Between Facts and Norms*, 135.

19. Habermas, *Between Facts and Norms*, 448.

20. Richard J. Bernstein, "The Retrieval of the Democratic Ethos," in *Habermas on Law and Democracy*, 289–90.

21. For a helpful discussion on this point, see Chambers, *Reasonable Democracy*, 197–202.

22. Habermas, *Between Facts and Norms*, 302; also see 358, 471, 489.

23. Habermas, "Reply to Symposium Participants," *Habermas on Law and Democracy*, 384–85.

24. For the fundamentals of this research program, see Jürgen Habermas, *Communication and the Evolution of Society*, trans. Thomas McCarthy (Boston: Beacon, 1979).

25. Hassen Ebrahim and Laurel E. Miller, "Creating the Birth Certificate of a New South Africa: Constitution Making After Apartheid," in *Framing the State in Times of Transition*, ed. Laurel E. Miller (Washington, D.C.: U.S. Institute of Peace, 2010), 133–34.

26. Jean-Jacques Rousseau, *The Social Contract*, in *The Social Contract and Other Later Political Writings*, ed. and trans. Victor Gourevitch (Cambridge: Cambridge University Press, 1997), 68. This remark is often read as a token of Rousseau's mistrust of the people. But the "blind multitude" of *The Social Contract* could as well be mirroring the "brave Corsicans" of the *Plan for a Constitution for Corsica*, especially if one considers the fact that Ebrahim and Miller's description of South Africa (a "largely illiterate rural population") as much applies to Rousseau's Corsica. In this reading, the "blind multitude" does not necessarily imply a pejorative remark but rather a sober diagnosis of the social and economic conditions constraining the agency of the common people. I am indebted to Rebecca Kingston for bringing this point to my attention.

27. Christina Murray, "Negotiating South Africa's New Constitution," in *Peace, Order, and Good Government*, ed. Clement Macintyre and John Williams (Kent Town: Wakefield, 2003), 80.

28. Heinz Klug, "South Africa's Experience in Constitution-Building," in *Reconstituting the Constitution*, ed. Caroline Morris, Jonathan Boston, and Petra Butler (Berlin: Springer-Verlag, 2011), 71.

29. Aristotle, *Nicomachean Ethics*, ed. and trans. Roger Crisp (Cambridge: Cambridge University Press, 2000), 1103a.

30. Simone Chambers, "Democracy, Popular Sovereignty, and Constitutional Legitimacy," *Constellations* 11, 2 (2004): 164.

31. Simone Chambers, "Open Versus Closed Constitutional Negotiation," in *Deliberative Democracy in Practice*, ed. David Kahane et al. (Vancouver: UBC Press, 2010), 85–86. For a detailed study of the importance and varieties of public rhetoric in the process of democratic founding in South Africa, see Joseph-Philippe Salazar, *An African Athens: Rhetoric and the Shaping of Democracy in South Africa* (Hillsdale, N.J.: Erlbaum, 2002).

32. Frank Michelman, "Constitutional Authorship," in *Constitutionalism: Philosophical Foundations*, ed. Larry Alexander (Cambridge: Cambridge University Press, 1998), 91.

33. Frank Michelman, "How Can the People Ever Make the Laws?" in *Deliberative Democracy: Essays on Reason and Politics*, ed. James Bohman and William Rehg (Cambridge, Mass.: MIT Press, 1997), 164.

34. Michelman, "How Can the People Ever Make the Laws?" 165.

35. Habermas, "Constitutional Democracy," 774. The exchange between Michelman and Habermas has sparked a number of commentaries and critical interventions, which add up to a small literature in itself. See Alessandro Ferrara, "Of Boats and Principles," *Political Theory* 29, 6 (2001): 782–91; Bonnie Honig, "Dead Rights, Live Futures," *Political Theory* 29, 6 (2001): 792–805; Ciaran Cronin, "On the Possibility of a Democratic Constitutional Founding," *Ratio Juris* 19, 3 (2006): 343–69; Kevin Olson, "Paradoxes of Constitutional Democracy," *American Journal of Political Science* 51, 2 (2007): 330–43; Christopher F. Zurn, "The Logic of Legitimacy," *Legal Theory* 16 (2010): 191–227.

36. Cronin, "On the Possibility of a Democratic Constitutional Founding," 356.

37. Habermas, "Constitutional Democracy," 774.

38. Habermas, "Constitutional Democracy," 774.

39. Habermas, "Constitutional Democracy," 776.

40. Habermas, "Constitutional Democracy," 775.

41. See Ferrara, "Of Boats and Principles," 787.

42. Cronin, "On the Possibility of a Democratic Constitutional Founding," 363.

43. Zurn, "The Logic of Legitimacy," 220–21.

44. See Honig, "Dead Rights, Live Futures," 799.

45. Especially see Jürgen Habermas, "Yet Again: German Identity—A Unified Nation of Angry DM-Burghers?" *New German Critique* 52 (1991): 84–101; "The Normative Deficits of Unification," in *The Past as Future*, trans. Max Pensky (Cambridge: Polity, 1994), 33–54.

46. Habermas, "Yet Again," 97.

47. In an assessment of Habermas's stance in the German unification debate, Matthew Specter critically writes: "Habermas appears to have been more concerned that future generations have a coherent *memory* of a founding moment, than that the current generation *experience* a significant act of political self-determination." See Matthew Specter, "Habermas's Political Thought, 1984–1996: A Historical Interpretation," *Modern Intellectual History* 6, 1 (2009): 108. It seems to me that Habermas was concerned with both aspects of the issue. Take, for instance, the following passage from "The Normative Deficits of Unification," 52: "Is it too much to demand that an effort be made in the medium of public communication, so that a *new* Federal Republic, composed of such unequal parts, can anchor itself in the consciousness of its citizens as something shared—and not experienced just as the by-product of the forced construction of an expanded currency zone?"

48. Jan-Werner Müller makes a similar observation regarding the Rousseauean undertones of Habermas's position in the German unification debate. Unlike the argument I present here, however, Müller finds that orientation somewhat problematic and standing in contrast to Habermas's criticism of the substantial conceptions of popular sovereignty;

see *Another Country: German Intellectuals, Unification, and National Identity* (New Haven, Conn.: Yale University Press, 2000), 112–17.

49. See, for instance, Kevin Olson's remarks about path dependence in constitutional development in "Paradoxes of Constitutional Democracy," 338–40.

50. Stephen Holmes and Cass R. Sunstein, "The Politics of Constitutional Revision in Eastern Europe," in *Responding to Imperfection: The Theory and Practice of Constitutional Amendment*, ed. Sanford Levinson (Princeton, N.J.: Princeton University Press, 1995), 276.

51. See Jon Elster, Claus Offe, and Ulrich Preuss, *Institutional Design in Post-Communist Societies* (Cambridge: Cambridge University Press, 1998); Andrew Arato, *Civil Society, Constitution, and Legitimacy* (Lanham, Md.: Rowman and Littlefield, 2000); Heinz Klug, *Constituting Democracy: Law, Globalism and South Africa's Political Reconstruction* (Cambridge: Cambridge University Press, 2000).

52. Holmes and Sunstein, "The Politics of Constitutional Revision in Eastern Europe," 285.

53. Andrew Arato, "Redeeming the Still Redeemable: Post Sovereign Constitution Making," *International Journal of Politics, Culture, and Society* 22 (2009): 428.

54. In what follows, I extensively draw on Arato's recent work, and bring it to bear on Michelman's challenge. In addition to "Redeeming the Still Redeemable," also see the following: Andrew Arato, "Constitutional Learning," *Theoria* 106 (2005): 1–36; "Multi-Track Constitutionalism Beyond Carl Schmitt," *Constellations* 18, 3 (2011): 324–51; "Conventions, Constituent Assemblies, and Round Tables: Models, Principles and Elements of Democratic Constitution-Making," *Global Constitutionalism* 1, 1 (2012): 173–200; Andrew Arato and Ertuğ Tombuş, "Learning from Success, Learning from Failure: South Africa, Hungary, Turkey and Egypt," *Philosophy and Social Criticism* 39, 4–5 (2013): 427–41.

55. Arato, "Redeeming the Still Redeemable," 432.

56. William Connolly, "Democracy and Territoriality," *Millennium* 20, 3 (1991): 466. The passage is omitted in the revised version of the essay in William Connolly, *The Ethos of Pluralization* (Minneapolis: University of Minnesota Press, 1995), 135–61, perhaps implying that Connolly no longer thinks there are other options "open for pursuit."

57. Honig, "Dead Rights Live Futures," 796; Jason Frank, *Constituent Moments: Enacting the People in Postrevolutionary America* (Durham, N.C.: Duke University Press, 2010), 237–54.

58. Habermas, "Constitutional Democracy," 768.

CONCLUSION. "THE ACT BY WHICH A PEOPLE IS A PEOPLE"

1. Jean-Jacques Rousseau, *The Social Contract*, in *The Social Contract and Other Later Political Writings*, ed. and trans. Victor Gourevitch (Cambridge: Cambridge University Press, 1997), 49.

2. For an important contemporary restatement of this longstanding view, see Cass R.

Sunstein, *Designing Democracy: What Constitutions Do* (Oxford: Oxford University Press, 2001).

3. John Searle, *Speech Acts* (Cambridge: Cambridge University Press, 1969), 33. Also see Stephen Holmes, "Precommitment and the Paradox of Democracy," in *Constitutionalism and Democracy*, ed. Jon Elster and Rune Slagstad (Cambridge: Cambridge University Press, 1993), 227.

4. Both Sheldon Wolin and Jacques Rancière, among others, offer vivid statements of this view. See the following essays by Sheldon Wolin: "Norm and Form: The Constitutionalizing of Democracy," in *Athenian Political Thought and the Reconstruction of American Democracy*, ed. Peter Euben, John R. Wallach, and Josiah Ober (Ithaca, N.Y.: Cornell University Press, 1994), 29–58; "Fugitive Democracy," in *Democracy and Difference*, ed. Seyla Benhabib (Princeton, N.J.: Princeton University Press, 1996), 31–45; "Transgression, Equality, and Voice," in *Dēmokratia: A Conversation on Democracies, Ancient and Modern*, ed. Josiah Ober and Charles Hedrick (Princeton, N.J.: Princeton University Press, 1996), 63–90. For Jacques Rancière's contributions, see in particular: "Democracy or Consensus," in *Disagreement*, trans. Julie Rose (Minneapolis: University of Minnesota Press, 1999), 99–121; "Democracy, Republic and Representation," *Hatred of Democracy*, trans. Steve Corcoran (London: Verso, 2006), 51–70; "Ten Theses on Politics," in *Dissensus*, ed. and trans. Steve Corcoran (London: Continuum, 2010), 27–44.

5. Wolin, "Fugitive Democracy," 37.

6. Rancière, *Dissensus*, 37, 33, respectively.

7. Wolin, "Norm and Form," 30.

8. For a similar view, see Antonio Negri, *Insurgencies: Constituent Power and the Modern State*, trans. Maurizia Boscagli (Minneapolis: University of Minnesota Press, 1999).

9. Hannah Arendt, *On Revolution*, rev. ed. (New York: Viking, 1965), 223: "To the extent that the greatest event in every revolution is the act of foundation, the spirit of revolution contains two elements which to us seem irreconcilable and even contradictory.... Perhaps the very fact that these two elements, the concern with stability and the spirit of the new have become opposites in political thought and terminology . . . must be recognized to be among the symptoms of our loss."

10. Patchen Markell, "The Rule of the People: Arendt, *Archē*, and Democracy," *American Political Science Review* 100, 1 (2006): 2.

11. I borrow the term "jurisgenesis" from Robert Cover, "Nomos and Narrative," *Harvard Law Review* 97, 4 (1983): 4–68. As I see it, the jurisgenerative potential of the event is a guiding trope of Bruce Ackerman's influential work *We the People: Foundations* (Cambridge, Mass.: Harvard University Press, 1991). Ackerman identifies three extraordinary (or if you like, "eventful") constitutional moments in the history of the United States—Founding, Reconstruction, and the New Deal—in which widespread mobilization of ordinary citizens resulted in popular acts of higher-lawmaking and altered the fundamental terms of the political association.

12. Jeremy Waldron, *Liberal Rights* (Cambridge: Cambridge University Press, 1993), 51–57.

13. Simone Chambers, "Theories of Political Justification," *Philosophy Compass* 5, 11 (2010): 894.

14. Seyla Benhabib, "Deliberative Rationality and Models of Democratic Legitimacy," *Constellations* 1, 1 (1994): 33. Also see *Situating the Self* (New York: Routledge, 1992), where Benhabib considers the epistemic value of deliberation through the lens of "enlarged mentality" as construed by Hannah Arendt. For a different view, offering a "strong" account of the epistemic value of deliberation, see David M. Estlund, *Democratic Authority: A Philosophical Framework* (Princeton, N.J.: Princeton University Press, 2009). Habermas stands somewhere in the middle, though having moved from a "relatively stronger" to a "relatively weaker" understanding of the epistemic value of deliberation. See, for example, his cautionary remarks on the "ideal speech situation" in *Between Facts and Norms*, trans. William Rehg (Cambridge, Mass.: MIT Press, 1996), 322–23.

15. Jon Elster, "Deliberation and Constitution Making," in *Deliberative Democracy*, ed. Jon Elster (Cambridge: Cambridge University Press, 1998), 111.

16. Jon Elster, "Forces and Mechanisms in the Constitution-Making Process," *Duke Law Journal* 45, 2 (1995): 388.

17. Elster, "Forces and Mechanisms in the Constitution-Making Process," 395.

18. See Andrew Arato, "Constitutional Learning," *Theoria* 106 (2005): 23–24.

19. For an illuminating discussion to this effect, see Simone Chambers, "Open Versus Closed Constitutional Negotiation," in *Deliberative Democracy in Practice*, ed. David Kahane et al. (Vancouver: UBC Press, 2010), 77–91.

20. Carl Schmitt, *Constitutional Theory*, trans. Jeffrey Seitzer (Durham, N.C.: Duke University Press, 2008), 132.

21. For a different view, see Andrew Arato, "Redeeming the Still Redeemable: Post Sovereign Constitution Making," *International Journal of Politics, Culture, and Society* 22 (2009): 431. Arato seems to think that the possibility of an "absolute veto" in the referendum is a remainder of the classical doctrine of constituent power and incompatible with the "post-sovereign paradigm" of democratic constitution-making. In my view, however, referendum is not necessarily tied to the paradigm of "sovereign decision" but can be incorporated into the deliberative model as a democratic check mechanism.

22. Jürgen Habermas, "Constitutional Democracy," *Political Theory* 29, 6 (2001): 774.

23. For a historical account, see Peter H. Russell, *Constitutional Odyssey*, 3rd ed. (Toronto: University of Toronto Press, 2004), 107–89.

24. Simone Chambers, "Contract or Conversation? Theoretical Lessons from the Canadian Constitutional Crisis," *Politics & Society* 26, 1 (1998): 161.

25. For an instructive assessment of the major problems and failures in the Egyptian process of constitution-making, see Ibrahim Awad, "Breaking out of Authoritarianism: 18 Months of Political Transition in Egypt," *Constellations* 20, 2 (2013): 275–92.

26. For an analysis of "tainted origins" from a developmentalist account of constitutional democracy, see Christopher F. Zurn, "The Logic of Legitimacy: Bootstrapping Paradoxes of Constitutional Democracy," *Legal Theory* 16 (2010): 191–226.

27. Alexis de Tocqueville, *Democracy in America*, trans. George Lawrence (New York: Anchor, 1969), 225.

28. Paul Pierson, *Politics in Time* (Princeton, N.J.: Princeton University Press, 2004), 64.

29. Kevin Olson, "Paradoxes of Constitutional Democracy," *American Journal of Political Science* 51, 2 (2007): 339.

30. Also consider in this regard the "entrenchment" mechanisms available to constitutional framers. Such mechanisms are especially powerful means to give the course of constitutional development a path-dependent direction. For a refined analysis and critique of entrenchment, see Melissa Schwartzberg, *Democracy and Legal Change* (Cambridge: Cambridge University Press, 2007).

Index

Ackerman, Bruce, 6, 187n11
Adams, John, 106
Amending power, 139–40
American Revolution, 2, 34, 97, 104–5; and the problem of constitutional authority, 39, 105–11. *See also* Arendt; Declaration of Independence
American Zionist Organization, 80
Arato, Andrew, 102, 105; post-sovereign constitution-making, 118, 140–42
Arendt, Hannah, 2, 12, 77–78; abyss of freedom, 112–13; action and world, 96–97; American and French Revolutions compared, 97–98, 104–8; American Revolution idealized, 97, 113, 116; authority, 104–17, 179n39; constituent power, 101–5; federal republic in Palestine, 85, 88–91; enlarged mentality, 88–91; ethnic and civic identities, 78–79, 82, 84, 87–88; founding as new beginning, 53, 95, 97, 105, 108–12, 115, 117; founding as world-building, 79, 85–88, 93, 97, 112; Jewish identity, 78, 80, 92–93; *The Jewish Writings*, 78–79, 91–93; nationalism, 79–83; natural law, 108, 111; novelty and permanence, 95–98, 110; *On Revolution*, 78, 95–98, 101, 108, 115–16; as phenomenologist, 77–78; power, 102–3, 106–7, 110, 112, 114, 178n35; principles of action, 95, 108–11, 116; promising, 110–15; public freedom, 98, 101–3, 115–18; totalitarianism, 77, 83, 95–96; yishuv, 85–88; Zionism, 79–83, 174n12
Aristotle, 60, 132, 146
Austin, J. L., 43–45
Autonomy, 8–9, 24, 37, 46–48; private and public, 121, 125–28; and respect, 150–51

Beiner, Ronald, 83
Ben-Gurion, David, 90
Benhabib, Seyla, 150, 188n14
Bennington, Geoffrey, 93
Bernstein, Richard, 91–93, 127–28
Boundary problem, 5, 160n8
Brit Shalom, 88
Burke, Edmund, 9, 46, 97

Canadian Constitution Act, 31–32, 155–56
Canovan, Margaret, 6, 75, 109
Chambers, Simone, 25, 120, 132, 163n16
Charlottetown Accord, 155
Cleisthenic revolution, 68, 182n85
Connolly, William, 11, 35, 42, 46–47, 59, 69, 142–43, 186n56
Consent, 3, 5; abstract vs. embedded, 87; critique of, 17–20; episodic vs. time-extended, 67; hypothetical, 20–23; and legitimacy vs. justification, 149; and power, 107
Constituent power: in American and French Revolutions, 104–5; classical theory of, 98–101; and contemporary constitution-making, 140, 188n21; critique of, 12, 78, 101–5, 118; and modern constitutionalism, 15, 163n3; and the paradox of founding, 38–39, 41, 50, 52. *See also* Sieyès; Schmitt
Constitutional democracy: as dynamic and open-ended project, 26–28, 133–38, 144–45, 154–58; and founding moments, 2–4, 6, 15–16, 25–28, 129–32, 139–42, 145, 154–58; normative foundations of, 9, 49, 123–25; and the people, 5–6; and popular sovereignty, 2, 35, 41–42; undemocratic beginnings of, 29–32. *See also* constitutionalism; constitution-making
Constitutionalism: ancient, 15; applied to constitution-making, 140; democratic, 2–4, 16, 25–26, 32, 42, 78, 133–38; dynamic,

Index

Constitutionalism: ancient (*cont.*) 26–28, 133–38, 144–45, 154–58; modern, 11, 15–16, 25, 106; and political culture, 27–28, 32, 129. *See also* constitutional democracy; constitution-making

Constitution-making: deliberative, 4, 119–20, 123–27, 129–32, 139–42, 149–53; and democratic legitimacy, 3–4, 16, 25, 29–32, 137, 141–42, 149–51, 159n2; "how" and "what" of, 2–4, 12, 25–32, 110–11, 119, 159n4; multi-stage model of, 140–42; and open vs. closed negotiation, 151–52; and organ sovereignty, 103; performative meaning of, 114, 116, 123–27; post-sovereign, 78, 98, 118, 140–42, 188n21. *See also* constitutional democracy; constitutionalism; infinite regress; paradox of founding

Dahl, Robert, 4
Declaration of Independence, 43–46, 107, 113, 179n51
Deliberative democracy, 4, 12, 23–24, 49–51; and dynamic constitutionalism, 154–58; and infinite regress, 49–51, 133–39; and law, 120–23; and legitimacy, 149–53; and the paradox of founding, 127–32. *See also* constitution-making; Habermas; public deliberation
Democratization, 74, 156
Derrida, Jacques, 11, 35, 70; Declaration of Independence, 43–46, 113; founding violence, 19–20, 45, 53, 94–95, 169n44; speech act theory, 43–46, 113
Dictatorship, 2, 101, 105, 116
Diversity, 3, 8, 24, 153,
Divine rights of kings, 17

Egyptian Revolution, 1–2, 9, 129, 141, 155–56
Elites, 6, 65–68, 130, 132
Elster, Jon, 151–52
Ethos, 35–37, 60, 115–17, 127–29, 131. *See also* political culture
Event and form, 2, 78, 98, 116, 146–49

Ferguson, Michaele L., 161n17
Filmer, Robert, 17–18
Foundationalism, 77, 108, 111, 183n14
Founding violence, 47, 72, 118, 168n40; obliteration of, 19, 169n44
Frank, Jason, 6, 162n28
French National Assembly, 45, 105, 152

French Revolution, 2, 34, 40, 82, 97, 101, 104, 113, 167n20. *See also* Arendt; French National Assembly; Sieyès

German Basic Law, 29–30, 165n43
German unification, 29–30, 137–39

Haam, Ahad, 88
Habermas, Jürgen, 4, 12, 23; *Between Facts and Norms*, 120, 123, 126, 127; communicative freedom, 124–25; communicative reciprocity, 125; constitutional history as learning process, 135–37, 142–43, 154–58; co-originality, 120–21, 123–26, 183n14; critique of Rawls, 24, 50; democratic ethos, 127–29; human rights, 121, 124–25; lifeworld, 127–28; and Michelman, 49–51, 133–39; performative meaning of constitution-making, 122–27; popular sovereignty, 120, 121, 124, 125; public and private autonomy, 121, 125, 126, 128; and Rousseau's paradox of founding, 127–29; system of rights, 120–22, 125–26, 135; on the unification of Germany, 137–39; pragmatic presuppositions of communication, 114, 125, 127, 183n14
Hegel, G. W. F., 5, 35, 40–42, 58, 60, 143, 167nn20, 25
Herzl, Theodor, 81–83, 90
Hobbes, Thomas, 3, 16, 21–22
Holmes, Stephen, 41–42, 139
Honig, Bonnie, 35, 42, 162n29; and Arendt, 112–14, 116–17; paradox of politics, 47–48, 53–55, 59, 171n72
Hume, David, 18–20, 72

Identity, 78, 94, 176n52; and action, 91–93; civic and ethnic, 79, 82, 87–88; and founding violence, 47; and humanity, 84; and *moeurs*, 60
Infinite regress, 51, 53, 133–39, 141
Ingram, David, 113–15, 170n61, 181n74
Israel, 81, 84–85

Japan: Constitution of, 29
Jefferson, Thomas, 107–8
Jewish Agency of Palestine, 81
Jurisgenesis, 148, 187n11
Justification and legitimacy, 149–50

Kalyvas, Andreas, 126, 170n69
Kant, Immanuel, 16, 18, 102, 109, 144;

founding violence, 72; gradual reform, 73–74; hypothetical popular sovereignty, 20–25; lawgiver, 72; original contract, 20–25, 73; and Rousseau, 61, 71–75, 138
Keenan, Alan, 48–49, 66
Kis, János, 41–42
Kohn, Margaret, 175n49
Kommers, Donald, 29

Lazare, Bernard, 81
Legal positivism, 51, 120–21, 167n23
Lessing, Ephraim, 80

Machiavelli, Niccolò, 69, 162n26, 168n40, 171n3
Madison, James, 34, 39, 48
Magnes, Judah, 88
Mandela, Nelson, 132
Markell, Patchen, 148
Marx, Karl, 107
McBride, Keally, 175n49
Meech Lake Accord, 155
Michelman, Frank, 11, 35, 42, 49–53, 133–39, 141, 164n33, 169n52
Montesquieu, 60, 109, 112
Mubarak, Hosni, 1
Murray, Christina, 130–31
Muslim Brotherhood, 2

Nationalism, 79–85, 87–88

Ober, Josiah, 68, 116–17
Ochoa Espejo, Paulina, 6, 164n34
Olson, Kevin, 157

Paine, Thomas, 98
Palestine, 78, 81, 84–91, 174n17
Paradox of founding, 7–11, 34–35; as category mistake, 35, 40–43; and deliberative democracy, 49–51, 127–32; displacement of, 54, 59; ethos- and procedure-based versions, 35–39; and hermeneutic circle, 54–55; as heuristic problem, 10–11, 35, 55–56, 75–76, 131, 143, 145; hypostatized, 51–55; and infinite regress, 51, 53, 133–35; and paradox of politics, 48, 52, 54, 59; and speech act theory, 43–46
Path dependency, 157
People: agency-centric conception of, 6–7, 60, 67–68, 76, 87, 93, 153, 161n17; as bounded community, 5–6; as corporate body, 6, 10, 17–18, 20, 75, 99, 147; as diverse and plural, 2–3, 8, 24–25, 102, 153; as macro-subject, 4, 6, 12, 98, 102, 106, 117, 152, 161n17; as multitude, 6, 10, 17–18, 36, 48, 57, 130, 147, 184n26; two bodies of, 10, 12, 75, 78. *See also* popular sovereignty
Philadelphia Convention, 39, 104, 152
Pierson, Paul, 157
Plato, 7, 66, 146
Plebiscitary politics, 132, 151–52
Political culture, 8, 28, 30, 32, 60–65, 68–69, 117, 127–28, 131, 154
Popular sovereignty, 16, 163n9; and boundary problem, 4–5, 92; constitutional claims of, 2–4, 11, 16, 25–26, 30, 149, 152; and deliberative democracy, 4, 12, 23–24, 120–21, 124–25, 153; hypothetical, 3, 11, 20–25, 163n16, 164n28; monological, 102, 115; objections to, 17–20; and the paradox of founding, 33, 35, 40–42, 47, 49, 164n34; and pluralism, 24–25; and popular insurgency, 148
Positive law, 61, 63, 99, 120–23, 126
Postmetaphysical, 74, 77, 120, 138, 182n3
Preuss, Ulrich, 41–42
Progress, 69, 73–75, 138
Public deliberation, 129–32, 141, 143, 149–53. *See also* deliberative democracy
Public reason, 150

Québec, 5, 31, 155–56

Rancière, Jacques, 6, 147
Rawls, John, 3, 23–24, 50, 122, 164n28
Referendum, 153, 188n21
Representation, 17–18, 39, 99–100, 103, 105, 141, 177n22
Ricoeur, Paul, 162n26, 168n40
Rorty, Richard, 51
Round table, 140–42
Rousseau, Jean-Jacques: deep voluntarism, 69; general will, 36–37, 47–48, 62, 99; and Kant, 22, 71–75, 138; lawgiver, 8, 10, 36–37, 39, 46–49, 57–60, 65–68, 72, 75, 129, 132, 169n47; *moeurs*, 60–65, 67–70; *Plan for a Constitution for Corsica*, 67, 184n26; paradox of founding, 7–8, 34–37, 46–49, 57–58, 90–91, 127–32, 142; popular agency, 10, 65–68, 94, 144, 148; *Social Contract*, 7, 34–35; time, 68–71
Royalists and Parliamentarians, 17–18
Rule of law, 120, 122, 124, 142

Schmitt, Carl, 12, 98–2, 105, 153, 178n25
Searle, John, 38
Sieyès, Emmanuel Joseph (Abbé), 12, 35, 37, 102, 166nn8, 9; constituent power, 38–39, 98–101, 139; representation, 39, 100, 105
Social contract, 20–22, 73, 99, 112, 122
South Africa, 9, 129–32, 140, 153
Speech act theory, 43–46, 113
Sunstein, Cass, 139

Tahrir Square, 1
Tocqueville, Alexis de, 97, 156, 167n18
Tully, James, 31

Waldron, Jeremy, 106, 179n45, 189n60
Weber, Max, 103, 178n35
Wellmer, Albrecht, 117, 182n84
Wolin, Sheldon, 66, 147

Yack, Bernard, 5, 87–88

Zionism, 79–83
Zurn, Christopher, 26–32

Acknowledgments

"But philosophy, some philosophy, starts at home," writes Avishai Margalit in his wonderful work, *Ethics of Memory*. Margalit's statement certainly holds true for the kind of theoretical inquiry undertaken in this book. To me "home" is Turkey, a country that has a decisive founding moment. It took place in the early 1920s, when a new republic was founded from the ashes of a collapsed empire. While it was far from the kind of democratic foundation that I argue for in this book, its effects have shaped the history of modern Turkey, for better and for worse, up to the present day. Hence the sense in which the central topic explored in this book—namely, the issue of founding—has for me an existential pull.

This book, however, actually began to take shape far from "home" at the University of Toronto. Ronald Beiner, Simone Chambers and Ryan Balot were encouraging, insightful and constructively critical mentors and interlocutors throughout that process. Their comments, questions and criticism did not only turn the agony of writing into an exciting endeavor of intellectual discovery but also taught me a lot about what it means to be a political theorist. My debt to them is beyond measure. I also would like to thank, especially, Peggy Kohn and William Scheuerman for their excellent feedback on the entire project. During my stay at the University of Toronto, I received generous support from the Department of Political Science, the prestigious Connaught Fund, and the Trinity College, for which I am grateful.

I was surrounded by a wonderful circle of friends and colleagues at the University of Toronto. Alex Livingston, Amy Nugent, Inder Marwah, Jakeet Singh, James McKee, Kiran Banarjee, Leah Soroko, Margaret Haderer, Mathias Thaler, Mihaela Mihai, Özgür Gürel, and Reuven Shlozberg not only made important contributions to this project in myriad ways, directly and indirectly, but also they made a difference in my life. Many of them were also among the participants of the Political Theory Reading Group. We regularly met for several years to discuss each other's work, and my own work benefited from their recommendations and critical scrutiny in more ways than I can possibly count here. Among those who made a difference in my life as I was working on this project, I must also mention Banu Doğan, Devrim Sezer, Emre Gönlügür, Fiona McCall, Merike Andre-Barrett, Paul Howard, and Sude Bahar Beltan.

On various occasions Alessandro Ferrara, Giuseppe Ballacci, Leigh Jenco, Rebecca Kingston and Valerio Nitrato Izzo read earlier versions of several chapters and provided very helpful feedback. Parts of the book were presented in "Semana da Filosofia Política" at the University of Coimbra, and at meetings of the American Political Science Association, Midwest Political Science Association, and Northeastern Political Science Association. I would like to thank my hosts, commentators and audiences in those venues.

Having returned "home" after what feels like a long and transformative journey, I completed writing this book in Izmir, Turkey, while at the same time teaching in the Department of Philosophy at Ege University. The current chair of the department, Nilgün Toker, generously took her time to read and comment on every single page. Her moral support and intellectual stimulation were invaluable in getting me through the final stage of writing. Damon Linker gently guided this project through the process of publication. I owe him a special debt of gratitude not only for his wise editorial advice, but also for the confidence he expressed in this project from the outset. I thank the anonymous reviewers of the Penn Press for their perceptive criticism and suggestions that significantly improved the manuscript.

Finally, I am indebted to my family beyond any measure. My parents, Cevdet and Güngör Tekin, have always made me feel at home in the world with their love and tremendous emotional support. My partner Ebru Dolunay is the best storyteller I ever met, and I really don't know how I could avoid paths of self-absorption without her love, her sense of humor, and her judgment about what really matters in life. She has been the best part of my life for more than a decade, and I am thoroughly grateful for that.